Denmark
Germany
Poland
Czech
Republic
Slovakia
Ukraine
Austria
Hungary
Romania
Croatia
Bosnia
Herzegovina
Yugoslavia
Bulgaria
Albania
FYROM
Aegean
Sea
Turkey
Greece
Athens
Crete
Tunisia

# European cuisine

The best in European food

R&R PUBLICATIONS MARKETING PTY LTD

Published by:
R&R Publications Marketing Pty Ltd
ABN 78 348 105 138
12 Edward Street
Brunswick, Victoria 3056
Australia
Phone: (61 3) 9381 2199
Fax: (61 3) 9381 2689
Australia-wide toll free: 1 800 063 296
E-mail: info@randrpublications.com.au
Web: www.randrpublications.com.au

European cuisine: the best in European food


Publisher: Richard Carroll
Production Manager: Anthony Carroll, Stephanie Souvlis (Italian)
Food Photography: Gary Smith, Warren Web (French), Andrew Elton
Photographic Assistant (French): Bill Holdsworth
Travel Text: Kerry Kenihan, Anna Maria Sabbione (Italian)
Food Stylists: Liz Nolan (French), Janet Lodge (French), Katrina Cleary (French, assisted on Spanish), Stephanie Souvlis (Italian, Greek)
Assisting Home Economist (Italian, Greek): Jenny Fanshaw
Recipe Development: Jenny Fanshaw, Ellen Argyriou (French), Mary Piggins (French), Janet Lodge (Spanish), Stephanie Souvlis (Italian), Amanda Cooper (Italian, Greek)
Creative Director: Aisling Gallagher
Cover Designer: Aisling Gallagher
Text Designers: Paul Simms, Lucy Adams and Elain Loh
Editors: Fiona Brodribb (French, Spanish), Samantha Carroll (Italian, Greek)
Proofreaders: Amber Parkinson, LoftCom; Diana Luger, U.S. Editors



Includes index
ISBN 1 74022 527 9
EAN 9 781740 225 274

This edition printed August 2005
Printed in China by Max Production Printing Limited

# Contents

# Introduction

Are you in a bind about what to plan for a special dinner party or celebration or simply how to break from the routine of cooking the same family meals repetitively? It's easy to fall into the trap of always falling back on tried and tested familiar recipes because you are busy and on the run. Pre-packaged, instant foods are a dangerous temptation lurking at the supermarket. These reduce the preparation time and challenge of home cooking, but don't provide the freshness, the cost savings, or the satisfaction of serving your own home made creations.

Here is a wide selection of excellent and beautifully photographed recipes, all with step-by-step instructions, which together represent the varied cuisines of France, Spain, Italy and Greece. Each section of recipes draws from a different set of culinary traditions and serves as a virtual cook's tour of each country. There are recipes to suit every budget and entice every type of guest, regardless of whether they are widely traveled gourmets or simply dining-room-chair travelers.

You will be delighted to hear that for those living on a Mediterranean-style diet, as exemplified in the Spanish, Italian and Greek recipes contained in this book, the risk of heart disease and cancer is considerably reduced. Mediterranean cuisine is based on olive oil rather than saturated fats, along with fish, poultry and other lean meat, vegetables, legumes, fruit and whole grains (cereals, bread and pasta), consumed with only moderate amounts of alcohol.

Turn to the section called *French food* for a dramatic contrast to the Mediterranean diet. From the 1800s to the 1970s' French chefs and French provincial cooks were the English-speaking world's greatest single influence on fine cooking. When people ate out, it was at a French restaurant. For many years, the inevitable way to make a good impression on guests at home was to prepare and serve French food.

A typical full menu would start with appetizers, soup, then an entrée of vegetables with sauce, eggs, fish or seafood, or pâté. To follow would be a main course of fish or seafood (unless it conflicted with the entrée), lamb, beef, pork, offal or poultry accompanied by vegetables and/or salad, then cheese. While other culinary traditions serve cheese as the last course with coffee and liqueurs, in the French tradition the cheese platter, consisting of a variety of soft and hard cheeses, should be served before dessert, accompanied by unbuttered dry biscuits or crackers. Dessert is the finale to the meal, which might vary from simple fruit to a rich soufflé. For a typical al fresco French lunch, cheese with crusty fresh bread and a light main course of soup and salad would be served.

The migration of the Italians, Greeks and other Europeans to newer worlds in the 1900s, along with the Spanish culinary influences that sifted through to the USA via Mexico, meant that traditional French cuisine suddenly had increased competition as a preferred style of dining. Following these new cuisines came an eruption of interest in Asian food. The introduction of nouvelle cuisine in the 1970s meant that traditional French cooking, with its reliance

LAMB CUTLETS WITH OLIVES AND ROSEMARY, PAGE 136

on cream-based sauces and longer cooking times, became almost passé. *Nouvelle cuisine* was healthier, looked lovely but was neither as filling, nor as hearty as provincial potages and *pots*. *French food* entices you to rediscover the traditional cuisines of France, from provincial cooking to *haute cuisine*, which were so much loved by earlier generations.

Within France, as indeed in most European countries, there is often much culinary exchange between neighboring regions. In the northeast of France, the cuisine of Alsace-Lorraine is a unique mixture of the neighboring French and German traditions. Other influences on French cuisine have been from Belgium, Luxembourg and the Netherlands. The island of Corsica may be administered by France, but its food traditions are influenced by Italy.

The cuisine described in the section called *Spanish food*, by contrast, reflects Spain's weather: dry and sunny except for the snowy winters of the center and north. The Pyrenees divide Spain from France and the tiny mountainous country of Andorra, restricting culinary interchange between these countries. It is difficult to imagine Spanish cuisine before the introduction of many of its key ingredients from its territories in South America, such as tomatoes, potatoes, chocolate and peppers. The Moors from northern Africa, who ruled Spain from the 700s and remained as a political force in Spain until the last Moorish rulers were routed from Granada at the end of the 15th century, also left their mark on Spanish food.

Tapas bars, which serve appetizers with alcohol before lunch or dinner, are located all over Spain and provide such an array of tempting morsels that it's difficult to tear yourself away for your planned restaurant meal.

# INTRODUCTION

The tapas concept is catching on internationally and many similar establishments are opening in many countries. A whole meal can focus on tapas, particularly when served with sangria. This writer and cook often serves sangria at brunches and lunches, regardless of the origin of the accompanying food. Sangria is light and refreshing and relatively low in alcohol. See the introduction to *Spanish food* for instructions on how to make it.

The Spanish are probably the world's most enthusiastic eaters of garlic, which is both rich in nutrients and beneficial for health and in preventing colds, while imparting a delightful pungency to Spanish food. Spanish-style salads and cold soups suit the hot climate perfectly. Meats and game are generally more popular in Spanish cuisine than poultry, but these are surpassed in popularity by seafood, particularly when combined with chicken in the national dish, paella. You pronounce this distinctive rice dish 'pa-eh-yuh' not as 'pay-ella'. This is an Arabic-style dish where all the diners traditionally share from the same communal dish. While expensive in restaurants, this delicious dish is not too expensive or difficult to prepare at home. See the two paella recipes in *Spanish food*.

Sharing the Mediterranean with Spain is the long coastline of Italy and the islands off its boot, Sicily and Sardinia. Italy has a colorful and ancient culinary history. The *Italian food* section embraces recipes including pasta, pizza, polenta, Parmesan, prosciutto, porcini and more. An enticing selection of antipasti (including vegetarian appetizers) is also included.

The rice and pasta dishes in these pages are easy yet innovative, so don't expect the old standards of spaghetti Bolognese, *spaghettini al burro* or *fettuccine ai funghi*. However, included for newcomers to Italian cooking are classics such as osso buco and veal saltimbocca *alla romana*. Tiramisu is currently about the most popular dessert offered at Italian restaurants; the secret to making it lies within these pages.

Greek food seems to offer more challenges to non-Greek cooks than many other European cuisines, yet it is well worth the effort. The section called *Greek food* contains every possible tantalizing, yet healthy, Hellenic-style course one could want to serve at lunch or dinner.

The origins of Greek cuisine are disputed. Centuries of rule by the Romans, followed by 440 years of rule under the Turkish Ottoman empire, have each left their mark on the cuisine. The Venetians brought their own flavors to the Greek island of Corfu, which they ruled for more than four centuries. Corfu is the only piece of Greek territory that was never occupied by the Turks, and as a result, Corfiot cuisine differs from that anywhere else in Greece.

Traditionally, Greeks never drink alcohol on an empty stomach. Hence *mezethes*, or appetizers, which can be as simple as olives or grilled octopus, always accompany an ouzo or other alcoholic drink, whether pre-meal or not. Greek soups range from light ones to hearty ones, which can constitute for a whole meal. The delicate and versatile filo pastry of Greece (available at supermarkets almost everywhere), used in the traditional Greek recipes of spanokopita and baklava, has been adopted by many cuisines to use with their own distinct ingredients. Recipes for popular Greek dishes such as souvlakia, moussaka and semolina cake have also been included in this section.

Fish and seafood are as popular in Greece as they are in Spain, France and Italy, whether harvested from the Mediterranean Sea (including the Aegean and Ionion Seas) or brought in from the North or Baltic Seas. Each of these countries has its own popular varieties of river fish.

You'll be sure to receive words of appreciation for your generous and exciting hospitality when serving your choice of recipes from each of these cuisines. I hope that your guests will be inspired to depart with a 'Merci beaucoup', 'Muchas gracias', 'Molte grazie', 'Efharisto poli' or a 'Thank you very much'!

Kerry Kenihan

POUSSINS PROVENÇALS, PAGE 56

# FRENCH
food

# the land AND ITS PEOPLE

| | |
|---|---|
| Status | People's Republic |
| Area | 338 004 sq mi |
| Population | 56 440 000 |
| Language | French |
| Religion | Roman Catholic |
| Currency | Euro |
| National Day | 14 July |

## LET THEM EAT CAKE

Regional French cuisine and *haute cuisine* have been infiltrating the world since restaurants came into existence around 1789, soon after the French Revolution. At this time, chefs in noble and upper class households whose employment was threatened by a diminishing aristocracy and political instability, obviously took Marie-Antoinette literally at her (reportedly) cynical words of the struggling, starving masses: 'Let them eat cake.' The chefs deserted palaces, châteaux and mansions to open their own establishments. Soon, more than cake was gracing the laden tables of all who could afford the kinds of dishes previously only created for royalty.

In the provinces, the thrust came from home cooks and their peasant food: family food raised from rich soil. This food was to share with and enliven anyone who valued time around a table and lively discussion over a *pot au feu* (France's national dish). It is only fairly recently that the gastronomic delights of provincial Provence, for example, have been revealed to the world beyond Europe.

My family and I traveled to Provence in the time before several TV documentary series and travel writers had extolled Provence's peaceful lifestyle, and before trendy foreign visitors had flocked to rent villas or country cottages in provincial France for cooking classes, wine tours or relaxing self-indulgence. On one occasion, we arrived at dusk in a village that had no name. The village was an inland place of rough stone houses, cobbled streets and an old stone church. If some of the buildings were shops, it was not evident as no merchandise was displayed. We were hungry and too tired to drive on in the descending darkness. Only one faded sign was evident in front of a dull façade: *auberge* (inn).

The only available room was cramped for me, my husband and my baby, but we were eager to try the fixed price, three-course house menu for two that we planned to share with our 12-month-old son. I had rejected the owner's suggestion to leave my son alone in the room while his parents dined. He was extremely well behaved, I assured the owner.

The first course was *magnifique*: pâté made in heaven, and little Myles thought so too. But our hostess flew into a fury when she saw him enjoying the pâté. 'My pâté is not for a child who cannot possibly appreciate it. My patrons come from as far as Paris for my pâté. I cannot make it quickly enough and you are wasting it on a baby,' she cried. 'I insist you and your husband only eat my pâté or I must ask you to leave.'

Astonished, I replied: 'Madame, we are paying guests, and teaching our son, so young, to be discerning in food choice. What better introduction to perfect pâté than from your superior table?'

She bustled away in a huff, but surprisingly, returned minutes later with an adequate serve, garnished with parsley and hot toast triangles. Gruffly she said: '*Pour l'enfant*.' I didn't dare ask for the recipe. I knew Madame would be the sort to maintain secrecy in order to preserve the mystique in which many French chefs and cooks have shrouded their traditions and innovations for centuries. '*Bof!*' she said when I tried to pay for the extra pâté—and finally she smiled at the baby.

This incident illustrated the pride the French have for their cuisine. It is not just the cuisine, but the individual cook's interpretation of the cuisine; their attention to attractive presentation and their desire to please patrons (even grudgingly, small people in strollers).

Provence is just one region to contribute to the varied, refined yet paradoxically hearty cuisines of France. Normandy, Burgundy, Périgord, Lyon, Alsace, Languedoc-Roussillon and French Basque Country in the Southwest produce the most distinctive provincial dishes. The local produce varies in each region. The sea yields more than beautiful beaches for beautiful people on the Riviera—it yields ocean fish.

Freshwater fish are found in the unpolluted reaches of the rivers Seine, Loire, Rhône, Garonne and Rhine and in countless streams.

France is shaped like a squat bell pepper. What divides it is an invisible line. Northern French cook in butter, while Southerners opt for olive oil. On the same day that northern snow-seekers ski in the Alps, southern sun-soakers can sauté their skins on the sands of the Atlantic and paddle in the pebbled shallows of the Mediterranean. In between are thick forests, undulating acres of vineyards, patchwork quilts of vegetables, the soaring white cliffs of Normandy, the perilous promontories of Brittany, and in almost every province in spring, fallow fields bright with laughing, wild, red poppies. No other European nation has such climatic and geographic variation, and such a huge diversity of produce. About 20 percent of France is forest clad with mainly pine, beech and oak and about 4 200 flower and plant species. Hundreds of mammal and bird species live there and more than 30 kinds of reptiles.

Within France lie treasures dating from 1st century Gallo-Roman times: aqueducts and bridges, Romanesque churches, as well as Gothic cathedrals, Renaissance structures, lavish baroque palaces,

France

# the land AND ITS

rococo, neoclassical, art nouveau and contemporary buildings, and beautiful art. Music, dance and literature are the essence of a rich past and the land and seascapes, quaint city quarters and villages are the transported riches of the present.

## PROVINCIAL PERFECTION

After the Crusades, southern France adopted garlic from the Middle East as a sacred herb, and combined with egg yolks and olive oil, it became known as *aioli,* which characterises many dishes of Provence. Any dish entitled *à la provençale* will inevitably have been prepared with garlic and tomatoes for which the province is renowned. With eggplant, zucchinis bell peppers, garlic and tomatoes, topped with a fresh herb such as oregano or parsley, ratatouille, the cooked vegetable salad of Provence, is born. Originating in Marseille, *bouillabaisse*, a thick fish soup, is famed in Provence, along with honey, goat's cheese, vegetables and truffles. The elusive truffles are sniffed out by trained dogs or pigs from November to March. Truffles grace dishes on the tables of the wealthy.

The adjoining province of Languedoc shares with Provence a passion for olive oil. The country's famed blue cheese is produced at Roquefort. *Cassoulet* is the province's most celebrated dish. Périgord is also praised for its truffles and its poultry, particularly goose, the liver of which translates into *pâté de fois gras* that is superb for stuffing into local freshwater fish. Crayfish, rabbit, beef, chestnuts, plums, grapes, pears, quinces and cherries are also prolific in Languedoc.

Normandy produces more than half of France's dairy products, from cream to Camembert, perfected in the province since William the Conqueror's time. Pâtés, tripe, duck, seafood, apples and apple brandy (calvados) are specialties of Normandy. France's famous crêpes Suzettes hail from Brittany.

*Bœuf bourguignon* is Burgundy's most famous dish and mustard is its most popular condiment, especially mustard from Dijon. Other Burgundy notables are its wine, black snails, blackcurrant jam and liqueur and surprisingly, gingerbread, which can take up to eight weeks to make. The city of Lyon is regarded as France's gastronomic temple where Lyonnaise mothers have forged Lyon's reputation for homely, wholesome fare in traditional restaurants operated by women. Burgundy cooking is at its best in Lyon.

In the Northeast of France, the fruits of the sea are legendary, while in Alsace, cooking has certain German influences. Many dishes of Alsace revolve around *charcuterie* (cooked meats). The people of Alsace love rich cakes and tarts and the local Riesling is enjoyed by the glass as well as in cooking. Alsace shares a beer-making tradition with Lorraine, where beer is frequently used in cooking.

The food of Basque, in the Southwest, is spiced with the local chili pepper. The food of this area has a Spanish influence. Trout, baby eels and wood pigeon are very popular here.

Paris offers all the regional food delights in its busy, buzzing markets and many specialty food shops. I recall one memorable Parisian *pique-nique* on the Champs Elysées—pâté and terrine, cured ham, moist cheeses, anchovies, pickled mussels, salad vegetables, baguette, Burgundy and fresh fruit—all bought from the market and far cheaper than at the nearby restaurant serving the same fare.

Of its almost 57 million people, more than 20 percent of French people live in sprawling metropolitan Paris, while populations in mountain and rural areas decline. Millions of immigrants and refugees from other parts of Europe arrived before and after both world wars to help rebuild a France that was crippled by war and short of workers. Then, as French colonialism collapsed in North and West Africa, as well as in Indochina in the late 1950s and early 1960s, French nationals returned from colonies and protectorates. To satisfy labor needs, they were followed by

# PEOPLE

workers from Africa, Indochina, India, the Middle East, the South Pacific and the Caribbean. The recipes they all brought continue to be prepared today.

The result of this immigration is a colorful combination of French men and women. The mix of nationalities means that there is an incredible variety of ethnic eateries in France, including Moroccan, Tunisian, Algerian, Asian (especially Vietnamese and Cambodian), and places featuring food from the Caribbean. In Paris, Marseilles and Strasbourg, there are many kosher restaurants to cater for Jewish patrons.

While several foreign cooking styles have absorbed French methods and ingredients, French cooking has not generally absorbed foreign cooking styles. Regardless of whether the style is *haute cuisine*, (descending from the courts of kings), *cuisine bourgeoise*, (dishes of high quality for the people), *cuisine de mère* (simple nourishing family fare such as mother used to make) or *nouvelle cuisine* (small portions emphasising textures and colors, but somewhat of a food fad), the French cook is an absolute purist. That is, unless he or she has succumbed to fusion cooking: the exciting eclectic method of taking a bit from this country and a bit from that. Yet fear not, the proud French cook will always admit to tampering with inherent tradition and confess that Greek moussaka, Moroccan couscous and Spanish paella have also crept onto modern French menus.

*people*

# Daily food IN FRANCE

## THE QUEEN OF CUISINES

Food is one of life's top priorities for the French. France's 21st century pace has led to the simplification of home cooking during the week because of time constraints. In defiance of tradition, fast food outlets are flourishing, but food and wine, particularly at the long Sunday lunch, remain very important.

American-inspired hypermarkets have put many little grocers on city outskirts out of business. These huge establishments in France are the largest in Europe and offer extensive, inexpensive, fresh and processed food choices. Despite the hypermarkets, the tradition of daily shopping has not died and fresh food markets are still crowded in most towns and cities. Old fashioned grocery shops (*épiceries*, meaning 'spice shops'), green groceries, fishmongers' shops and butcheries still exist. Some butcheries still sell horse meat, which remains popular in France.

The French are fanatical about fresh food. Going to market is a social occasion in smaller communities. Fresh bread is baked several times a day in *boulangeries* so baguettes, soft *pain* (bread) and heavier breads are always available. Sometimes attached to bakeries are patisseries offering glorious pastries, tarts, cakes and cookies. A French delicatessen is known as a *charcuterie*.

The French adore cheese. French cheeses can roughly be categorized into fresh cheese, including home made cream cheese, fermented cheese, such as Camembert and Brie, and cooked cheese, such as Gruyère. Emmental, Gruyère and Cheddar are classified as hard

MONKFISH BOURGUIGNON, PAGE 50

cheeses. Semi-soft cheeses are appreciated at the French table. For a festive Sunday lunch or dinner, the French share with the Swiss a love of fondue.

While cheese can be bought at supermarkets and hypermarkets, most French trust the expertise of the owner of a *fromagerie* (cheese shop) or *crémerie* (dairy shop).

### LE PETIT DEJEUNER

'The little lunch' or breakfast in France is similar to that taken throughout continental Europe. The French begin the day with one, or several, of the following: a flaky, buttery croissant; a muffin-shaped brioche; a piece of baguette; a bread roll with butter (butter is usually unsalted unless from Brittany or Normandy) and jelly; a pastry bought from a patisserie. This is served with *café au lait* (hot, milky coffee), a small black coffee or hot chocolate. A section of baguette with butter and jelly may also include a melted square of chocolate!

### LE DEJEUNER

In the past, lingering over lunch took up the whole afternoon, particularly in the South where Mediterranean dining habits, including siesta, have come in from Spain, Portugal, Italy, Greece and Corsica. These days, the traditional big midday meal is served only in rural areas, with the exception of Sunday lunch.

Those French who still consider the midday lunch as their main meal often opt for two courses, but rather than serve a main course and dessert, the French cook prefers the main to be preceded by an appetizer and the dessert course is dropped.

In cities and towns, lunch is likely to be a sandwich, a salad, an omelette or a steak at a café or at home. It could also be a fast-food take-away, a crêpe from a kiosk or *crêperie*, or a light meal at a Vietnamese, Chinese or North African restaurant. Lunch is also served at restaurants, wine bars, cafeterias, bistros and brasseries (big bustling places selling beer).

The urban lunchtime trend is against richly sauced restaurant food. The French have now become more health conscious. The attitude change was aided by the popularity of *nouvelle cuisine* during the 1980s. Light sauces replaced cream sauces. Portions became small. But the new cuisine, with its rejection of flour and heaviness and with its emphasis on artistry in presentation and garnish, was somewhat contrived, and particularly at dinner, left people hungry.

BOUILLABAISSE, PAGE 36

### LE DINER

A traditional French *dîner*, the main meal of the day, usually features at least three courses. If large and elaborate, dinner may include sorbet, which is served as a palate cleanser, as well as a dessert. Dinner begins with an entrée or hors d'œuvre. This course may be a series of appetizers such as nibbles on crackers or pâté or it could be a soup, a salad, an egg dish or a terrine; the possibilities are endless.

*Le plat* or the main course comprises fish, meat, poultry, game or offal, usually with a sauce. This is served with potatoes, pasta or rice and vegetables and/or salad. A five-course meal is likely to include: hors d'œuvres; an entrée or a fish dish; a main course; a cheese platter; and a dessert. The style of the main course dictates whether dessert will be light or substantial.

Techniques of French wine-making date back to pre-Roman times. The most important vineyards were established in the Middle Ages around monasteries, as wine was needed for monks to celebrate the Mass. Later, cultivation was moved closer to French ports so that wine could be exported more easily. Key wine

districts are Bordeaux, Burgundy, Beaujolais, Champagne, Alsace, the Loire Valley, Provence, Jura and Savoie, the Southwest, Languedoc-Roussillon and Rhône. Imported French wine is expensive. If you can't afford it, choose an amiable local, or a cheaper import to accompany the main course.

When entertaining family or close friends, French hosts often inform guests of what they propose to serve. This is so that if a guest intends to give a gift of wine, cheese or another food contribution, the gift will complement the cook's planned menu.

## FESTIVE FRANCE

Christmas and Easter are big festival days in the essentially Christian France. (eighty percent of the population are Roman Catholic.) Easter is traditionally celebrated with a marinated, boned, roasted leg of lamb served with warm, puréed garlic sauce, fresh herbs, spring salad and vegetables. Red wine accompanies the meal.

Lamb, although hideously expensive in France, is also the preferred main dish for a wedding party and is inevitably followed by *croquembouche*, the impressive witch's hat-shaped tower of *crème pâtissière*-filled profiteroles, decorated with sugar-almonds or crystallized violets and gleaming with caramel and spun sugar. This anniversary gâteau is also made for other special celebrations.

Until turkey was discovered in the Americas, most French families ate roast goose at Christmas. Many still do, and Périgord province is a prolific producer of geese. Sophisticated French begin Christmas day with caviar and champagne, followed by a special breakfast such as smoked salmon with scrambled eggs. If the main Christmas course is roast turkey, it will be stuffed with chestnuts or apples. After the cheese, the light yet rich, beautifully decorated *bûche de Noël* (traditional French Christmas log) is the festive centerpiece. Called *merveilles* (wonders) or *frivolités* (small frivolities), depending on the region, crisp fritters, sweetened with orange blossom water and crystallized sugar, with an optional few drops of brandy or liqueur, are treats served at Christmas, carnivals, weddings, christenings, birthdays or on Sundays.

The national Bastille Day on July 14 commemorates the 1789 French Revolution and is always remembered with great gusto and feasting. Saints' days are celebrated by devout Christian communities, particularly in the provinces, where tradespeople and individuals named after saints are the inspiration for special meals. For example, a carpenter's family rejoices around the table on the day of St. Joseph, the carpenter; or a man in the shoemaking industry may share his craft's achievements over a festive meal with loved ones and friends on the day of St. Thomas, the cobbler. It's all wonderfully quaint and yet just another excuse to plan a very special meal.

On Purification Day, February 2, and on Shrove Tuesday, the French eat all the wicked foods they are supposed to give up until Easter Sunday: wicked food in the form of crêpes. In Northeastern France, buttery, egg-enriched brioche is eaten on St. Nicholas Day, December 6. It is also eaten on New Year's Day.

Is French cooking the doyen, the epitome, the jewel in the world crown of food creativity? The most complicated or the simplest? *Ah, mon Dieu*. French cooking has been adopted by the world since the 18th century, and yet some non-French home cooks in the 21st century are still hesitant to try out the fundamentals of peasant cooking, or to be challenged by the queen of cuisines.

These recipes should help you overcome any hesitation in preparing and serving French food at your table.

*Kerry Kenihan*

# *entrées & salads*

# Beautiful BEGINNINGS

The French have created a vast variety of entrées that stimulate visual interest, as well as the palate. Pâté (literally, 'paste') is available from many stores and in many forms. As a mousse, pâté is an easily spreadable hors d'œuvre or appetizer to offer with drinks. It is served as an entrée when firmer in individual pots. More substantial is a coarser country-style pâté.

*Crudités*, which are raw fresh vegetables, such as baby tomatoes, champignons, celery, cauliflower florets, scallions, celery, carrot sticks and radishes (to name a few), are served on lettuce leaves with an onion and cheese mousse or just with vinaigrette.

While the French aren't into eggs for breakfast, they excel at presenting them as entrées in the form of flans and quiches, or as omelettes and savory soufflés. Baked on a bed of spinach or served alone with cream and butter, eggs sprinkled with fresh herbs and chopped mushrooms make a stunning starter.

The French also specialize in wonderful salads. Cooked potatoes and green beans are added to sliced fresh celery, bell pepper, cucumber, hard-boiled egg, olives and anchovy fillets, and dressed with vinaigrette to create *salade niçoise*, the famed salad from Nice. Avocado, artichokes, snow peas, scallions, chilies, a variety of lettuces, bean sprouts, fresh herbs, blanched zucchini, leek and turnip, cold cooked brains, poultry slices, sliced pâté, shellfish, smoked fish and even violet petals are used imaginatively in French salads with vinaigrette combinations of fruit vinegars and oils.

## COCKTAIL CHEESE TOASTS

**Ingredients**

1 pound Gruyère cheese, grated
1 tablespoon dry white wine
1/4 cup plain yogurt
1/4 cup scallion leaves, minced
1 teaspoon garlic, minced
3 teaspoons lemon zest, grated
1/4 cup red onion, finely minced
1/4 cup parsley, finely minced
48 bread rounds (1/4 inch thick) cut from a French style baguette

**Method**

1. In a medium bowl combine cheese, wine, yogurt, scallion, garlic and 2 teaspoons lemon zest. Cover and chill overnight or for up to 2 days.
2. Preheat grill. In a small bowl combine the remaining 1 teaspoon lemon zest, red onion, and parsley. Arrange bread rounds on a baking sheet and spread liberally with cheese mixture. Grill until cheese browns and bubbles (2–3 minutes). Garnish with parsley mixture. Serve hot.

Makes 4 dozen cocktail-sized toasts

## CELERIAC AND HERB REMOULADE

### Ingredients

1 celery root (about 1 pound)
3 tablespoons lemon juice
½ cup green onion stalks, minced
¼ cup scallion, minced
¼ cup Dijon-style mustard
½ cup olive oil
2 tablespoons whipping cream
¼ cup fresh mint, minced
salt and freshly ground pepper

### Method

1. Peel celery root; julienne with a mandoline or by hand, or grate coarsely. Immediately transfer to a stainless steel, glass or enamel bowl; add lemon juice and toss. Add onions and toss again.
2. Place mustard in a small bowl. Whisk in olive oil in a slow, steady stream to make a thick, creamy mixture. Whisk in cream and mint. Add dressing to vegetables and toss to blend. Season to taste with salt and pepper. Chill well before serving.

*Note:* Salad may be made up to 2 days ahead. Before serving, taste and adjust seasoning.

Serves 6

## CHILLED MUSSELS WITH CITRUS RELISH

(opposite)

### Ingredients

3 dozen mussels
1 cup dry white wine
1 ½ cups water
1 bay leaf
1 tablespoon fresh thyme, minced, or
1 teaspoon dried thyme
2 shallots, minced
1 tablespoon plus 1 teaspoon orange zest, grated
1 tablespoon plus 1 teaspoon lemon zest, grated
flesh of 1 small orange (pith, seeds and membranes removed), finely diced
2 tablespoons parsley, finely minced
salt and freshly ground pepper
lemon juice and orange juice, as needed
hearts of butter lettuce

### Method

1. Scrub mussels well; pull out hairy beard that protrudes from shell.
2. In a large pot combine wine, water, bay leaf, thyme, shallots, 1 tablespoon of orange zest and 1 tablespoon of lemon zest. Bring to a boil over high heat. Add mussels and cover. Cook over high heat for 1 minute, then uncover and remove any opened mussels to a separate bowl. Cover pot and continue cooking, shaking pot vigorously once or twice and uncovering every 20–30 seconds to check for opened mussels. Discard any mussels that don't open after 5 minutes of cooking.
3. After removing all mussels from pot, reduce liquid over high heat to ¾ cup. Strain through dampened cheesecloth into a large stainless steel, glass or ceramic bowl. Add orange and scallion, and remaining orange and lemon zest. Remove mussels from shells, reserving 12 half shells, and add to bowl. Stir to blend, then cover and refrigerate for at least 2 hours or up to 1 day. Remove from refrigerator 20 minutes before serving. Season to taste with salt and pepper. Add more lemon or orange juice if necessary.
4. To serve, spoon a mussel and some of its liquid into each of the 12 reserved shells. Line a large serving platter or individual salad plates with cup-shaped leaves of butter lettuce. Spoon remaining mussels into lettuce cups.

Serves 6 as an appetizer or 3 as a first course

## GOAT'S CHEESE SOUFFLE WITH WATERCRESS SALAD

### Ingredients

1 tablespoon unsalted butter, for greasing soufflé cups
2 tablespoons walnuts, finely ground
4 large eggs, separated
3 oz mild goat's cheese, at room temperature
2 tablespoons chives, minced
salt and freshly ground pepper
2 bunches watercress
2 tablespoons lemon juice
6 tablespoons walnut oil
½ cup walnut halves, toasted

### Method

1. Preheat oven to 400°F. Butter six ½-cup soufflé cups and dust bottom and sides with ground walnuts.
2. In a large bowl beat egg yolks, 2 ounces of the cheese, chives, salt, and pepper with a wire whisk until blended; cheese need not be totally smooth. Beat egg whites with a pinch of salt until stiff, but not dry. Gently fold beaten whites into cheese mixture. Spoon into prepared soufflé cups. Bury a small chunk of the remaining goat's cheese in the center of each soufflé. Bake until puffed and browned (about 12 minutes).
3. Meanwhile, wash and dry watercress and remove tough stems. In a small bowl, whisk together lemon juice and walnut oil to make dressing. Season to taste with salt and pepper.
4. When soufflés are ready, quickly toss watercress with walnuts and dressing. Put soufflé cups in the center of 6 large salad plates and surround each with watercress salad.

Serves 6

## WARM SALMON SALAD WITH GREEN BEANS

**Ingredients**

1 salmon fillet (2½ pounds), skin attached
2 cups dry white wine
8 oz green beans, ends trimmed, halved if large
1 heart (pale inner leaves only) cos lettuce
1 scallion, green part only, minced, for garnish

*Sauce*

1 egg yolk
juice of 1 lime
2 tablespoons white wine vinegar
6 scallions (white and pale green part only), coarsely chopped
1 cup olive oil
salt and freshly ground pepper

**Method**

1. In a blender or food processor, combine egg yolk, lime juice, vinegar and chopped scallions. Blend until smooth. With motor running, add oil drop by drop until sauce thickens, then add oil faster until all is used. Sauce should be thick and green. Remove to a bowl; stir in salt and pepper to taste. Sauce may be made up to 1 day ahead, covered and refrigerated.
2. Cut salmon crosswise into strips about 1 inch wide. Season with salt and pepper. In each of two 9 inch skillets over moderate heat, bring 1 cup wine to a simmer. Divide salmon between the skillets, return to a simmer, then adjust heat to maintain a simmer. Cover and cook for 3 minutes. Turn fillets over, cover, and cook for an additional 3 minutes. Check that fish is cooked. (Fish should be bright pink and firm, but still moist in the center.) With a slotted flat spatula, transfer fillets to clean kitchen towels to drain.
3. While fish is cooking, steam green beans over, not in, boiling salted water until tender-crisp (6–10 minutes, depending on size). On a large serving platter or on individual plates, arrange poached salmon, bundles of green beans, and heart of cos lettuce. Garnish platter with minced scallion. Pass sauce separately or drizzle some of sauce over salad and pass remaining sauce separately.

Serves 6

## SALADE NIÇOISE

**Ingredients**

4 small new potatoes
8 oz French green beans
3 medium eggs
4 tomatoes
½ white onion, thinly sliced
7 oz can tuna in oil, drained
8 black olives, halved
6 anchovy fillets (optional), halved
1 head cos lettuce, leaves separated

*Dressing*

4 tablespoons olive oil
1 tablespoon white wine vinegar
salt and black pepper to taste

*Garnish*

watercress sprigs

**Method**

1. After peeling, boil potatoes in a saucepan of salted water for 15–20 minutes, until tender. Drain and set aside until cool enough to handle, then dice. Meanwhile, cook beans in another saucepan of boiling salted water for 5 minutes or until tender. Drain and halve.
2. Put eggs into a saucepan of cold water. Bring to a boil, then cook for 10 minutes. Peel eggs under cold running water and cut into quarters lengthwise. Place tomatoes in a bowl and cover with boiling water. Leave for 30 seconds, then peel and cut into wedges.
3. Place potatoes, green beans, eggs, tomatoes, onion, tuna, olives and anchovies, if using, in a large bowl. Mix together dressing ingredients, pour over salad and toss lightly. Line platter with lettuce leaves and spoon salad on top.

Serves 4

## PICKLED BEET SALAD

**Ingredients**

8 medium beets
2 cups white wine vinegar
grated zest and juice of 1 lemon
½ cup sugar
6 sprigs thyme (each 3 inches long)
1 bay leaf
3 large cloves garlic, peeled and left whole
1 cup onion, thinly sliced
salt and freshly ground pepper
2 small heads curly endive
½ cup olive oil
3 tablespoons chives, minced, for garnish

**Method**

1. Scrub beets well. Place in a covered steamer and steam over boiling water until beets can be pierced easily with a knife (20–25 minutes). Add more water to steamer as necessary. Drain beets; when cool enough to handle, peel and slice into ¼ inch thick rounds.
2. In a medium saucepan over high heat, bring vinegar, lemon zest, lemon juice and sugar to a boil. Simmer for 3 minutes. Add sliced beets, turn to coat with liquid, and cook for 2 minutes. Transfer beets to a stainless steel, glass or enamel bowl, using a slotted spoon. Add thyme, bay leaf, garlic cloves and onion.
3. Over high heat, reduce liquid in saucepan to 1 cup. Pour over beets and toss to coat. Cool to room temperature, then transfer to a covered container and refrigerate for at least 3 days or for up to 2 weeks.
4. Remove beets from refrigerator 15 minutes before serving. Discard garlic, bay leaf and thyme. Season to taste with salt and pepper. Wash and dry endive and separate into leaves. Line individual salad plates or a large serving platter with endive. Top with beets and onions. Drizzle salad lightly with beets liquid then drizzle with olive oil and garnish with chives.

Serves 6

## CAMEMBERT FILO PARCELS

### Ingredients

9 sheets filo pastry, cut into 12 inch squares
5 oz butter, melted
3 tablespoons fresh rosemary, chopped plus extra to garnish
3 x 8 oz round Camembert cheeses
black pepper
3 tablespoons ready-made smooth apple sauce

### Method

1. Lay a sheet of filo pastry on a work surface, and brush lightly with butter. Take second sheet and place on top of first sheet at an angle to form a star shape with 8 points. Brush with butter. Take a third sheet and place again at an angle, to add 4 more points to the star shape, then brush with butter.
2. Sprinkle a little rosemary over the star and place Camembert in the center. Top with black pepper, 1 tablespoon of apple sauce and a little more rosemary.
3. Bring edges of the filo up over cheese, scrunch together to close at the top and brush with butter. Repeat for the other parcels. Cover loosely with plastic wrap and refrigerate for 2 hours.
4. Preheat oven to 400°F. Lightly butter a large baking sheet. Put parcels on sheet and bake for 25 minutes or until crisp and golden. Cool for 15 minutes, then serve warm with rosemary sprinkled over. Cut into quarters and serve as finger food.

Serves 12

## LOBSTER CREPES

### Ingredients

*Filling*

2 cups lobster meat, fresh or frozen
¼ cup butter
2 tablespoons onion, chopped
2 cups mushrooms
¼ cup flour
½ teaspoon salt
⅛ teaspoon pepper
1 cup milk
¼ cup butter, melted
¼ cup Gruyère cheese, grated

*Crêpes*

2 eggs
¾ cup flour
½ teaspoon salt
1 teaspoon dried parsley
1 teaspoon dried chives
1 cup milk

### Method

1. If frozen, thaw and chop lobster into bite-sized pieces. Melt butter and sauté onion and mushrooms 3–5 minutes. Stir in flour and seasonings; add milk and cook, stirring constantly, until thickened. Add lobster.
2. To make crêpes, beat eggs then add flour, salt and herbs. Add milk and beat until smooth. Refrigerate for 2 hours. For each crêpe, pour 2–3 tablespoons of batter in a heated, oiled pan. Brown lightly on each side.
3. Spoon 3 tablespoons of filling into each crêpe, roll up and arrange in a baking dish. Brush with half the melted butter and sprinkle with grated cheese. Bake at 425°F for 5–8 minutes. Stir remaining melted butter into remaining filling and serve over crêpes.

Serves 4

# French breads

# Beautiful BREAD

Few home cooks ever make their own bread in France because good bread is so readily available at nearby *boulangeries*. In most homes, bread is a daily—and sometimes twice daily—purchase. Because it is such a large part of the French diet, especially in poor regions, the government regulates the content, size, and price of the most basic loaves.

The basic daily bread of the French is the long, slender, white flour loaf known as a baguette. It contains nothing but flour, water, yeast and salt and thus stays fresh for only one day. The same dough is made into other popular shapes, such as the skinny *ficelle* or the short, plump *bâtard*.

Some bakeries make a denser, chewier bread using a sourdough starter. This type of bread is generally known as *pain de campagne* (country bread); it may contain whole wheat or rye flour. Thanks to the starter, these breads stay fresh for at least a couple of days.

Both baguettes and *pain de campagne* are suitable for serving as an accompaniment to a French meal. However, the baguette, with its mild flavor, is possibly a better choice when the meal is somewhat formal; the full-flavored *pain de campagne* is more appropriate when the food is rustic and hearty.

## BRIOCHE

**Ingredients**

¼ cup superfine sugar
2 teaspoons salt
1 tablespoon yeast
½ cup warm water
5 cups unbleached bread flour
6 eggs, at room temperature
8 oz unsalted butter, cut into dice
1 egg yolk, beaten

**Method**

1. Combine sugar, salt, yeast, warm water and 1 cup of flour in a bowl and beat with a wooden spoon until well mixed. Transfer mixture to the bowl of a mixer and add eggs, one at a time, beating well after each addition. Gradually add 2 more cups of flour.
2. With mixer on low speed, add pieces of butter, several at a time. When all butter has been added, begin sprinkling remaining 2 cups of flour over dough slowly, using only as much as is necessary to give the dough a very creamy, butterly texture. When it has this consistency, it is ready to rise.
3. Gently place dough in a well-oiled bowl and cover tightly with plastic wrap. Place in a cool place to rise until doubled in size (approximately 2 hours). Gently deflate the dough, re-form into a circle and return to the bowl. Allow to rise for about 10 hours or overnight in the refrigerator.
4. Gently turn dough out onto a well-floured benchtop and divide dough into twelve equal pieces. Pinch a small amount of dough from each piece and roll both large and small pieces into ball shapes. Place large ball in very well-greased fluted tins and then carefully push your finger through center of dough to the bottom. Elongate bottom of small ball and gently place this into the hole created by your finger.
5. Allow brioche dough to rise in a cool place until doubled in size. This should take about 45 minutes. Be careful that dough does not over-rise. Glaze with well-beaten egg yolk and bake in a 400°F oven for 10–15 minutes for small brioche, and 25–30 minutes for large ones. When cooked, remove from tins and cool completely on a wire rack.

***Note:*** Any leftover brioche (if you should be so lucky) makes fabulous French toast or a sublime bread and butter pudding.

Makes 12 small brioche or 2 loaves

## HOLIDAY SPICE BREAD

### Ingredients

2 tablespoons unsalted butter, melted
all-purpose flour for dusting pan
1 cup almonds, coarsely chopped
½ cup golden raisins
¼ teaspoon salt
¼ teaspoon nutmeg
1 teaspoon ground ginger
1½ teaspoon cinnamon
1 teaspoon anise seed
pinch of ground cloves
1½ teaspoon dried orange peel, minced
1 teaspoon baking powder
2 teaspoons baking soda
1 cup water
1 cup honey
¼ cup brown sugar
1 large egg, lightly beaten
⅓ cup dark rum
1 cup rye flour
1 cup whole wheat flour
1 cup bread flour

### Method

1. Preheat oven to 400°F. Use butter to grease one 8-cup loaf pan (6 x 10 inch) or two 4½-cup loaf pans (3 x 6 inch). Dust bottom and sides with flour, shaking out excess.
2. In a large mixing bowl, combine almonds, golden raisins, salt, nutmeg, ginger, cinnamon, anise seed, cloves, orange peel, baking powder and baking soda. Bring water to a boil in a medium saucepan over moderate heat. Add honey and stir to dissolve. Add brown sugar and stir to dissolve. Remove from heat; allow to cool for 5 minutes.
3. Add egg and rum to honey and sugar mixture and whisk to blend. Add to spice mixture and stir to blend. Add flours and stir just until flour is absorbed (about 50 strokes). Transfer batter to prepared pan and bake for 10 minutes. Reduce heat to 350°F and bake until a cake tester inserted in center comes out dry (about 30 more minutes for one large pan; 20–25 more minutes for smaller pans). Bread will be very dark.
4. Let bread cool in pan on a rack for 5 minutes. Remove from tin and finish cooling on rack. Wrap tightly with plastic wrap and store at room temperature for 2–3 days before serving. Thinly slice to serve.

Makes one 6 x 10 inch loaf or two 3 x 6 inch loaves

## CROISSANTS

**Ingredients**

7–8 cups unbleached bread flour
1 level tablespoon malt extract
4 tablespoons sugar
2 teaspoons salt
2 tablespoons yeast
1½ oz evaporated milk
1½ oz warm water
1 pound unsalted butter, chilled
a little milk, to glaze

**Method**

1. Place flour, malt extract, sugar, salt, yeast, milk and warm water in a mixing bowl and combine with a wooden spoon.
2. When ingredients begin to stick together, turn out mass of dough and knead mixture gently on a well-floured surface until all ingredients are incorporated and dough is smooth and elastic (about 10 minutes). Shape into a rough square, flour well and place on a flat oven tray, covered loosely with plastic wrap. Place in refrigerator for a minimum of 2 hours, or overnight.
3. When chilled, remove dough from refrigerator and roll out to a rectangular shape approximately 12 x 24 inches. Using a vegetable peeler or cheese slicer, cut slices of chilled butter and lay them on the bottom two thirds of dough.
4. Carefully seal seam, turn dough so seam is at the side and gently, but firmly, roll out dough to a large rectangle. Fold dough as before, bringing top third down and the bottom third up, then flour well and place on tray and chill for at least 2 hours. Repeat the above rolling, buttering, folding and rolling process again, using remaining butter. Again, chill for a minimum of 2 hours.
5. When ready to shape croissants, flour bench well and firmly. Gently roll out dough to a thickness of about ⅛ inch and about 24 x 16 inches. With a sharp knife, cut dough in half so that you have two pieces (each 24 x 8 inch).
6. Mark out triangles with base of about 3 inches and height of 8 inches so that full width of dough is used and each triangle joins the one before, with no waste. Cut out these triangles. Place a small cut in middle of base of each triangle then roll triangles up gently, but firmly, from base towards point of triangle. Continue rolling croissants up to form croissant shape and place them on an oiled baking sheet, making sure that each point lies under the croissant.
7. Gently curve corners to resemble a croissant. Allow to rise at room temperature until doubled in size and carefully glaze with milk. Allow to rest for 30 minutes then bake at 475°F for approximately 10 minutes, watching for signs of burning. When baked, allow to cool on wire rack.

Serves 6

## FRENCH SOURDOUGH WITH CARAMELIZED ONIONS

**Ingredients**

1 cup whole wheat flour
1 cup plain yogurt
1 teaspoon sugar
1 teaspoon yeast
¼ cup warm water
1 ½ oz butter
4 large onions, sliced
1 tablespoon dried yeast
¼ cup warm water
1 teaspoon sugar
1 ½ teaspoons salt
1 teaspoon baking soda
2–3 cups whole wheat flour

**Method**

1. In a large mixing bowl, combine flour, yogurt, sugar, yeast and warm water. Mix well, then set aside and allow to ferment at room temperature for 24 hours.
2. The next day, melt butter in large skillet and add sliced onions. Stir to coat with butter and cook over medium heat until onions are translucent. Cover saucepan with lid and continue to cook on low heat for about 40 minutes or until onions are golden brown. Set aside to cool.
3. Mix yeast, water and sugar together and allow to sit for 5 minutes. Mix this mixture into prepared starter dough along with salt, half the caramelized onions and baking soda. Slowly add more flour until dough forms a shaggy mass.
4. When dough is quite smooth and manageable, allow it to rise for 30 minutes at room temperature. Remove dough from bowl and divide in half. Shape each piece of dough into a flat oval loaf, about ¾ inch thick, using your fingertips to add texture to dough. Scatter remaining onions over surface of dough then drizzle dough with some olive oil and allow to rest again for 30 minutes. Preheat oven to 400°F. Spray dough with water and bake 25–30 minutes, or until crusty and golden.

Serves 6

## FRENCH OLIVE LADDER BREAD

**Ingredients**

1 tablespoon yeast
3 cups warm water
4 cups bread flour
2 cups whole wheat flour
$\frac{1}{4}$ cup buckwheat flour
2 tablespoons olive oil
2 teaspoons sea salt
1–2 cups black olives, chopped
olive oil and sea salt to garnish

**Method**

1. Combine yeast, water and 2 cups of bread flour and mix well with a wooden spoon for 3 minutes, until mixture resembles a thick batter. Cover with plastic wrap and allow to rest for 2–3 hours at room temperature.
2. Add all remaining ingredients, except garnish, and mix to form a soft dough. Turn out onto a floured bench and knead well for about 10 minutes, adding a little extra flour if dough is too sticky. Return dough to an oiled bowl and allow to rise once more for 1 hour.
3. Remove dough from bowl and divide into four even pieces. Working with one piece at a time, flatten dough to a thickness of $\frac{1}{2}$ inch and approximately 12 x 4 inches. With a sharp knife, make deep cuts in dough $\frac{1}{2}$ inch inside each edge and extending from one side of dough to other. When you have made four cuts, gently pull top and bottom of dough to stretch cuts, making cuts look like rungs on a ladder. Complete other pieces of dough in same manner. Transfer breads to oiled baking sheets and allow to rise for 30 minutes at room temperature. Brush with olive oil and scatter a little sea salt over surface.
4. Bake at 400°F for 20–25 minutes, until loaves are crisp and golden.

***Variation:*** This dough also makes a fabulous loaf or small rolls. To make loaf, shape dough into a tight ball and allow to rise at room temperature on oiled baking sheet until almost doubled. Score surface with sharp knife then bake at 400°F for 40 minutes. To make rolls, divide dough into 16 pieces and roll each into small ovals. Allow to rise at room temperature until doubled then bake at 400°F for 20 minutes.

Serves 6

## FRENCH BAGUETTES

**Ingredients**

1 tablespoon dried yeast
1 tablespoon sugar
1 tablespoon salt
5–6 cups unbleached bread flour
2 cups warm water
1 egg white, beaten, for glazing

**Method**

1. Mix yeast, sugar, salt and 4 cups of flour with water, adding remaining flour, half a cup at a time, until dough is very soft, but still manageable enough to knead. Turn dough out onto a floured surface and incorporate only as much flour as needed to prevent sticking, then knead very well until dough is soft and satiny. Place in oiled bowl and allow to rise at room temperature until doubled in size (about 2 hours). If you have time, this dough would benefit from a longer rise.
2. Turn dough out and cut into three or four equal portions (depending on required size of baguettes). Roll dough out to an oval shape and roll up tightly, Swiss-roll fashion. Roll shaped dough back and forth to lengthen baguette.
3. Brush surface with beaten egg white or water then sprinkle with flour. With a very sharp knife, slash tops of baguettes diagonally at 4 inch intervals and allow dough to rise at room temperature until doubled in size (about 30 minutes). Bake at 425°F for 20–30 minutes, until crisp and pale golden.

*Note:* For crispier crust, spray loaves with water at 10 minute intervals during baking.

Serves 4

## FOUGASSE PROVENÇALE

**Ingredients**

2 cups bread flour
1 tablespoon yeast
1 ½ cups warm water
3 pounds all-purpose flour
1 ½ tablespoon salt
1 tablespoon yeast
8 cloves garlic, freshly minced
4 oz olive oil
1 cup warm water
sea salt to garnish

**Method**

1. To make starter, mix flour, yeast and water together until mixture resembles a semi-thick batter. Allow to prove at room temperature, covered, in a non-reactive bowl for up to 3 days (8 hours minimum) to develop a lovely mature flavor.

2. To make dough, mix the starter, 2 pounds of flour and salt, yeast, garlic and half the oil with warm water to make a soft dough. Knead on floured surface until dough is silky smooth, adding remaining flour as necessary until dough is no longer sticky. Allow dough to rise at room temperature in an oiled bowl until doubled in size (about 2 hours).

3. Divide dough into 12 pieces and, using your fingertips or rolling pin, shape into ovals about ½ inch thick. With a sharp knife, make diagonal cuts through dough and then gently stretch to open up holes. Brush with remaining oil and sprinkle with a little sea salt if desired.

4. Allow to rise for 30 minutes at room temperature then bake at 250°F for 15–20 minutes, spraying with water twice during baking, (If you prefer, place baking pan of boiling water in bottom of oven to create steam.) Remove from oven and brush once more with olive oil before cooling.

Serves 6

# soups

# A hearty meal OR REFINED STARTER

In the provinces, a workman who says, 'I'm going for some soup,' means he is heading home for the evening meal. Families who have enjoyed a full lunch are often content with a thick creamed vegetable soup or broth with vegetables and meat plus a baguette for dinner.

*Bouillabaisse*, the thick fish soup from Provence, can be a meal in itself. Some call it a stew. Authentically, *bouillabaisse* contains at least six fish types and becomes a real party *potage* (soup) if other seafood is added. If *bouillabaisse* is part of a lunch or dinner, other courses should be light.

French onion soup is also an appetizing starter, particularly if topped with dried bread and grated cheese; grilled to become a gratinée; or given a pastry hat and baked—another real party piece.

Most popular of all are creamed vegetable soups such as *vichyssoise*, or potato and leek soup. This soup is delicious hot or cold. Cold soups, like iced cucumber soup, are refreshing summer starters. Cauliflower, pumpkin, peas, Brussels sprouts, celery, zucchini, mushrooms, spinach, asparagus, watercress, carrots (terrific with orange juice added), leek (thickened and sweetened with pears), garlic, broccoli and tomatoes make wonderful creamed soups.

Another style of French soup is consommé, a broth yielded from boiled meat and vegetables that are removed before the soup is clarifed. It has a distinctive flavor, without grease or cloudiness.

## EASY FRENCH ONION SOUP

**Ingredients**

2 oz butter
1½ pound onions, peeled and thinly sliced
1 clove garlic, peeled and crushed
2 teaspoons all-purpose flour
5 cups beef bouillon,
fresh or made with bouillon cubes
salt and black pepper
4 slices French bread, about 1 inch thick
3 oz Gruyère cheese, grated

**Method**

1. Heat butter in large heavy saucepan over low heat until it melts and begins to foam. Add onions and garlic, cover pan, and cook, stirring often, for 30–35 minutes, until onions are golden brown.
2. Add flour and cook, stirring constantly, for 2–3 minutes. Pour in bouillon little by little, stirring all the time, and bring to a boil. Reduce heat and simmer, covered, for 30 minutes. Season to taste with salt and black pepper.
3. Preheat grill to high. Place French bread on one side under grill, then top uncooked side with grated cheese. Grill until cheese has melted and browned. Pour soup into individual bowls and place a piece of 'cheese on toast' on top of each serving.

Serves 4

## LOBSTER BISQUE

### Ingredients

1 small lobster, cooked
1 large carrot, peeled and diced
1 small onion, finely chopped
4 oz butter
¾ cup dry white wine
bouquet garni (see page 82)
6½ cups fish or chicken bouillon
⅓–¾ cup rice
salt, pepper and ground cayenne pepper
½ cup cream
2 tablespoons brandy
parsley, chopped, to garnish

### Method

1. Cut lobster in half, lengthwise, and remove flesh from shell. Set aside. Wrap shell in an old tea towel, crush with a hammer and set aside. Sauté carrot and onion in half the butter until softened, but without coloring (about 5 minutes). Add crushed shell, sauté for a further minute, then add wine. Boil until reduced by half. Add bouquet garni, bouillon and rice.
2. After about 20 minutes, when rice is tender, remove large pieces of shell and bouquet garni. Purée in a food processor with the remainder of the butter, doing so in small batches. Pour through a strainer. Rinse out food processor to remove every trace of shell and purée strained liquid again, this time with lobster flesh, saving a few pieces for garnish. Reheat gently.
3. Add salt, pepper and cayenne to taste then stir in cream, brandy and reserved lobster pieces, cut into thin slices. Serve very hot garnished with parsley.

Serves 4

## BOUILLABAISSE

**Ingredients**

6 pounds mixed fish and seafood, including firm white fish fillets, shrimp, mussels, crab and squid rings
1/4 cup olive oil
2 cloves garlic, crushed
2 large onions, chopped
2 leeks, sliced
2 x 14 oz canned tomatoes, undrained and mashed
1 tablespoon fresh thyme, chopped or 1 teaspoon dried thyme
2 tablespoons fresh basil, chopped or 1 1/2 teaspoons dried basil
2 tablespoons fresh parsley, chopped
2 bay leaves
2 tablespoons orange rind, finely grated
1 teaspoon saffron threads
1 cup dry white wine
1 cup fish bouillon
black pepper, freshly ground

**Method**

1. Remove bones and skin from fish fillets and cut into 1 inch cubes. Peel and devein shrimp, leaving tails intact. Scrub and remove beards from mussels. Cut crab into quarters. Set aside.
2. Heat oil in a large saucepan over medium heat. Add garlic, onions and leeks and cook for 5 minutes or until onions are golden. Add tomatoes, thyme, basil, parsley, bay leaves, orange rind, saffron, wine and bouillon and bring to a boil. Reduce heat and simmer for 30 minutes.
3. Add fish and crab and cook for 10 minutes. Add remaining seafood and cook for 5 minutes longer or until fish and seafood are cooked. Season to taste with black pepper.
4. To serve, place in a soup tureen and allow your guests to serve themselves.

Serves 6

## VEGETABLE SOUP WITH BASIL PUREE

### Ingredients

½ cup small dried white beans

12 cups *fond de volaille* (see page 82)

1 onion, cut into ½ inch dice

1 leek (white part only), sliced ⅓ inch thick

1 stalk celery, cut into ½ inch dice

½ large potato, peeled and cut into ⅓ inch dice

2 carrots, cut into ½ inch dice

1 cup tomato, peeled, seeded and coarsely chopped

¾ cup green beans, cut into 1 inch lengths

2 small zucchini, cut into ⅓ inch dice

½ cup dried macaroni

1 cup Gruyère cheese, grated

*Pistou*

2 tablespoons garlic, minced

4 tablespoons olive oil

1 cup fresh basil leaves

½ cup Gruyère cheese, grated

### Method

1. Put white beans in a bowl and cover with 1 inch of cold water. Let soak overnight. Drain.

2. In a large pot over moderate heat, bring bouillon to a boil. Add white beans, reduce heat to low, and simmer for 35 minutes. Add onion, leek, celery, potato and carrots. Simmer for 20 minutes. Add tomato, green beans, zucchini and macaroni and simmer until all vegetables are tender (about 20 minutes more).

3. Meanwhile, make *pistou*. Place all ingredients in a blender or food processor and blend until smooth. Makes about ½ cup.

4. Serve soup in warm bowls; garnish each serving with 2 teaspoons *pistou*. Place extra *pistou* and Gruyère on the table.

Serves 6

## PROVENÇAL FISH SOUP WITH GARLIC MAYONNAISE

**Ingredients**

3 tablespoons olive oil
1 ½ cups onion, chopped
1 leek (white and pale green part only), cleaned and cut into ½ inch rounds
1 stalk celery, chopped
1 carrot, chopped
3 pounds meaty fish bones
1 cup dry white wine
2 cups water
zest of ½ orange (removed with a sharp vegetable peeler)
3 large sprigs thyme or ½ teaspoon dried thyme
3 bay leaves
1 teaspoon pepper, freshly ground
1 teaspoon fennel seeds
salt
2½ pounds fish fillets (preferably a mixture of sea bass, cod, snapper, halibut), cut into 1½ inch cubes
croutons
3 tablespoons minced chives for garnish

*Aioli*

1½ tablespoons garlic, coarsely chopped
1 teaspoon salt, plus extra salt to taste
3 egg yolks
1 cup olive oil
lemon juice

**Method**

1. In large pot over moderate heat, heat olive oil. Add onion, leek, celery and carrot. Reduce heat to low and cook gently until vegetables are soft (about 15 minutes). Add fish bones, wine, water, orange zest, thyme, bay leaves, pepper and fennel seeds. Raise heat to moderate and bring mixture to a boil, skimming any scum that rises to the surface. Reduce heat to maintain a simmer and cook for 35 minutes. Strain soup into a clean pot. Season to taste with salt.

2. Meanwhile, to make *aioli*, process garlic, salt and yolks in food processor until smooth. With motor running, begin adding oil, drop by drop through feed tube. When mixture is thick and smooth, add oil faster. Transfer to a bowl and season to taste with lemon juice, adding more salt if necessary. Makes 2 cups.

3. Return broth to a simmer over moderate heat. Add fish cubes. If using only one type of fish, add all at once, otherwise add firm fish first and more delicate fish about 2 minutes later. Cook until fish just begins to flake (3–4 minutes total). Remove fish with a slotted spoon to a warm platter. Moisten with ¼ cup broth, cover and keep warm in a low oven.

4. Put 1 cup of *aioli* in a medium bowl. Whisk in ½ cup hot broth. Whisk this mixture back into pot. Cook over low heat, stirring constantly with a wooden spoon, until visibly thickened (about 3 minutes). Do not allow soup to boil or it will curdle. Serve garnished with croutons and chives.

Serves 6

# meat

# Cuts above THE REST

All parts of the sheep are used in French cooking, including sweetbreads: the thymus gland of milk-fed lamb or veal. Difficult to obtain in some countries, sweetbreads remain France's favorite offal. Lamb from Normandy and Brittany is the crème de la crème of French meats and is priced accordingly. Lamb and mutton are interchangeable in French recipes, but cheaper mutton cuts, full of flavor, are preferred for stewing.

Every part of beef cattle, including the tongue and brains, can be utilized, and all pig parts can be roasted or salted. The head of the calf and pig are bought to make brawn. Roast pork is usually marinated for several hours before cooking, or left overnight after rubbing with salt, garlic and oil. Goat and horsemeat are also eaten in France and rabbit is regarded as a delicacy. Offal, particularly liver and kidney, is prepared frequently as it is less expensive.

French butchering methods are different from those in many other countries. Meat cuts are separated along the muscles. Roast dinners also differ in France. Most legs of meat are boned and roasted in butter, yielding meat sediments and juices on which to base a sauce. While *nouvelle cuisine* has reduced the reliance on cream, flour and cheese in sauces, taste traditions are hard to break.

Whichever way they cook it, the French make meat taste marvellous.

## COLD ROAST PORK WITH PRUNES

**Ingredients**

8 oz large prunes, pitted
2 cups slightly sweet white wine
2 teaspoons dried thyme
2 tablespoons paprika
1 tablespoons dried savory
2 bay leaves, coarsely crumbled, or
 1 teaspoon bay leaf, ground
1 tablespoon salt
2 teaspoons black peppercorns
6 pound center-cut pork loin, boned but not tied
4 large cloves garlic, peeled and thinly sliced

**Method**

1. Soak prunes in wine overnight. Drain, reserving wine.
2. Grind thyme, paprika, savory, bay leaf, salt and peppercorns to a fine powder in a spice grinder.
3. Trim away all but 1/8 inch fat on surface of pork. Butterfly roast by making a long, lengthwise cut through the center, not quite all the way through. The loin should open like a book. Rub cut surfaces with 2 teaspoons of spice mixture, then cover with prunes. Using kitchen string, tie roast at 1 inch intervals. With a small, sharp knife, cut slits about 1/3 inch deep in fat side of pork. Roll garlic slivers in spice mixture and insert in slits. Coat roast with any remaining spice mixture. Place on a plate, cover with plastic wrap and refrigerate for 12 hours.
4. Preheat oven to 350°F. Transfer roast to a rack in a roasting pan and cook until meat thermometer registers 150°F (about 2 hours), basting every 25 minutes with reserved wine. Remove roast from oven, cool to room temperature, then cover and refrigerate. Slice thinly to serve.

Serves 12

## LEG OF LAMB WITH WHITE BEANS

**Ingredients**

2½ cups dried white beans
1 cup salt pork, diced (⅓ inch cubes)
butter (optional)
½ cup carrot, minced
½ cup onion, minced
½ cup celery, minced
bouquet garni (see page 82)
2 cups plus 2 tablespoons dry white wine
3½ cups *fond de volaille* (see page 82)
1 leg lamb (4½ pounds), boned and butterflied
2 cloves garlic, peeled and thinly sliced
2 teaspoons salt
1 teaspoon pepper, freshly ground
1 teaspoon fresh thyme, minced
  or ½ teaspoon dried thyme
1 bay leaf, crumbled
2 tablespoons olive oil
2 tablespoons parsley, finely minced for garnish

**Method**

1. Put beans in large pot; cover with 8 cups cold water and let soak overnight. (To quick-soak, bring beans and water to a boil for 1 minute, then cover and let stand for 1 hour.) Drain beans and set aside.
2. In an ovenproof casserole large enough to hold both lamb and beans, render pork over low heat until crisp. With a slotted spoon, transfer pork to paper towels to drain. Pour off all but 3 tablespoons fat in pan, or add enough butter to make 3 tablespoons. Add carrots, onions and celery and sauté over moderately low heat until softened (about 10 minutes). Add drained beans, salt pork, bouquet garni, 2 cups wine, and just enough *fond de volaille* to barely cover.
3. Bring mixture to a simmer over moderately high heat, stirring. Cover, reduce heat to maintain a simmer, and cook until beans are just tender. Depending on age of beans, cooking may take up to 3 hours.
4. With a small, sharp knife, cut 10 slits in lamb about ⅓ inch long and ¼ inch deep. Insert a garlic sliver in each slit. In a blender combine remaining garlic, salt, pepper, thyme, bay leaf, oil and remaining 2 tablespoons wine. Blend to mix. Rub mixture evenly over meat. Cover lamb and marinate in refrigerator for at least 5 hours or overnight.
5. Preheat oven to 350°F. Make a space in center of beans large enough to hold lamb. Transfer lamb to casserole. Sprinkle beans with just enough bouillon (about 1 cup) to moisten them. Roast, uncovered, until lamb is done to your liking (about 1 hour and 10 minutes for rare meat). Let stand for 10 minutes before carving.
6. To serve, arrange sliced lamb on a warm serving platter. Serve beans in a separate dish or surround lamb with beans. Garnish beans with minced parsley.

Serves 6

## CHAMPAGNE SAUSAGES WITH MUSTARD SAUCE

### Ingredients

1/3 cup soft bread crumbs
2 pound pork shoulder
1 shallot, peeled and halved
2 cloves garlic, peeled and coarsely chopped
1 large egg
1/2 teaspoon pepper, freshly ground
1 teaspoon ground ginger
1 teaspoon cloves, ground
pinch of nutmeg
1/2 teaspoon salt
1/2 cup champagne
1/4 cup scallion, chopped

*Sauce moutarde*

1/4 cup stone-ground honey mustard
3/4 cup sour cream or crème fraîche (see page 82)
salt and freshly ground pepper

### Method

1. Preheat oven to 350°F. Toast breadcrumbs for 5 minutes, then set aside. Bone pork and cut meat into 2 inch cubes; do not trim away fat.
2. To make sausages, combine breadcrumbs, pork, shallot, garlic, egg, pepper, ginger, cloves, nutmeg, salt and champagne in a food processor. Process until meat is well chopped, but not pasty. Add scallion and process for 2 seconds just to blend.
3. Form mixture into 6 patties. Transfer to a large plate, cover with plastic wrap and refrigerate for 4–8 hours.
4. To make *sauce moutarde*, whisk together mustard and sour cream. Season to taste with salt and pepper. Makes 1 cup.
5. Prepare a medium-hot charcoal fire. Grill patties, turning once, until done throughout (about 15 minutes total cooking time). Serve on a warm platter with a small dollop of *sauce moutarde* in the center.

Serves 6

## FRESH PORK AND SPINACH SAUSAGE

### Ingredients

2 tablespoons unsalted butter
4 oz chicken liver
1 pound pork, coarsely ground
1 egg
1 cup onion, minced
2 tablespoons garlic, minced
2 cups fresh spinach leaves, coarsely chopped and tightly packed
2 teaspoons fresh sage, minced, or 1 teaspoon dried sage
2 tablespoons all-purpose flour
1 cup soft breadcrumbs
½ teaspoon salt
1 teaspoon pepper, freshly ground
pinch of nutmeg
8 oz caul fat (see note)
sage sprigs for garnish

### Method

1. Melt butter in a large skillet over moderate heat. Add liver and sauté until lightly browned (about 1½ minutes on each side). Transfer liver to a plate. Add pork and sauté until it is no longer pink (about 3 minutes).
2. Transfer pork and liver to a food processor and process 2 seconds. Add egg, onion, garlic, spinach, sage, flour, breadcrumbs, salt, pepper and nutmeg. Pulse several times until blended.
3. Preheat oven to 375°F. Shape sausage into 6 large or 12 small patties. Cut caul into squares and wrap each patty in caul. Bake on lightly oiled baking sheet until browned (10–15 minutes for small sausages or 25 minutes for large ones). To serve, transfer to a warm platter and garnish with sage.

*Note*: Caul fat is a lacy, net-like fat that surrounds a cow's stomach. Most specialty butchers can get it for you with a few days' notice.

Serves 6

## PROVENÇAL BEEF STEW

**Ingredients**

3 pound beef chuck steak
1 1/3 cups white wine vinegar
4 tablespoons olive oil
1 teaspoon salt
1/2 teaspoon pepper, freshly ground
1 bay leaf
2 cloves garlic, peeled and crushed with flat side of knife
1 teaspoon fresh thyme, minced or 1/2 teaspoon dried thyme
2 narrow strips orange zest
2 cups dry red wine
2 tablespoons parsley, minced for garnish
hot buttered noodles to serve

**Method**

1. Trim meat of excess fat and cut into 2 inch cubes. In a large bowl whisk together vinegar, 2 tablespoons of oil, salt, pepper, bay leaf, garlic, thyme and orange zest. Add meat, cover bowl with plastic wrap and refrigerate for 12–18 hours. Drain meat, reserving marinade. Pat meat dry with paper towels.
2. In a Dutch oven or a large skillet with a lid, heat remaining 2 tablespoons olive oil over moderately high heat. Brown meat well on all sides. Add wine and reserved marinade. Bring to a simmer and cook, uncovered, for 3 minutes. Reduce heat to maintain a bare simmer. Cover and cook until meat is meltingly tender (about 3 hours). For best flavor, allow to cool to room temperature then refrigerate, covered, overnight. Reheat gently to serve. Ladle stew into warm soup bowls or over buttered noodles if desired, and garnish each serving with parsley.

Serves 6

## LAMB SHANKS WITH GARLIC SAUCE

**Ingredients**

6 lamb shanks (about 1–1½ pounds each), cut into 3–4 pieces
2 bulbs garlic, separated into unpeeled cloves
6 large tomatoes, cored
3 tablespoons olive oil
1 tablespoon salt
1½ teaspoon pepper, freshly ground
½ cup shallots, minced
4 large sprigs fresh thyme or 1 teaspoon dried thyme
1½ cups dry red wine

**Method**

1. Preheat oven to 300°F. Trim shanks of any visible fat; reserve. In a large roasting pan, drizzle garlic cloves and tomatoes with oil. Roast, uncovered, for 45 minutes. Transfer tomatoes and garlic to a bowl. When cool enough to handle, peel tomatoes and garlic. Chop tomatoes coarsely.
2. Raise oven temperature to 400°F. Season shanks with salt and pepper. Roast for 30 minutes; turn shanks, add shallots, and cook for 15 minutes.
3. Spoon off all but 2 tablespoons fat. Add tomatoes, garlic, thyme and red wine to pan. Cover and bake for 30 minutes. Uncover and continue baking for 30 minutes. Turn shanks and continue cooking until they are fork-tender (20–30 minutes more). Remove from oven, discard thyme.
4. Transfer shanks to a warm platter, cover loosely with aluminum foil and keep warm in a low oven. Pour contents of pan into a measuring cup and let settle for 5 minutes. Spoon off any fat that floats to surface. Place contents of cup in a blender or food processor and blend until smooth and silky. Reheat sauce and spoon over and around shanks to serve.

Serves 6

## CASSEROLE OF PRESERVED DUCK, PORK AND BEANS

**Ingredients**

2 pounds small dried white beans
1 teaspoon dried thyme or
 2 teaspoons fresh thyme, minced
2 onions, peeled and halved,
 each half stuck with a clove
1 bay leaf
1 bulb garlic, halved crosswise
2 ham hocks
2 teaspoons pepper, freshly ground
salt
6 duck legs
2 tablespoons fat
2 cups onion, coarsely chopped
1 tablespoon garlic, minced
2 pounds garlic pork sausage links,
 cut into 2 inch chunks
$\frac{1}{2}$ cup day-old breadcrumbs

**Method**

1. Cover beans with cold water and soak overnight. Drain beans and place in a large pot. Add thyme, onion halves, bay leaf, garlic bulb, ham hocks and black pepper. Add cold water to cover by 1 inch. Bring to a simmer over moderately high heat. Reduce heat to low and cook for 2 hours, adding water as necessary to keep beans barely covered. Taste beans and add salt if necessary. Remove onion halves and garlic bulb. Transfer beans, bay leaf, and ham hocks to a large earthenware casserole.
2. Bring duck legs to room temperature, letting excess fat drip off. Wipe duck legs with paper towels.
3. Preheat oven to 300°F. In a medium skillet over low heat, melt 2 tablespoons fat. Add chopped onion and minced garlic and sauté for 10 minutes. Add to beans along with sausage and duck legs. Cover loosely with aluminum foil and bake for $1\frac{1}{4}$ hours. Uncover and sprinkle with breadcrumbs. Bake for 30 minutes more. Serve directly from the casserole dish.

Serves 6

# seafood & fish

# Fruits of sea AND RIVER

France's most prized seafood is the yabbie (*écrevisse*). These lowly freshwater crustaceans are now served at top tables. Australia exports yabbies to France as does Canada and Turkey, because the French have largely fished out their own supplies.

Most French recipes alter according to region, but seafood is often served raw (oysters *naturel*) or boiled (mussels, yabbies and lobster) throughout France. A pre-cooked lobster should be eaten cold and never reheated or the texture will be rubbery and the flavor diminished. Scallops, fish and other seafood are often sautéed, pan- or deep fried in egg and breadcrumbs or in batter. Squid is lovely when braised and oysters, with tidbits or sauces in their shells, may be lightly grilled.

Trout with almonds is a commonly ordered fish dish in French restaurants. If trout is unavailable, home cooks can prepare trout recipes with whiting, bream or flounder. For grilling, choose fish that will not break up when turned, such as red mullet, garfish, pike, mackerel, or tuna steaks.

Bream, snapper, perch, yellow belly, whiting and trout (wonderful stuffed), lend themselves well to baking whole in minimal butter, white wine, cider, fish bouillon, cider, milk or cream. These liquids are also suitable for poaching fish such as garfish, snapper, perch and whiting. Steaming maintains the natural flavor of fish and is also gentle for delicate fish that can break up while cooking.

Fish rissoles or quenelles are never more delicious than when served Lyonnaise-style in choux pastry.

## SALT COD–STUFFED BELL PEPPERS

**Ingredients**

3 pound salt cod
5 1/2 cups milk
3 tablespoons olive oil
1 medium red onion, thinly sliced
6 cloves garlic, thinly sliced
1 1/2 cups whipping cream
1 pound potatoes, peeled and diced
3 tablespoons red wine vinegar
3/4 teaspoon cayenne pepper
6 tablespoons capers
6 tablespoons parsley, minced
1 large bunch scallions, chopped
8 green bell peppers
8 red bell peppers

**Method**

1. Cover cod with cold water. Refrigerate for 24 hours, changing water 3 times. The last time, add 4 cups of milk to water. Drain and cut cod into 10 pieces.
2. Preheat oven to 350°F. In a large skillet over moderate heat, heat oil. Add onion and garlic and toss to coat with oil. Add salt cod, 1 1/2 cups milk, cream and potatoes. Bring to a simmer, reduce heat to low and cook for 5 minutes, turning fish occasionally. Remove fish to a bowl with a slotted spoon. Cover skillet and simmer until potatoes are tender (8–10 minutes longer).
3. Lightly break fish apart with a fork. When potatoes are tender, add contents of skillet to bowl, along with vinegar, cayenne, capers, parsley and scallions. Stir to blend.
4. Cut tops off bell peppers and reserve. Remove seeds and cut out ribs. Stuff each bell pepper with 3/4 cup salt cod mixture. Replace tops of bell peppers. Place bell peppers in a roasting pan, cover with aluminum foil and bake until soft (30–35 minutes). Serve hot or warm.

Serves 16

## SAUMON EN CROUTE

### Ingredients

6 skinless salmon fillets, about 7 oz each
salt and black pepper
1 pound pack frozen puff pastry, thawed
2 tablespoons semolina
½ oz butter
finely grated rind and juice of ½ lemon
1 tablespoon each fresh dill, parsley and tarragon, chopped
1 large egg yolk mixed with 1 tablespoon milk, for glazing

*Herb sauce*

1½ oz chilled butter, cubed
1 tablespoon all-purpose flour
7 oz fish bouillon
3 tablespoons white wine
1 tablespoon heavy cream or whipping cream
1 tablespoon each fresh parsley, dill and tarragon, chopped
salt and pepper

### Method

1. Preheat oven to 425°F. Lay fillets side by side on baking paper, season and refrigerate. Cut pastry into 2 pieces, one slightly larger than the other. Roll smaller pieces into a rectangle just larger than fillets. Place on dampened baking sheet and prick. Refrigerate for 15 minutes.
2. Cook pastry sheets for 8–10 minutes until golden. Cool for a few minutes, then sprinkle with semolina. Lay fillets on pastry, dot with butter and sprinkle with lemon rind and juice, dill, parsley and tarragon. Season and set aside.
3. Roll rest of pastry in to a rectangle slightly larger than base. Place over fillets, tuck edges under base, score and brush with egg mixture. Cook for 15 minutes, then turn heat down to 325°F. Cook for a further 15 minutes. Cover with foil if pastry starts to burn.
4. Meanwhile, make sauce. Melt half the butter in pan. Add flour and stir for 1 minute, then add bouillon and wine and bring to a boil, stirring. Simmer, stirring occasionally, for 5 minutes or until thickened. Add cream, herbs and seasoning, then whisk in remaining melted butter. Serve with salmon.

Serves 6

## MONKFISH BOURGUIGNON

**Ingredients**

2 tablespoons vegetable oil
1½ oz butter
1 onion, chopped
7 oz rindless streaky bacon, chopped
7 oz button mushrooms, 2 oz chopped, the rest left whole
2 tablespoons all-purpose flour
2 cups red wine
1⅕ cups fish or chicken bouillon
1 dried bay leaf
fresh thyme sprigs
salt and black pepper
12 pickling onions
1 pound monkfish fillet, cut into cubes
fresh parsley, chopped, to garnish

**Method**

1. To make sauce, heat 1 tablespoon of oil and ½ oz of butter in a pan. Cook onion, 2 oz of bacon and chopped mushrooms for 5 minutes or until onion is golden. Stir in flour and cook for 1 minute. Stir in wine and bouillon. Add herbs and pepper. Simmer, covered, for 30 minutes, stirring occasionally.
2. Put pickling onions into boiling water for 2 minutes, then drain, dry and skin them. Heat remaining oil and ½ oz of butter in a skillet and fry onions for 5 minutes. Add remaining bacon and cook for 5 minutes. Remove from pan. Cook fish in 2 batches for 1 minute, browning on all sides, then remove from pan. Melt rest of butter and cook whole mushrooms for 2–3 minutes.
3. Strain sauce into a clean pan and add pickling onions and bacon. Cook gently for 10 minutes, then add monkfish and mushrooms and cook for a further 5 minutes, until fish is cooked through. Season and serve garnished with parsley.

Serves 4

## CRAB AU GRATIN

**Ingredients**

4 small crabs

1 tablespoon scallions, chopped

½ cup mushrooms, chopped

1 tablespoon butter or margarine

seasoning, to taste

2 tablespoons Cognac

*Gratin sauce*

2 tablespoons butter or margarine

2 tablespoons flour

1½ cups fish bouillon

½ cup cream

1 teaspoon Dijon mustard

1 teaspoon cayenne pepper

½ cup cheese, grated

**Method**

1. Prepare crab meat by taking the meat from the shell and legs and set to one side, being careful to keep the body shells intact. Sauté scallions and mushrooms in butter, season and add warmed ignited Cognac. Remove from heat.

2. Make sauce by melting butter in a saucepan and stirring in flour over low heat for 1–2 minutes. Gradually add fish bouillon and stir until sauce thickens then stir in cream, mustard and seasoning. Allow to simmer for 2–3 minutes then remove from heat and stir in crab meat and mushrooms. Spoon mixture into crab shells, sprinkle with cheese and bake at 300°F for 5 minutes.

Serves 4

## SCALLOPS MARINATED IN CITRUS JUICES

(opposite)

**Ingredients**

1 pound sea or bay scallops
juice of 2 limes
juice of 1 orange
grated rind of 1 lemon, 1 lime, ½ orange
salt and freshly cracked pepper
2 tablespoons orange liqueur
4–6 lime slices

**Method**

1. Slice raw scallops thinly. Combine with remaining ingredients, except lime slices. Let sit covered in the refrigerator overnight. (The acid in citrus juice will cook scallops.) To serve, arrange, your favorite green lettuce and top with mound of scallops. Garnish with slice of lime. This recipe should be made one day prior to serving.

Serves 4–6

## SEAFOOD WITH GREEN VEGETABLES

**Ingredients**

4 oz snow peas
8 oz broccoli, broken into small florets
8 oz asparagus spears, trimmed
1½ cups fish bouillon
8 oz large uncooked shrimp, shelled and deveined, tails intact
8 oz firm white fish fillets, cut into 1 inch cubes
8 oz scallops
½ cup heavy cream
½ cup tomato paste
1 tablespoon fresh tarragon, chopped, or 1 teaspoon dried tarragon
freshly ground black pepper

**Method**

1. Steam or microwave snow peas, broccoli and asparagus, separately, until just tender. Drain, refresh under cold running water and set aside.
2. Place bouillon in a large saucepan and bring to a boil. Add shrimp, fish and scallops to bouillon and cook for 5 minutes or just until cooked. Using a slotted spoon remove and set aside.
3. Stir in cream, tomato paste and tarragon, and bring to a boil. Reduce heat and simmer for 10 minutes or until liquid is reduced by one-third. Add reserved vegetables and seafood to sauce and cook for 1–2 minutes or until heated through. Season to taste with black pepper and serve immediately.

Serves 4

## SALMON ROLLS WITH TOMATO BUTTER

**Ingredients**

4 oz low-fat ricotta or cottage cheese, drained
1 tablespoon fresh dill, chopped
2 teaspoons lime juice
1 tablespoon lime rind, finely grated
freshly ground black pepper
1 pound salmon fillet, boned and skinned
½ bunch watercress, broken into sprigs

*Tomato butter*

4 ripe tomatoes
sea salt
1 oz butter

**Method**

1. To make tomato butter, cut tomatoes in half lengthwise and place on a lightly greased baking tray. Sprinkle with salt and bake for 30 minutes or until tomatoes are very soft. Remove tomatoes from oven and set aside to cool slightly. Place warm tomatoes and butter in a food processor or blender and process until smooth.
2. Place ricotta or cottage cheese, dill, lime juice, lime rind and black pepper in a food processor or blender and process until smooth.
3. Cut salmon in four 1 inch wide strips. Spread each strip with some of the ricotta mixture, roll up and secure with wooden toothpicks or cocktail sticks. Place rolls on a lightly greased baking tray, cover and bake at 350°F for 15 minutes or until fish is cooked.
4. To serve, divide watercress among four serving plates and top with a salmon roll. Serve immediately drizzled with tomato butter.

Serves 4

## GRILLED LOBSTER WITH THREE SAUCES

### Ingredients

2 live lobsters (2 pounds each)
1/4 cup (approximately) melted unsalted butter

*Basil cream sauce*

1 cup sour cream or crème fraîche (see page 78)
1/4 cup fresh basil, minced
2 teaspoons lemon juice
salt and freshly ground pepper

*Shallot tarragon butter*

1 cup plus 1 tablespoon unsalted butter
1 shallot, minced
2 tablespoons dry white wine
2 heaping tablespoons fresh tarragon, minced
1/4 teaspoon salt
1/2 teaspoon pepper, freshly cracked

*Summer garden vinaigrette*

2 tablespoons apple cider vinegar
1 tablespoon lemon juice
1 teaspoon Dijon mustard
2 tablespoons parsley, minced
3/4 cup olive oil
1/2 cup fresh tomato, diced
2 teaspoons chives, minced
salt and freshly ground pepper

### Method

1. Bring a large pot of salted water to a boil over high heat. Plunge lobsters into boiling water for 2 minutes. Drain. When lobsters are cool enough to handle, cut them in half lengthwise with a heavy knife. Remove and discard any viscera, including the intestinal vein in the tail.
2. Brush lobsters with melted butter and place them on grill, shell-side up. Grill over a medium-high fire for 8–10 minutes, then turn, brush with butter, and continue grilling until tails are firm and white (about 5 minutes more). Remove to a warm serving platter. Twist off claws and return the claws to grill for an additional 3–4 minutes. Serve on platter accompanied by the three sauces below.

Serves 4

*Basil cream sauce*

1. In a small bowl, whisk together sour cream, basil and lemon juice. Season to taste with salt and pepper. Cover and refrigerate for at least 1 hour or up to 1 day. Remove from refrigerator 30 minutes before serving.

Makes about 1 1/4 cups

*Shallot tarragon butter*

1. In a small skillet over moderately low heat, melt 1 tablespoon of butter. Add shallot and sauté until softened (about 3 minutes). Add wine and reduce until most of wine has evaporated. Place contents of skillet in food processor with the remaining 1 cup butter and tarragon. Process until smooth.
2. Season to taste with salt and pepper. Pack seasoned butter into serving ramekin(s) and chill for at least 1 hour or up to 1 day. Bring to room temperature before serving.

Makes about 1 cup

*Summer garden vinaigrette*

1. Whisk together vinegar, lemon juice, mustard and parsley in a medium bowl. Add oil in a slow, steady stream, whisking constantly; mixture should be thick and creamy. Stir in tomatoes and chives. Season to taste with salt and pepper.

Makes about 1 1/4 cups

# chicken & poultry

# Anything BUT PALTRY

Legend has it that Julius Caesar was delivered a scrawny rooster from the Gauls, with whom his Roman troops were warring in about 52BC. Round its neck was a taunting message, '*Bon appétit!*' With humor, Caesar summoned the leaders of his adversaries to dine with him. The Gauls were so thrilled with the coq au vin, simmered in wine and herbs, that they adopted it, sending the recipe down through the centuries in the land now known as France.

Poultry, French-style, has always been praiseworthy. The French have elevated chicken, the most economical and prolifically bred bird on earth, to a special status.

French cooks roast poultry similarly to their counterparts in other Western countries, but chicken is served, not with gravy, but with unthickened *jus de viande* (its own juices). Roast duck is often dressed up and tantalizingly tasty with fruit; who has not enjoyed duck à l'orange? Pan-fried poultry is also good with added fruit, and in a casserole or stew, is so full of flavor.

Chicken, duckling, wild duck, squab and pheasant, the latter of which can be tough when roasted, braise beautifully. The secret in the sauce is to brown the bird well first so the color will be darkly rich. In France, braising is done by slow cooking over a long period in a heavy lidded pot with minimal liquid; similar to pot roasting. Chicken also poaches nicely and can be coated in aspic for a special salad.

Whether it is grilled, cubed for kebabs, folded into a fricassé, crêpe or soufflé, poultry in all its guises is the most versatile of meats—suitable for simple family meals or for a banquet for VIPs.

## POUSSINS PROVENÇALS

**Ingredients**

4 cloves garlic, halved lengthwise
6 fresh rosemary sprigs, 4 whole and 2 chopped, plus extra to garnish
4 oven-ready poussins (baby chickens)
4 tablespoons olive oil
salt and black pepper
2 teaspoons all-purpose flour
1 1/5 cups chicken bouillon or white wine
juice of 1/2 lemon
1 teaspoon Dijon mustard

**Method**

1. Preheat oven to 400°F. Place 2 pieces of garlic and 1 rosemary sprig in cavity of each poussin, then place them on a rack in a roasting tin.
2. Brush each bird with 1 tablespoon of oil and sprinkle with chopped rosemary. Season and roast for 50 minutes or until cooked through and tender. Remove from oven, then loosely cover with foil to keep warm.
3. Remove rack, then pour cooking juices into a small saucepan. Stir in flour, then stir for 1–2 minutes until smooth. Pour in bouillon or wine and bring to a boil, stirring. Add lemon juice and simmer for 2–3 minutes, stirring, until thickened. Add mustard and season. Garnish with rosemary and serve with gravy.

Serves 4

## CHICKEN FLORENTINE

### Ingredients

2 pound chicken legs
1 small onion
1 stick celery, roughly chopped
1 carrot, roughly chopped
2 cups hot water
1 chicken bouillon cube
3 peppercorns
salt to taste
1 tablespoon oil
1 medium onion, finely chopped
2 lb frozen spinach, thawed
salt, pepper, nutmeg
2 tablespoons cream
2 tablespoons butter
4 tablespoons all-purpose flour
½ cup cream (optional)
2 tablespoons tasty cheese, grated
lemon to garnish

### Method

1. Place chicken legs in a saucepan, add onion, celery, carrot and enough hot water to just cover (about 3 cups). Crumble in bouillon cube, peppercorns and salt. Bring to a boil, then turn down immediately and simmer slowly for 45 minutes.

2. To prepare spinach, heat oil in medium saucepan and sauté onion until soft. Add spinach, stir well, and simmer spinach in its own juices for 10 minutes. Add seasonings and stir in cream. Spread spinach on serving platter. Lift legs from pan and arrange over spinach in a single layer. Cover with foil and keep hot. Strain bouillon and measure quantity; there should be about 2 cups. If there is more than 2 cups of bouillon, place in clean saucepan and reduce by boiling. Melt butter in a saucepan, stir in flour and cook, stirring, for 1 minute. Remove from heat and gradually add chicken bouillon. Return to heat and stir until sauce boils and thickens. Remove from heat and stir in cream and cheese. Spoon sauce over each leg and garnish with lemon. Serve immediately.

Serves 4

## CHICKEN AND APRICOT ROULADE

### Ingredients

2 pounds ground chicken
1 cup soft breadcrumbs
1 small clove garlic, crushed
1 teaspoon salt
1/4 teaspoon pepper
2 tablespoons lemon juice
1 tablespoon water
2 tablespoons parsley, chopped

*Filling*

4 oz dried apricots, chopped
3/4 cup water
1 teaspoon sugar
1 small onion, finely chopped
1 stick celery, diced
1 cup soft breadcrumbs

*Glaze*

2 tablespoons apricot jelly
1 tablespoon water
2 teaspoons teriyaki sauce

### Method

1. In a large bowl, combine all ingredients for chicken mince mixture and knead well by hand. Set aside.
2. To make filling, reserve 5 apricots for garnish and place remainder with water and sugar in small saucepan. Cover and cool until apricots are soft. Uncover and allow most of the water to evaporate. Stir well then mix in remaining ingredients.
3. Preheat oven to 350°F. Place a 14 inch length of plastic wrap on work bench. Spread chicken mince mixture onto wrap to form a rectangle approximately 12 x 9 inches. Spread apricot filling over ground chicken. Lift the plastic wrap in front of you, holding it towards the ends, and fold over meat 2 inches. Pull off wrap towards the end, rolling mince up as you pull. Discard plastic wrap and place roulade on greased oven slide. Press 5 apricots along the top. Brush with combined glaze ingredients and place in preheated oven for 40 minutes, brushing with glaze every 10 minutes. Serve roulade hot with vegetable accompaniments, or cold with salad.

Serves 8

## CHICKEN A LA KING

**Ingredients**

1 pound chicken breasts
1 ½ tablespoons butter
5 oz mushrooms, thinly sliced
2 tablespoons all-purpose flour
salt and pepper
½ cup chicken bouillon
1 cup cream
2 eggs yolks
1 teaspoon onion, grated
2 tablespoons lemon juice
2 tablespoons dry sherry
½ red bell pepper, finely chopped
hot buttered noodles to serve

**Method**

1. Poach chicken, allow to cool slightly then remove meat from bones and cut into ⅓ inch dice. Melt butter in a saucepan, add mushrooms and sauté for 3 minutes. Stir in flour and add salt and pepper. Remove from heat and gradually add bouillon and cream, stirring after each addition. Return to low heat and stir until mixture thickens. Remove from heat and stir in egg yolks, onion, lemon juice and sherry. Add chicken and stir to combine. Simmer uncovered on low heat to heat chicken through (about 10 minutes), stirring occasionally. Stir in bell pepper. Serve immediately with hot buttered noodles or on toast.

Serves 4

## COQ AU VIN

### Ingredients

2 pounds chicken breasts
2 tablespoons butter
1 tablespoon olive oil
7 oz thick-cut bacon
12 pickling or pearl onions
4 oz button mushrooms, sliced
6 shallots, sliced
3 tablespoons seasoned all-purpose flour
2 tablespoons brandy
1 1/2 cups good red wine
1 teaspoon sugar
salt and pepper
1 sprig fresh thyme and 2 bay leaves
2 tablespoons parsley, chopped

### Method

1. Cut chicken breasts through the bone into 2–3 pieces. Set aside. Remove rind from bacon and cut into 1/4 inch cubes. Heat butter and oil in a large skillet, add bacon and cook until it begins to brown. Add onions and sauté for 2 minutes. Add mushrooms and shallots and sauté until mushrooms brown slightly. Using a slotted spoon, move bacon and vegetables to an ovenproof casserole dish.
2. Dip chicken in seasoned flour and place in pan. Brown a few pieces at a time on all sides and place in casserole dish. Drain oil from pan. Reduce heat, pour brandy into pan, tilt to ignite brandy then pour in wine. Simmer wine while scraping up brown pan juices. Add sugar and pour gravy into casserole. Add salt, pepper, thyme, bay leaves and parsley. Sprinkle in remaining seasoned flour. Cover casserole and place in preheated oven at 350°F. Cook for 40 minutes until chicken is tender and sauce thickens. Garnish with parsley and serve from casserole.

Serves 4–6

## CHICKEN NOISETTES WITH PESTO FILLING

**Ingredients**

5 thick-cut bacon
2 pounds chicken breast fillets
1 tablespoon lemon juice
salt and pepper
10 small bamboo skewers
melted butter

*Filling*

1 cup fresh breadcrumbs
1 clove garlic, crushed
¼ cup pine nuts
1 tablespoon lemon juice
salt and pepper
½ cup parsley or basil, finely chopped
bacon trimmings

**Method**

1. Cut rind and some of fat from bacon. Trim wide part of bacon to same width as streaky part; set aside. Reserve timmings. Pound out each chicken fillet thinly, between 2 sheets of plastic wrap. Sprinkle with lemon juice, salt and pepper. Soak skewers in water to prevent burning in oven.
2. Preheat oven to 350°F. Place all filling ingredients in food processor or blender and process for 60 seconds to produce a paste consistency. Place chicken fillets on work surface with wide side in front of you. Divide filling among fillets, spread along upper half almost to top edge, then fold lower half over filling. Roll fillets left end over right end and stand upright. Wrap a bacon strip around the side of each noisette and overlap ends. Insert a skewer through the overlap and through the center of each noisette. Grease a shallow baking dish with butter, place the noisettes in dish and brush with melted butter. Bake in oven for 30 minutes. Remove skewers and serve with vegetable accompaniments.

Serves 4

## ROASTED CORNISH HENS WITH MUSHROOMS

**Ingredients**

2 oz dried cèpe (porcini) mushrooms
3 Rock Cornish hens (about 1½ pounds each)
3 tablespoons unsalted butter, softened
2 tablespoons fresh thyme, minced
or 2 teaspoon dried thyme
1 tablespoon salt
2 teaspoons pepper, freshly ground
½ teaspoon bay leaf, ground
1 tablespoon garlic, minced
1 cup dry white wine
3 tablespoons olive oil
1 pound fresh mushrooms, sliced 2 inches thick

**Method**

1. Cover dried mushrooms in warm water; soak for 20 minutes. Meanwhile, wash hens inside and out; pat dry. Remove wing tips.
2. Lift mushrooms out of water with a slotted spoon and check carefully for any grit. Strain soaking liquid through a double thickness of dampened cheesecloth into a small saucepan. Add rehydrated mushrooms and 1 tablespoon of butter. Simmer over moderately low heat until all liquid evaporates (about 7 minutes). Divide mushroom mixture among hen cavities.
3. In a small bowl, make a paste of the remaining 2 tablespoons of butter along with thyme, salt, pepper and ground bay leaf. Rub mixture over birds. Cover with plastic wrap and refrigerate at least 4 hours or overnight.
4. Preheat oven to 375°F. Bring birds to room temperature and place on a rack in a roasting pan. Whisk together garlic, wine and olive oil. Roast birds, basting with wine mixture and pan drippings every 15 minutes. Add sliced fresh mushrooms and continue baking, until hens are golden brown and juices run clear when birds are pierced with a knife (about 25 more minutes). Remove from oven and let stand for 5 minutes. Using a sharp, heavy knife or a cleaver, cut hens in half. Transfer to warm serving plates. Surround each half with fresh and dried mushrooms.

Serves 6

# *vegetables*

# Here comes THE CRUNCH

The French revere vegetables and take great pride in preparing them as individual dishes and not mere addendums to a plate of meat, fish or poultry. The French prefer to shop for fresh produce at markets instead of supermarkets, because small growers supply markets with their freshest and best.

Home cooks will be familiar with the term *al dente* as applied to Italian food. The French equivalent is *croquant*, meaning crunchy. Greens must retain their color in French cooking: immerse them in cold water until the pot boils. Then plunge the produce into the boiling water, cook until done, run veggies under cold water, then reheat in a little butter.

As with many meats and fish, the French like to dress their vegetables with vinaigrette, *aioli*, butter or mayonnaise. Alternatively, they sauce them with hollandaise. Ratatouille is a favorite vegetable dish featuring eggplant.

## STUFFED CABBAGE WITH GRAINS

**Ingredients**

1/3 cup soft breadcrumbs
2 medium-sized red cabbages
1/2 cup unsalted butter
1/4 cup shallot, finely minced
1 1/2 cups carrot, finely minced
1/2 cup long-grain white rice
1/2 cup buckwheat groats
4 1/2 cups *fond de volaille* (see page 82)
1 cup tomato paste
2 teaspoons salt
1 teaspoon pepper, freshly ground
1 cup parsley, minced
2 tablespoons olive oil
2 onions, minced
1 cup celery, sliced
3 cups dry white wine
2 tablespoons red wine vinegar

**Method**

1. Preheat oven to 350°F. Toast breadcrumbs on a baking sheet until lightly browned (about 10 minutes). Set aside.
2. Raise oven temperature to 375°F. Remove large outer leaves from cabbage heads. Set aside 12 well-formed leaves. Quarter remaining cabbage and core. Shred enough of cored cabbage to yield 2 cups.
3. In a medium saucepan over moderate heat, melt 4 tablespoons of butter. Add shallot and 1/2 cup of carrot and sauté for 1 minute. Add shredded cabbage and sauté for 3 minutes. Add rice and buckwheat groats. Sauté for 2 minutes. Add 2 1/2 cups bouillon, tomato paste, salt and pepper. Bring to a boil, then cover, reduce heat to low and cook for 15 minutes. Grains will be almost tender. Cool slightly, then stir in 3/4 cup of parsley.
4. In a roasting pan or straight-sided skillet just large enough to hold 12 cabbage rolls side by side, heat 2 tablespoons of butter with olive oil over moderate heat. Add onion, celery and remaining cup of carrot and sauté for 5 minutes. Add wine and remaining 2 cups of bouillon and bring to simmering point. Cook for 15 minutes, then remove from heat.
5. Bring a large pot of salted water to a boil over high heat. Add wine vinegar. Parboil reserved cabbage leaves until slightly softened (about 5–7 minutes). Remove with a slotted spoon. When cool enough to handle, cut away the center rib of each leaf to make them easier to roll.
6. Place 1/4–1/3 cup stuffing near bottom of each leaf. Roll up halfway, then fold in sides and continue rolling to make a short, plump log. Place seam side down in roasting pan.
7. Melt remaining 2 tablespoons butter and brush over surface of cabbage rolls. Sprinkle with breadcrumbs. Cover and bake for 15 minutes. Uncover and bake for 15 minutes more.

Serves 6

## SAUERKRAUT

### Ingredients

10 pound green cabbage, halved, cored and shredded
½ cup, plus 4 teaspoons, non-iodized salt

### Method

1. Combine 4 cups cabbage and ¼ cup of salt in a stainless steel bowl. Let stand for 1 hour.
2. Transfer salted cabbage to a large earthenware crock. Add remaining cabbage and salt in layers, leaving at least 3–4 inches of space at top of crock. Put a small plate directly on surface of cabbage, then put a 2 pound weight on the plate. Cover crock well with plastic wrap, making sure it is sealed tightly.
3. Set crock in a cool, dark place, no warmer than 65°F. Cabbage will begin to ferment after 7–10 days. Allow it to ferment for 4–6 weeks.
4. Transfer fermented cabbage and any liquid to a large pot. Bring to a simmer over moderately high heat. Pack sauerkraut into sterilized canning jars and cover with a little juice. Cover with lids and rings and process in a boiling water bath for 20 minutes. Store sauerkraut in a cool place. It will keep for up to 1 year.

Makes 1.2 litres

## SPINACH SOUFFLE

**Ingredients**

1 pound fresh spinach
1 oz sunflower spread, plus extra for greasing
1 tablespoon Parmesan cheese, finely grated
1 oz all-purpose flour
1 cup reduced fat milk
4 medium eggs, separated, plus 1 extra egg white
4 oz reduced fat mature Cheddar, finely grated
black pepper
large pinch of ground nutmeg

**Method**

1. Rinse spinach, remove any coarse stalks or leaves and place in a large saucepan. Cover and cook over low heat for 4–5 minutes or until it has wilted. Drain and squeeze out any excess water. Chop roughly and set aside.
2. Preheat oven to 375°F. Grease a 6 cup, 8 inch soufflé dish, sprinkle with Parmesan and set aside. Gently heat sunflower spread, flour and milk in pan, whisking continuously, until sauce boils. Simmer for 3 minutes, stirring. Transfer to a large bowl, add spinach and mix well. Gradually beat in egg yolks and 2½ oz of cheddar, then season with pepper and nutmeg. Whisk egg whites in a clean, dry bowl until stiff (this is easiest with an electric mixer), then fold into spinach mixture.
3. Spoon mixture into prepared dish and sprinkle with remaining cheddar. Bake for 30 minutes or until well risen and lightly set. Serve directly from the soufflé dish.

Serves 4

## RATATOUILLE

### Ingredients

1 large eggplant (about 1 pound)
1 tablespoon salt, plus extra salt to taste
2 pounds ripe tomatoes, peeled, halved, and seeded
½ cup olive oil
8 oz zucchini, sliced ⅓ inch thick
8 oz yellow squash, sliced ⅓ inch thick
1 green bell pepper, seeded, ribs removed, and cut in ¾ inch wide strips
1½ cups onion, coarsely chopped
1 tablespoon garlic, minced
3 sprigs thyme or ½ teaspoon dried thyme
6 tablespoons parsley, coarsely chopped
6 tablespoons fresh basil, coarsely chopped
freshly ground pepper

### Method

1. Cut unpeeled eggplant into 1 inch cubes. In a medium bowl toss cubes with 1 tablespoon salt, then transfer to a sieve or colander and allow to drain for 30 minutes.
2. Cut each tomato half in quarters and let drain in a colander or sieve for 30 minutes.
3. In a large skillet over moderate heat, heat 2 tablespoons of oil. Add zucchini and squash and sauté until lightly browned (about 5 minutes). Using a slotted spoon, transfer to a bowl. Add 2 more tablespoons of oil to pan and sauté bell pepper for 5 minutes. Add to bowl.
4. Rinse eggplant, drain and pat dry. Add 4 tablespoons of olive oil to skillet; when oil is hot, add eggplant. Sauté, stirring often to prevent sticking, until eggplant is lightly colored and softened (about 7 minutes). Transfer to bowl with other vegetables.
5. Add remaining 3 tablespoons of oil to skillet. Sauté onion and garlic until garlic is fragrant (about 3 minutes). Add tomatoes, thyme and 2 tablespoons parsley. Simmer for 10 minutes. Return sautéed vegetables to skillet and simmer for 10 minutes. Vegetables should be tender, but not mushy. Remove from heat and gently stir in remaining parsley and 4 tablespoons of basil. Season, to taste, with salt and pepper. Serve warm, at room temperature, or cold. Add remaining basil and adjust seasoning just before serving.

Serves 6

## ASPARAGUS WITH VINAIGRETTE

**Ingredients**

1 tablespoon Dijon mustard
4 tablespoons red wine vinegar
1 teaspoon sugar
1 teaspoon salt
½ teaspoon black pepper, ground
parsley, finely chopped
fresh chives, snipped
½ cup olive oil
1 bunch asparagus

**Method**

1. For vinaigrette, place mustard into a bowl. Whisk in vinegar and sugar, and salt, pepper and herbs to taste.
2. Continue whisking, slowly adding oil until mixture thickens. Cover until ready to use.
3. Prepare asparagus by cutting or breaking off the hard end and steaming for 5 minutes or until tender, but still crisp.
4. Arrange asparagus on a plate and drizzle with vinaigrette. Serve warm or cold.

Serves 2–4

## GREEN BEANS AND MUSTARD SAUCE

**Ingredients**

3 egg yolks
1 tablespoon Dijon mustard
2 teaspoons butter
1/4 cup cream
2 teaspoons vinegar
1 pound green beans

**Method**

1. To make sauce, heat egg yolks, mustard and butter in a double boiler over simmering water. Mix continuously until mixture is frothy.
2. Add cream and mix for 3 minutes. Add vinegar. Sauce can be set aside at this stage and reheated over simmering water when beans are cooked.
3. Wash, top and tail beans. Steam until tender, but still crisp.
4. Pour sauce over beans and serve.

Serves 6

## EGGPLANT PROVENÇAL

**Ingredients**

2 medium eggplants
salt
2 tablespoons olive oil
4 shallots, finely chopped
1 clove garlic, crushed
1 tomato, diced
2 cups cooked rice
½ teaspoon dried oregano
1 cup tomato juice
1 tablespoon parsley, chopped

**Method**

1. Cut eggplants into halves lengthwise. Scoop out flesh, leaving a 1 inch shell, and dice. Sprinkle salt over shells and allow to stand for 30 minutes.
2. Meanwhile, heat 1 tablespoon of oil in skillet. Cook diced eggplant flesh, shallots, garlic and tomato until eggplant is just tender. Stir in rice and oregano. Season to taste. Preheat oven to 350°F.
3. Drain any liquid from eggplant shells. Pat dry with paper towel and brush outside of shell with remaining oil. Spoon rice mixture evenly into cavities. Arrange in a shallow ovenproof dish. Pour tomato juice over. Bake in oven for 35–40 minutes or until tender. Serve sprinkled with parsley.

Serves 6

# desserts

# All sweetness AND LIGHT

The French are the world's greatest dessert creators. They offer a range of sweet delicacies from custards and creams to the commanding *croquembouche*: the crowning glory on a wedding party table.

Mousses and cold soufflés are not difficult to make. Cold soufflés are always refreshing when made with fruit. Hot sweet soufflé recipes frighten off some cooks, but following directions to the letter with confidence will produce a successful soufflé and applause from guests.

Tarts are French favorites and home cooks who master them are highly regarded. Tarts can feature pre-cooked or raw fruit on an unbaked or blind-baked base and can be served as is or glazed. Custard is a tempting filling on its own, or can be topped with extra ingredients.

Ice cream and parfaits are so important to the French that they have even created a fruity Christmas parfait, laced with rum, as an alternative to the Christmas log cake. Champagne sorbet, for example, may be served between courses. As a finale to a large repast, lemon, tropical fruit and berry sorbets are sweeter alternatives. Coulis can be used as a garnish or to drizzle over a dessert such as a crêpe.

Few desserts beat fresh fruit cooked in wine or macerated in liqueurs or wine. Attractively served and with the colors complementing each other, fresh unadulterated fruits fanned on a serving plate are ideal after a big meal and/or for guests with simple dessert tastes.

## TROPICAL TOUCH PARFAIT

**Ingredients**

2 cups cooked rice
16 oz canned pineapple pieces
  or fruit salad (reserve liquid)
grated rind and juice of 2 oranges
1 tablespoon honey or sugar, to taste
1 tablespoon butter
1 cup cream, whipped
3 passionfruit
1 banana, sliced and soaked in lemon juice

**Method**

1. Combine rice with pineapple liquid, rind and juice of oranges, honey and butter. Place over moderate heat and stir occasionally until liquid is almost absorbed. Allow to cool. Fold in half the cream and half the passionfruit. Add pineapple and blend thoroughly. Spoon into parfait glasses. Decorate with remaining cream and top with banana slices and remaining passionfruit.

Serves 4

## POUND CAKE WITH BERRIES AND CREME FRAICHE

### Ingredients

butter for greasing pan, plus
½ cup unsalted butter, slightly softened
granulated sugar for dusting pan
and for sweetening berries if needed
1 cup dark brown sugar
4 large eggs
pinch of salt
1 teaspoon vanilla extract
1 teaspoon grated lemon zest
½ teaspoon allspice
2 cups all-purpose flour
3 tablespoons sour cream
or crème fraîche (see page 82)
½ cup almonds, toasted, ground medium-fine
3 cups mixed summer berries (strawberries, raspberries, blackberries, blueberries)
¼ cup raspberry eau-de-vie or Cognac

### Method

1. Preheat oven to 350°F. Lightly butter a 9 inch (6-cup capacity) loaf pan. Sprinkle bottom and sides with granulated sugar, shaking out excess.
2. With an electric mixer, cream butter until smooth. Add brown sugar, gradually, and beat until light. Add eggs one at a time, beating well after each addition. Beat in salt, vanilla, lemon zest and allspice. On lowest speed add 1 cup of flour and beat just until blended. Add sour cream and beat to blend. Add remaining flour and almonds, beating just to blend. Batter will be very thick and sticky.
3. Pour batter into prepared pan and smooth the top. Bake until top is firm and a cake tester inserted in the center comes out dry (about 1¼ hours). Cool in pan for 2 minutes, then remove from pan and finish cooling right-side-up on rack.
4. In a medium bowl, combine berries and eau-de-vie. Add sugar if berries are not sufficiently sweet. Let macerate at room temperature for 15 minutes. Serve pound cake in thin slices with berries on the side or on top. Provide a pitcher of cold crème fraîche.

Makes one 23cm loaf cake

## PEAR TART WITH CORNMEAL CRUST

**Ingredients**

zest of 1 lemon

2 tablespoons lemon juice

½ cup honey

2½ cups water

½ cup dry white wine

1 cinnamon stick

2 cloves

½ vanilla bean, split

2 large ripe pears, peeled, halved and cored

3 large eggs

¾ cup whipping cream

¼ teaspoon freshly grated nutmeg

*Cornmeal tart dough*

1 cup all-purpose flour, plus 2 tablespoons extra if necessary

⅓ cup yellow cornmeal

2 tablespoons sugar

½ teaspoon salt

6 tablespoons unsalted butter, chilled, cut into small pieces

1 large egg, beaten with 1 tablespoon water

**Method**

1. In a large pot combine lemon zest, lemon juice, honey, water, wine, cinnamon and cloves. With the tip of a small, sharp knife, scrape vanilla seeds into liquid, then add bean to pot. Bring mixture to a simmer over moderate heat. Add pears and poach just until a knife can be slipped in and out easily (15–25 minutes depending on size and ripeness). Cool in liquid.
2. To make cornmeal dough, place 1 cup flour and cornmeal, sugar and salt in bowl of food processor. Process until mixed (about 3 seconds). Add butter and process until blended (about 4 seconds). Add egg and water mixture and process until dough barely forms a ball.
3. Turn out onto a lightly floured surface; knead lightly to form a ball, sprinkling with up to 2 more tablespoons of flour if necessary. Pat into a square, cover with plastic wrap, and refrigerate for at least 1 hour or up to 1 day (if more than 2 hours, remove from refrigerator 20 minutes before pressing out).
4. With your fingers, press cornmeal tart dough into a 9 inch tart tin, covering bottom and sides. Prick dough all over with a fork. Chill for 45 minutes.
5. Preheat oven to 375°F. Cut each pear in half and half again, lengthwise. Arrange pear sections neatly in tart shell, with one of the cut sides facing down. In a medium bowl, whisk together eggs, cream, ¼ cup of pear poaching liquid, and nutmeg. Carefully pour mixture around and over pears. Bake until custard is firm to the touch and lightly browned (about 35 minutes). Cool on rack. Serve at room temperature.

Serves 4–6

# BLUEBERRIES AND CHAMPAGNE SABAYON

## Ingredients

16 oz canned blueberries, drained
4 egg yolks
2 tablespoons superfine sugar
½ cup champagne or sparkling white wine

## Method

1. Spoon blueberries into individual serving dishes or glasses and refrigerate. Place egg yolks, sugar and champagne into top of a double boiler and beat over medium heat, until mixture thickens and becomes light and fluffy.
2. Pour sabayon over blueberries and serve at once with home made shortbread.

Serves 4–6

## FRENCH BREAD PUDDING

**Ingredients**

1 loaf brioche (see page 26), sliced
6 eggs, lightly beaten
1 ½ cups milk
1 teaspoon vanilla essence extract
1 teaspoon nutmeg, ground

*Fruit filling*

4 oz dried figs, chopped
4 oz dried dates, pitted and chopped
½ cup orange juice
⅓ cup brandy
1 cinnamon stick

**Method**

1. To make filling, place figs, dates, orange juice, brandy and cinnamon stick in a saucepan and cook over low heat, stirring, for 15–20 minutes or until fruit is soft and mixture is thick. Remove cinnamon stick.
2. To assemble pudding, place one-third of the brioche slices in the base of a greased 4 x 8 inch loaf tin. Top with half the filling. Repeat layers, ending with a layer of brioche.
3. Place eggs, milk, vanilla and nutmeg in a bowl and whisk to combine. Carefully pour egg mixture over brioche and fruit and set aside to stand for 5 minutes. Place tin in a baking dish with enough boiling water to come halfway up the sides of the tin. Bake for 45 minutes or until firm. Stand pudding in tin for 10 minutes, then turn out of tin and cut into slices. Serve with cream.

*Note:* This dessert is best eaten shortly after it is turned out of the tin.

Serves 6–8

## APRICOT AND LIME SOUFFLE

### Ingredients

8 oz dried apricots
1 mint tea bag
finely grated zest and juice of 2 limes
butter for greasing
6 tablespoons superfine sugar, plus extra for coating
6 large egg whites
pinch of salt
confectioner's sugar for dusting

### Method

1. Place apricots and tea bag in bowl, cover with boiling water and leave to soak for 1 hour. Drain, reserving 2½ tablespoons of liquid, and discard tea bag. Put apricots in a food processor with reserved liquid, lime zest and juice, and blend to a slightly chunky purée. Transfer to a large bowl.
2. Grease a 8 inch soufflé dish with butter and dust with superfine sugar. Preheat the oven to 375°F. Whisk egg whites with a tiny pinch of salt until they form soft peaks (this is easiest with an electric beater). Gradually sprinkle in sugar and whisk again until mixture is thick and glossy.
3. Using a large metal spoon, fold a spoonful of whisked egg whites into apricot purée to loosen it, then gently fold in rest of egg whites. Spoon mixture into soufflé dish. Cook for 30–35 minutes until just firm and well risen. Dust soufflé with confectioner's sugar and serve immediately.

Serves 6

## GRAND MARNIER SOUFFLE

**Ingredients**

½ cup orange juice
1 teaspoon grated orange rind
¾ cup cooked long-grain rice
4 egg yolks
1 tablespoon superfine sugar
1 tablespoon cornstarch
1 ¼ cups milk
4 tablespoons Grand Marnier
5 egg whites
⅓ cup superfine sugar, extra

**Method**

1. Place orange juice, rind and rice in a saucepan and bring to a boil. Reduce heat and allow to simmer, stirring occasionally, until all liquid has been absorbed. Set aside.
2. Whisk together egg yolks, superfine sugar and cornstarch. Heat milk in a saucepan until just at boiling point. Add to egg yolk mixture, whisk, then return mixture to saucepan. Stir over medium heat until custard boils and thickens. Reduce heat and simmer for 3–4 minutes, stirring constantly. Remove from heat. Stir in Grand Marnier and rice mixture. Cool slightly.
2. Preheat oven to 425°F. Beat egg whites until stiff peaks form. Add extra sugar, a tablespoon at a time, beating after each addition. Stir a little beaten egg white into rice custard then lightly fold in remaining whites. Spoon into prepared soufflé dish. Bake for 20–25 minutes until soufflé is puffed and golden. Serve immediately.

Serves 4

## CREPES SUZETTE WITH STRAWBERRIES

### Ingredients

1 pint strawberries, sliced
½ cup orange juice, warmed
2 tablespoons superfine sugar
1 tablespoon orange-flavored liqueur
1 tablespoon brandy

crêpes
4 oz all-purpose flour
milk
½ cup water
2 eggs
½ oz butter, melted
1 tablespoon sugar

### Method

1. To make crêpes, place flour, milk, water, eggs, butter and sugar in a food processor or blender and process until smooth. Cover and let stand for 1 hour.
2. Pour 2–3 tablespoons of batter into a heated, lightly greased 8 inch crêpe pan and tilt pan so batter covers base thinly and evenly. Cook over high heat for 1 minute or until lightly browned. Turn crêpe and cook on other side for 30 seconds. Remove from pan, set aside and keep warm. Repeat with remaining batter to make 12 crêpes.
3. Slice strawberries and place on crêpes. Fold crêpes into quarters and arrange, overlapping, in a heatproof dish. Pour orange juice over and sprinkle with superfine sugar. Place orange liqueur and brandy in a small saucepan and warm over low heat, ignite and pour over crêpes. Serve immediately.

Serves 4

## SERVING FRENCH CHEESES

In the minds of most French people, a meal is incomplete without cheese. At home, the cheese course may be no more than a wedge of Camembert. In restaurants, the cheese selection is typically presented on a platter or wheeled to the table on a cart, and diners are encouraged to choose as many varieties as they wish to try. The waiter cuts appropriate portions and presents them on one plate.

Cheese is almost never served before a meal in France. At a traditional lunch or dinner, the main course is followed by a small green salad. The cheese course is served after the salad. Fruit may be offered at the same time as the cheeses, but it is meant to be eaten afterwards for good reason. French red wines that go so beautifully with cheese are not compatible with fruit. When planning a cheese course, bear in mind that it's fine to present just one or two perfectly ripe cheeses. If you'd like to offer a more varied platter, the important consideration is balance. Contrast soft cheeses with hard ones; pungent with mild; fresh cheeses with aged; cow's milk cheeses with goat's milk cheeses.

The following cheeses are among France's best known and are widely available in this country.

## BRIE

A soft cow's milk cheese with a powdery white rind. A ripe Brie will be smooth and creamy throughout; under ripe Brie is chalky in the middle. The texture should be soft but not excessively runny. Avoid Brie with an ammonia odor.

## CAMEMBERT

A soft cow's milk cheese with a powdery white rind, in small rounds. A perfectly ripe Camembert can have an aroma of mushrooms. Select as for Brie.

## CANTAL

A firm cow's milk cheese with a nutty flavor. Young Cantal is smooth and mellow; as it ages the flavor becomes sharper and the texture more crumbly.

## CHEVRE

The generic term for goat's milk cheese. Chèvres come in a nearly endless variety of shapes and flavors. When very young, they can be quite mild and creamy. As they age, chèvres become sharper and drier. The French goat cheeses commonly available overseas are Montrachet, *bûcheron* and Sainte-Maure. Goat milk cheeses are delicious with wine.

## COMTE

A firm cow's milk cheese. The French equivalent of the Swiss Gruyère, Comté is an excellent mild grating cheese for use in cooking.

## EPOISSES

A small round cow's milk cheese from Burgundy. Epoisses has a creamy, moderately pungent interior and a reddish rind washed with brandy made from Burgundy wine.

## FOURME D'AMBERT

A blue cheese made from cow's milk. The classic Fourme d'Ambert is a cylinder about twice as high as it is wide. The rind is golden orange and the interior strong in flavor and slightly crumbly.

## FROMAGE DES PYRENEES

A generic name for cheeses from the *Pyrénées* region. *Doux de montagne* is often found in the United States and has a semi-soft interior and a mild, nutty flavor. Most of the *fromage des Pyrénées* exported to the United States are made of cow's milk, but sheep's milk cheeses are also made in France.

## MUNSTER

A soft cow's milk cheese from Alsace, Munster is superb with beer. In France, it is sometimes served with caraway or cumin seeds. This round cheese has a yellow-gold rind and a pale, creamy interior; when fully ripe it can be agreeably pungent.

## PETIT-SUISSE

A fresh cow's milk cheese, usually packaged in single-serving plastic containers. Petit-Suisses are enjoyed throughout France as dessert cheeses; typically they are spooned out of their containers, sweetened with sugar and eaten with fruit.

## PONT-L'EVEQUE

A soft cow's milk cheese from Normandy. Pont-l'Evêque is fabricated in a small square and it has a powdery orange rind and a creamy, golden interior with a strong flavor. Enjoy it with cider or a full-bodied red wine.

## REBLOCHON

A soft cow's milk cheese from the Savoy region, Reblochon is made in small rounds. Its rind is pale orange with a powdery white coat. The interior is pale, creamy and full-flavored when ripe. Try it with Beaujolais, Chinon or Bourgeuil.

## ROQUEFORT

A blue cheese traditionally made from sheep's milk. To select a good Roquefort, look for a cheese that's creamy, pale and well marbled with blue veins. Avoid cheeses that are excessively salty or crumbly. Some diners like to mute the pungent character of Roquefort by eating it with butter. On its own, the cheese is a challenge for wines. Sturdy red wines can work with it, but some say that the ideal match is a sweet Sauterne.

## BASIC VINAIGRETTE

**Ingredients**

1/4 cup red wine vinegar

salt

freshly ground pepper

3/4 cup olive oil

**Method**

1. In a small bowl, combine vinegar, salt and pepper. Whisk in oil and let stand 5 minutes. Whisk again, then taste and adjust seasoning. Keeps in refrigerator for 1–2 weeks.

Makes 1 cup

## BOUQUET GARNI

**Ingredients**

4 sprigs parsley

1 bay leaf

1 teaspoon dried thyme or 4 sprigs thyme

10 black peppercorns, lightly crushed

**Method**

1. Combine all ingredients in a cheesecloth bag and tie securely.

## CRÈME FRAICHE

**Ingredients**

1 cup whipping cream, not ultra-pasteurized

1 tablespoon buttermilk

**Method**

1. In a clean glass jar, combine cream and buttermilk. Cover jar and shake for 30 seconds to blend. Store at room temperature until thickened (24–36 hours), then refrigerate. Crème fraîche will keep for 5–7 days in the refrigerator.

Makes 1 cup

## FOND DE VOLAILLE (CHICKEN BOUILLON)

**Ingredients**

5 1/2 lb chicken parts
(backs, necks, wings, wing tips)

2 carrots, coarsely chopped

2 cloves garlic, peeled and lightly crushed

1 large stalk celery

2 large leeks, well washed and chopped

1 large onion, halved

2 whole cloves

bouquet garni (see above)

10 black peppercorns, lightly crushed

**Method**

1. Put chicken parts in a large pot and add 10 cups cold water. Bring slowly to a simmer over moderate heat, skimming as necessary with a slotted spoon to remove any scum that rises to the surface.

2. When mixture begins to simmer, add carrots, crushed garlic, celery, leeks and bouquet garni. Pierce each onion half with a clove and add to pot. Return to a simmer, then reduce heat to maintain a simmer. Cook for 3 hours, uncovered. Cook to room temperature, then strain and refrigerate. When ready to use, lift off any congealed fat on the surface. Bouillon may be kept in refrigerator for up to 1 week or frozen for up to 3 months.

Makes about 8 cups

## FOND DE VEAU (VEAL BOUILLON)

**Ingredients**

2 lb veal shanks

2 lb veal bones

1 onion, halved

2 whole cloves

8 oz carrots, coarsely chopped

2 leeks, well washed and coarsely chopped

10 cups water

bouquet garni

**Method**

1. Preheat oven to 450°F. Place veal shanks and bones in a large roasting pan and bake for 45 minutes. Pierce each onion half with a clove. Add onion, carrots and leeks to pan and bake for an additional 30 minutes. Transfer bones and vegetables to a large pot.

2. Add 4 cups water to roasting pan and bring to a boil on top of the stove, scraping bottom of pan with a wooden spoon to release any deposits. Pour into pot. Add 6 cups of cold water and bouquet garni. Bring slowly to a simmer, skimming as necessary with a slotted spoon to remove any scum that rises to the surface. Reduce heat to maintain a simmer and cook for 12 hours.

3. Cool bouillon to room temperature, then strain and refrigerate. When ready to use, lift off any congealed fat from the surface. Bouillon may be kept in refrigerator for up to 1 week or frozen for up to 3 months.

Makes about 8 cups

# ITALIAN
## food

# the land AND ITS PEOPLE

| | |
|---|---|
| Status | Republic |
| Area | 187 205 sq mi |
| Population | 58 138 000 |
| Language | Italian |
| Religion | Roman Catholic 83% |
| Currency | Euro |
| National Day | Republic Day, 2 June |

Another set of Italian recipes? Yes! As long as people have taste buds there will be room for books on cooking, and Italian cooking, with its vast repertoire of recipes, with its origin pre-dating ancient Rome, and with its influence on the rest of the world, is an ideal subject and a special gift to our palates.

Four of our senses—sight, smell, taste and touch (texture)—are in full swing when performing one of the most essential acts of our lives, that of eating. We enjoy looking at brightly colored and beautifully presented dishes, we enjoy the smell of freshly baked bread, and we get a sense of immense satisfaction when eating a perfectly cooked meal. Add some music, and we are also using the sense of hearing, thus completing the full range of sensory experience.

For Italians, food is not a means to survive: food is an art and an act of celebration. These recipes exemplify the simple delicious flavors of Italian cuisine. Happy cooking and *buon appetito*!

Italy, after the fall of the Roman Empire in 476 AD, was a geographical expression rather than a nation. It was not politically united until 1861, and did not become the modern Republic with which we are familiar until after World War II.

Today, Italy is made up of 20 regions (including Sicily and Sardinia). Each region has its own geographical and climatic characteristics varying from the chilly alpine north to the warm coastal south. Each region has its distinctive political and social history. Over the centuries, these various histories have contributed to the development and refinement of particular cuisines.

There are often small variations of the same dish within the same region (as is the case with the Ligurian pesto), but there are also more distinctive variations which can be interpreted as the great gastronomical divisions of Italy; oil and butter fall into this category. Although olive oil has become the standard condiment of Italian cuisine, butter is still more often used in the north than in the south of Italy.

Furthermore, from a socio-economic point of view (excluding the culinary excesses of the Roman Empire and of the Renaissance), Italian eating habits since Roman times for the less-affluent social classes consisted mainly of only one dish at any meal, whereas more than one dish was served at the tables of the wealthier classes.

The socio-economic changes that took place in Italy after World War II also influenced local eating habits. Dried pasta, which had become popular in Naples towards the end of the 18th century, has spread throughout the rest of the Italian peninsula.

There has also been a revival of what Italian cookery books sometimes refer to as 'poorer' cuisine. In a rather romantic fashion, these recipes bring to mind images of bygone times, with an almost obsessive emphasis on the genuine quality of products. Because of this love for the 'genuine', traditional markets are still the center of shopping for the household chef, despite modern mega-markets and frozen foods.

# Italy

# Daily life IN ITALY

## ITALIAN COOKING

Italian cooking, in the minds of some people, is still synonymous with pasta. It is true that pasta is very popular in Italy, but so too is rice, which grows in northern Italy. Soups are also very popular, varying from region to region, and from season to season. Meats, fish, crustaceans and shellfish with vegetables (either cooked or served as salads) make up the *secondo piatto* (second course). Fresh fruit and a variety of cheeses complete the meal, which is then finished with a cup of *espresso* coffee.

## EATING HABITS

Traditionally, the main meal in Italy is lunch. With most offices, shops and schools closed between 1pm and 4pm, and with some public offices closing down for the day at 2pm, lunch in an Italian household, is on the table any time after 1pm. For those who only have a one-hour break, lunch is still a very important meal. Whether at home, in the restaurant around the corner from the office, or at the *mensa* (the office refectory or canteen), lunch is comprised of the *primo piatto* (first course) of soup, rice or pasta, followed by the *secondo piatto* (second course) of meat or fish together with cheeses, vegetables or salad, and finally, fruit.

The evening meal, taken at any time after 8 pm, can be a lighter version of lunch. However, the pasta is often replaced by a light soup with very small pasta-shapes cooked for only a few minutes, and a frittata might replace the meat dish. For the evening meal, the emphasis is on easily digestible foods: vegetables, salads, cheeses and fruit. Bread (but not butter) is part of every meal.

Italians prefer to have a very light breakfast: a cappuccino or an *espresso* coffee, and perhaps a small cake from the local coffee-bar on the way to work. Caffè latte and cookies, a thick slice of home made cake, or bread and butter with jam, make up a usual Italian breakfast at home.

## THE DAILY BREAD

Bread has an almost transcendental role in Italian eating habits, and bakers are the high priests of Italian cooking. During the 1950s and 1960s there were attempts to replace the local *panetteria* (bread shop) with mass-produced bread, but common sense, and the Italian love for traditional bread-making, defeated the invading industrial moguls. The *panettieri* (bakers) retained their traditional role in the lives of Italians. Today, thousands of *panettieri* prepare regional breads, differing in shape, taste, texture and ingredients, and continue the tradition that started soon after 168 BC, when Macedonian freed slaves baked bread for the Roman Empire.

The popular *pasta dura* bread, typical of Emilia-Romagna, is considered to be the oldest type of bread, going back to Egypt, via Rome. The most extraordinary breads come from the two largest Italian islands—Sicily and Sardinia. Sicilian bread, with its unusual shapes and sprinkling of sesame seeds, bears the marks of the Saracen occupation, but perhaps the most unusual bread is the *carta da musica* ('music paperbread') from Sardinia. Made from unleavened dough, this wafer-thin bread was originally used by Sardinian shepherds during their lengthy periods away from home. Today, however, the *carta da musica* (so-called because, in the eating, it sounds like music) has become a symbol of refined living and discerning cuisine.

It has been said that music is food for the soul. If so, Italians, with their love of music, and their culinary repertoire, must have found the perfect formula for happiness of body and soul! Be it the lively tarantella or a majestic opera, be it a regional folk-song or a modern pop-tune, there is always some music that can add to the success of a meal.

The use of music and other forms of entertainment at mealtimes is not, after all, such a modern accomplishment. During the Italian High Renaissance, Cristoforo di Messisbugo (the meat-carver for the Duke of Ferrara) added to his recipe book instructions for enhancing banquets. Those instructions included music, dancing and theatrical presentations. A few centuries later, once opera had become a fashionable form of public entertainment, food and drinks were taken to the opera. Before the La Scala theatre opened in Milan in 1778, opera lovers attended the old Ducal Opera House, taking their food with them. This was then heated in the restaurant inside the building. La Cannobiana, another Milanese opera house, opened in 1779 and served whole dinners that the public consumed while the singers performed on stage. Hector Berlioz, recalling his visits to the Ducal Opera House, complained bitterly because the clatter of plates submerged the voices of the singers!

In more recent times, Filippo Tommaso Marinetti, in his book *Cucina futurista* (*Futurist Cooking*, 1932), required all sorts of sounds for his banquets. Classical music was definitely 'out' but the 'invigorating and masculine' sounds of guns firing, or the revving-up of engines, were definitely 'in'!

Things have changed decidedly since those days at the opera, and from the days of Marinetti's recipe book. Today, snacks and drinks are served only during intervals, and dinners (at home or at the restaurant) are enriched by the sounds of music rather than by the deafening sounds of Marinetti's guns!

## ROMANCING THE VINE

There are hundreds of regional and local Italian wines that reflect the climatic and geographical diversity of the country.

One can enjoy the golden Cinqueterre wines from Liguria where vines cling onto slopes dipping into the sea, or the Brolio Chianti from the picturesque hills between Florence and Siena. One can become euphoric with a bottle of Bardolino, a light dry red from the cool shores of Lake Garda (not too far from Verona), or with the dark, ruby-red and subtly scented Falerno from Campi Flegrei (near Naples). The latter is not to

be confused with the Falerno Laziale, which looks like liquid amber. Complete your meals with a glass of Monica, a sweet velvety red with amber highlights (from the area of the same name near Cagliari, in Sardinia), or have a platter of the local fish with a chilled Capri, the straw-colored, dry white wine from the Isle of Capri. You may prefer a Sicilian cassata followed by Moscato di Pantelleria, the sweet, generous and soft white from the isle of Pantelleria. For more robust meals, choose the austere, full-bodied red Barolo (from Piedmont), the orange-red, dry Brunello from Montalcino (near Siena), or the aristocratic Gattinara (from Vercelli), a full-bodied red wine with a distinctive aroma.

Basically, there is a wine to suit all tastes, moods and feelings. It's just a matter of personal choice: 'Cincin!'

(DOC, which stands for Denominazione di Origine Controllata, indicates that the wine is 100 percent genuine, that it has been checked for its purity, and that it has the official blessing of Italian œnologists.

# traditional ITALIAN FOOD

## STEPPING BACK IN TIME

The history of Italian gastronomy goes back to pre-Roman times, and consists of a long list of 'imported' and 'exported' foods.

The first Romans were shepherds and farmers who soon learned how to evaporate sea water to produce salt for their sheep. When the production of salt was surplus to their needs they started to export to Greek settlements in the south, and to the Etruscans in the north. It was the beginning of a very profitable trade, as testified by the name of one of the main roads leading to Rome—the Via Salaria (salt road)—which was used by Roman salt exporters.

By the second century BC, Roman cuisine had become more complex. Herbs and spices brought back to Rome by Roman legionnaires were added to basic foods, and different sauces were developed—including the garum sauce (a fish-based sauce) and the *agrodolce* sauce, still in use today. These sauces were indiscriminately splashed on every dish.

CHAR-GRILLED VEGETABLES WITH PESTO, PAGE 101

The extravagant and excessive cooking/eating habits of the newly rich from the dying days of the Roman Empire are sarcastically (but graphically) depicted by Petronio in his *Satyricon*. We have to wait until the banquets of the Renaissance to again see such incredible gastronomical extravagance.

The Crusaders introduced buckwheat to Italy, and then to Europe. They also reintroduced lemons and spices, many of which had been known to the Romans. Marco Polo did not introduce noodles to Italy, but his trip to the east eventually led to the opening up of a direct route to the spices of the *Far East*, and his countrymen, the Venetians, became wealthy importers and exporters of spices and coffee. With the discovery of the New World, peppers, tomatoes and potatoes (among other palatable foods) were introduced to Italy and soon became part of Italian culinary traditions. Maize, which is now used to make polenta, was accepted by Italian palates in 1650. By the end of the 16th century, Italian cooking and eating habits had reached full maturity.

There are more recently imported foods—such as the Big Mac—which can be bought in locations strategically positioned in the very heart of touristic Italy. In addition, certain Italian regional foods have migrated from their places of origin. Such was the destiny of the Neapolitan pizza, which at first crawled rather slowly to other parts of Italy, and then zapped throughout the planet, and thence into international cookery books!

## TOWARDS THE FUTURE

It took centuries to perfect the cooking habits and techniques that we now recognise as 'Italian cooking'; centuries to move from the plain, the bland and the basic to the extravagant, the astonishing and the complex.

Roman soldiers and citizens of the second century BC ate basic polenta-type dishes, but the

time of the declining Roman Empire was marked by the extraordinary banquets of the rich and famous.

With the fall of the Roman Empire, hordes of barbarians invaded the peninsula, and cooking again became plain and bland, with very few herbs used to enhance flavors. The monks of the Middle Ages had to learn how to elevate the taste of the humble turnip they relied on to make their meals a little more interesting and appetizing.

During the Renaissance, culinary excess (such as the five banquets and three days of celebration for Lorenzo il Magnifico's wedding in 1469) was counter-balanced by the less flamboyant meals of the *signori* and wealthy Florentine merchants, and the less rich Florentines who enjoyed an even simpler form of cooking. In fact, apart from festivities or celebrations, the Florentines of the

Italy

# INTRODUCTION

Renaissance generally preferred a rather uncomplicated style of cooking. In so doing, they were following the advice of Platina, librarian of the Vatican. In his book, *De Honesta Voluptate ac Valetudine* (*Concerning Honest Pleasure and Well-Being*), Platina, whose real name was Bartolomeo Sacchi, recommended moderation. The book was first published in 1475 and was reprinted six times within 30 years. The success of Platina's book clearly indicates the importance of the art of cooking during the 15th century.

The increasing interest in gastronomy during this period is further illustrated by the foundation of the first modern cooking academy, the *Compagnia del Paiolo* (Company of the Cauldron) in Florence. One of its most famous members was the painter Andrea del Sarto (1486–1531), who prepared for the Compagnia a dish representing a temple resting on a multi-colored gelatin. Sausages and wedges of Parmesan cheese were used to represent the temple's columns. Inside the temple was a music-stand holding a book, with pages made of sheets of pasta, and the musical notes represented by grains of pepper. It is this sort of extravagant combination of ingredients (and richness of color) that we find again, four centuries later, in Marinetti's *Futurist Cookbook*.

It is also rather interesting (and slightly amusing) to see that a cooking utensil was used as a icon for one of the most formal institutions of the 16th century: the *Accademia della Crusca* (Academy of the Bran). Founded in 1582, the very name of the academy suggests food, but, in fact, the *Accademia della Crusca* was founded in order to establish and safeguard the correct use of the Tuscan language. One of the symbols used by the academy was, and still is, the wooden shovel used by bakers. It represents the 'sifting' of the good usage of the language from the bad.

Florence was the cradle of the Renaissance in every field, including gastronomy, and the influence of Florence on the rest of the then-known world was unchallenged. But it was not the uncomplicated and healthy cooking habits recommended by Platina that conquered French palates. It was the rich, voluptuous and sumptuous cuisine of the Florentine court that appealed to Francis I, and which his daughter-in-law (Catherine de' Medici) took back to France. A new gastronomical era was beginning for the French court, through the subtleties and variations of Italian cuisine.

LINGUINE WITH SHRIMP AND SCALLOPS IN A ROASTED TOMATO SAUCE, PAGE 123

# basic recipes

# Basic RECIPES

Of all the exotic spices, the one that has been universally accepted throughout Italy is pepper, and of all the herbs available, the most popular is rosemary, that ancient aromatic Mediterranean herb. By contrast, the use of all other herbs and spices varies greatly from region to region, and even within the same region. Lombardy loves nutmeg, but does not use it when preparing the traditional Christmas turkey. Tuscany can produce a four-course meal with a strong reliance on sage leaves. The south of Italy is attached to the use of oregano. Sicily uses the green tips of (wild) fennel for a popular pasta dish. The isle of Sardinia resorts to saffron for its tiny saffron-flavored pasta balls cooked in consommé, and wraps a boiled chicken in myrtle leaves for 24 hours before serving it as a cold dish.

Through the ages, two flavors have become intrinsically connected with Italian cuisine—the tomato and the *tartufo* (truffle). Truffles were well known and much loved by the ancient Romans. There are two types of truffle in Italy—the white truffle from Piedmont and the black truffle from Umbria, which has a less pungent scent but is more piquant in flavor. Whether white or black, truffles are buried treasures and are rather difficult to find, so they are hunted by specially trained dogs. Once found, the expensive truffles must be treated with great respect, and are used with great parsimony, for only a few shavings are needed to enhance any dish.

The tomato is a much more recent acquisition. Despite the fact that it did not reach Italian soil until the 16th century (when Cortés brought it back from Mexico), the tomato is now as much a part of Italian gastronomy as any native product. It took a couple of centuries of careful cultivation for the small golden *pomodoro* ('apple of gold') to turn into today's bright-red, meaty tomato. And the rest, of course, is history.

## BASIL AIOLI

**Ingredients**

1 cup basil leaves
1/2 cup olive oil
1 clove garlic, minced
2 egg yolks
3 teaspoons lemon juice
1 tablespoon water
pepper, freshly ground
salt, to taste

**Method**

1. In a food processor, place basil, one tablespoon oil, garlic, egg yolks and lemon juice. Process until well combined.
2. With processor running, add remaining oil in a thin stream and process until thick. Add water to make a thinner aioli.
3. Add salt and pepper to taste.

Makes 1 1/2 cups

## BALSAMIC DRESSING

**Ingredients**

1/4 cup olive oil
1 tablespoon balsamic vinegar
1/2 teaspoon sugar
2 teaspoons sesame oil
salt and pepper

**Method**

1. Combine all ingredients in a bowl, and whisk until thick.
2. Use as desired, or store in an airtight container in the refrigerator. It will last about a week.

Makes 1/4 cup

## PESTO SAUCE

### Ingredients

1 ½ cups basil leaves
¼ cup pine nuts, toasted
2 cloves garlic, roughly chopped
¼ cup Parmesan cheese, grated
¼ cup pecorino cheese, grated
⅓ cup olive oil
salt and freshly ground black pepper

### Method

1. Place the basil, pine nuts, garlic and cheeses in a food processor and process until a paste.
2. With the motor still running, add oil in a steady stream until well combined.
3. Season with salt and pepper, to taste.
4. Store in refrigerator, with a little olive oil over the top to prevent basil from going brown.

*Note:* Pesto can be frozen.

Makes ¾ cup

## PIZZA DOUGH

### Ingredients

2 cups warm water
½ sachet dried yeast (⅛ oz)
1 teaspoon superfine sugar
2 pounds bread flour (1 ¾ pounds for dough; ¼ pound extra)
1 tablespoon extra virgin olive oil
2 teaspoons sea salt

### Method

1. Combine water, yeast and sugar in a bowl, add 14 oz of the flour, and stir until mixture is a sloppy paste.
2. Gradually add another 1 pound flour, then the oil and salt, and work together with your hands until the mixture forms a ball. Knead the dough with your hands for 10 minutes, until mixture is very elastic and smooth. (Alternatively, use an electric mixer with a dough hook, and knead on a low speed for 10 minutes.)
3. Take a piece of dough and roll, with your hands, into a ball the size of an orange. Place on a floured tray and repeat, until all the dough is used up. Cover tray with a damp cloth and leave in a warm place for 2 hours, or until dough has doubled in size.

Makes 8–10 mini pizzas

## POLENTA

### Ingredients

1 ½ cups water
1 teaspoon salt
1 cup polenta
2 cloves garlic, minced
⅔ cup Parmesan cheese, grated
salt and freshly ground pepper

### Method

1. Lightly grease a 10 x 12 inch dish.
2. In a saucepan, bring water and salt to a boil, and gradually add polenta, stirring continuously for 3–5 minutes, or until polenta becomes thick and comes together like glue. Take off heat. Add garlic and Parmesan.
3. Pour into a greased dish and press polenta into base of dish Leave to cool. Cut into wedges.

Makes 8 wedges

## SUN-DRIED TOMATO PESTO

### Ingredients

2 oz sun-dried tomatoes, drained
2 cloves garlic, roughly chopped
2 oz capers, drained
1 tablespoon lemon juice
¼ cup basil
¼ cup parsley
¼ cup Italian parsley
⅓ cup olive oil
salt and freshly ground black pepper

### Method

1. Place sun-dried tomatoes, garlic, capers, lemon juice, and basil and parsley in a food processor, and process until mixture resembles a paste.
2. Slowly add olive oil in a steady stream, until the paste is smooth.
3. Add salt and pepper to taste.

Makes ¾ cup, use within 24 hours

## BASIL AND GARLIC BAKED POLENTA

### Ingredients

3 cups chicken bouillon
1 cup instant polenta
1 clove garlic, minced
2 tablespoons basil, chopped
⅓ cup pecorino cheese, grated
salt and pepper, to taste

### Method

1. Grease a 10 x 12 inch dish, and preheat oven to 350°F.
2. Pour bouillon into a saucepan, bring to a boil, and gradually pour in polenta, stirring continuously for 5–10 minutes, or until it comes away from saucepan
3. Take off the heat and add the garlic, basil, cheese, and salt and pepper. Pour the polenta into a greased dish, and press the polenta evenly over the base.
4. Bake at 350°F for 30 minutes.
5. Serve polenta cut into triangles.

Makes 8 triangles

## PESTO CREME FRAICHE

### Ingredients

¼ cup thickened cream
¼ cup sour cream
2 tablespoons pesto sauce
1 teaspoon lemon juice
salt and freshly ground black pepper, to taste

### Method

1. Place all ingredients in a bowl and mix together until smooth.

Makes ¾ cup, use within 24 hours

## ROASTED GARLIC WITH THYME

### Ingredients

3 whole bulbs of garlic
¼ cup olive oil
1 tablespoon thyme, chopped

### Method

1. To roast garlic, slice off enough of the tops of bulbs to expose tips of the cloves. Place the heads cut-side up in a roasting pan, drizzle with a little olive oil, and sprinkle with thyme.
2. Cover with foil and roast at 350°F until soft, golden brown and quite fragrant, 45–60 minutes.
3. Let cool, then squeeze garlic out of the cloves and wrap in plastic wrap. Keeps in refrigerator for up to 1 week.

Serves 4

## PARMESAN POTATOES

**Ingredients**

14 oz washed potatoes, peeled and cubed
1 tablespoon olive oil
1 tablespoon butter
1 tablespoon Parmesan, grated

**Method**

1. Place potatoes in a saucepan with salted water and boil until potatoes are almost cooked, but still a little hard in the center. Drain.
2. Heat the oil and butter in a pan, add potatoes, and cook until brown. Add cheese, and cook, until potatoes are crisp.

Serves 4

## BAKED POTATOES WITH ROSEMARY

**Ingredients**

2 pounds potatoes, peeled and cubed
1 tablespoon olive oil
½ teaspoon sea salt
1 tablespoon rosemary, chopped

**Method**

1. Preheat the oven to 400°F.
2. Place potatoes in a baking dish, and toss in the oil, salt and rosemary.
3. Bake in the oven for 45–60 minutes.

Serves 4

## BASIC CHICKEN BOUILLON

**Ingredients**

4 pound chicken bones
8 pints of water
8 oz chicken wings
3 onions, chopped
2 carrots, chopped
1 leek, sliced
3 stems of parsley
1 celery stick, chopped
6 mushrooms
1 bay leaf
1 sprig thyme
a few black peppercorns

**Method**

1. Place chicken bones and wings in a large pot, and cover with cold water. Bring to simmering point and skim well.
2. Add the rest of the ingredients and simmer for 3–4 hours on low heat. Strain bouillon, and allow to cool. Remove any fat that has risen to the surface, or solidified. Boil to reduce bouillon, thus concentrating the flavor.
3. Can be kept in refrigerator for 2–3 days, and in freezer for 2 months.

Makes about 8 pints

## CHILI OIL

**Ingredients**

¼ cup extra virgin olive oil
2 red chilies, seeded and finely chopped
1 clove garlic, crushed
2 sprigs rosemary, chopped
black pepper, freshly ground
sea salt

**Method**

1. In a small saucepan, heat oil over low heat, turn off heat, add chili and garlic, before leaving for 10 minutes to allow the flavors to infuse through the oil.
2. Add the rosemary, pepper and salt, and leave to cool.
3. Store in airtight container.

Makes ⅓ cup

## BASIC BROWN VEAL AND BEEF BOUILLON

**Ingredients**

2 onions, chopped
2 carrots, chopped
1 leek, sliced
3 cloves garlic, crushed
4 pounds mixed veal and beef bones, cut into pieces
6 mushrooms, chopped
4 firm tomatoes, chopped
2 sticks of celery, chopped
3 sprigs of parsley
1 bay leaf
1 sprig of time
a few black peppercorns
cold water to cover (8 pints)

**Method**

1. Preheat oven to 400F°. Place onions, carrots, leek, garlic and bones in a roasting pan, and roast for 45 minutes until well colored but not burnt. Drain any fat from pan, then transfer bones and vegetables to a large saucepan, and add rest of the ingredients and enough cold water to cover.
2. Bring to a boil, then reduce heat and simmer gently, uncovered, for approximately 4 hours, skimming scum off surface of bouillon as it rises. Remove from heat, and strain, before allowing to cool. Remove any fat that has risen to the surface, or solidified. Boil to reduce bouillon, thus concentrating the flavor.
3. Can be kept in refrigerator for 2–3 days and in freezer for 30 days.

Makes about 4 pints

# appetizers

# Mouthwatering MORSELS

The custom of serving appetizers was one of the novelties introduced during the Renaissance and was reserved for extravagant banquets. Historically, antipasti were leftovers turned into delicious morsels by skillful and imaginative cooks. The Renaissance custom continues today—mouthwatering antipasti are reserved for dinner parties, Sunday lunches and special festivities. Italian restaurants, however, take great pride in the daily display of trays heaped with cheeses, vegetables (fresh, cooked or grilled), meats (cured or cold), seafood and tiny pastries.

There are three basic types of antipasti. The first of these are the *affettati,* which are sliced, cured meats, such as prosciutto and various regional salami. The second are the *antipasto misto*, which (as the name suggests) combine different types of food from olives to shavings of Parmesan cheese; from rolled anchovies to wedges of tomatoes with capers; from tiny artichokes to stuffed peppers. The third and final type is the *antipasto di mare* in all its glory. This colorful mixed seafood antipasto is a mosaic of delicate mussels nestled in their shining black shells, small white pieces of baby octopus and pink shrimps, cubes of fleshy lobsters and other tantalizing fish—it is the virtuoso of all appetizers!

## BRUSCHETTA WITH TOMATO AND BASIL

**Ingredients**

1 ciabatta loaf or French baguette, sliced into 1 inch slices
olive oil, for brushing
2 garlic cloves, roasted and puréed; (see roasted garlic recipe page 93)
1 pound plum tomatoes, diced
1 small red onion, finely chopped
1 tablespoon basil, chopped
1 tablespoon balsamic vinegar
2 tablespoons olive oil
salt
black pepper, freshly ground

**Method**

1. Grill bread slices for 2–3 minutes on each side.
2. Brush with a little olive oil and spread a thin layer of roasted puréed garlic on each slice.
3. In a bowl, mix together tomatoes, onions, basil, vinegar and olive oil and season with salt and pepper.
4. Serve grilled bread with tomato mixture on top.

Serves 4–6

## BRUSCHETTA WITH FRESH MOZZARELLA AND BASIL

### Ingredients

1 ciabatta loaf, sliced in 1 inch slices

¼ cup olive oil

⅓ cup sun-dried tomato paste

7 oz fresh mozzarella, each ball sliced into 5 slices

½ cup basil leaves, shredded or whole

### Method

1. Grill ciabatta slices on each side for 2–3 minutes.
2. Brush with olive oil, spread with sun-dried tomato paste, top with cheese slices and shredded basil leaves, or whole leaves, if preferred.

Serves 6

## ASPARAGUS WITH PECORINO AND PANCETTA

**Ingredients**

1 pound asparagus spears
juice of 1 lemon
4 oz extra virgin olive oil
sea salt
black pepper, freshly ground
8 thin slices of pancetta, cut into pieces
pecorino cheese, shaved

**Method**

1. Trim off the thick asparagus ends and cook asparagus in boiling water for 4 minutes, until tender, but still crisp. Run under cold water until asparagus is cool, then dry with paper towels.
2. To make the dressing, place the lemon in a bowl then slowly add the oil, whisking, until dressing is thick. Season with salt and pepper.
3. Pour the dressing over asparagus and serve with the pancetta and pecorino cheese shavings.

Serves 4–6

## POLENTA AND CORN FRITTERS

**Ingredients**

1 ½ cups water
½ teaspoon salt
½ cup polenta
½ cup corn kernels or
  ½ cup red bell pepper, diced
¼ cup scallions, finely sliced
1 tablespoon parsley, finely chopped
1 small clove garlic, minced
⅓ cup all-purpose flour
¼ teaspoon baking powder
1 egg, lightly beaten
salt and pepper to taste
olive oil, enough to cover base of pan

**Method**

1. In a saucepan, bring water and salt to a boil, gradually add polenta, stirring continuously for 3–5 minutes (or until polenta becomes thick and sticks together like glue).
2. Take off heat and add corn, scallions, parsley and garlic. Stir until combined. Transfer to a bowl and leave to cool.
3. Sift flour and baking powder together and combine with polenta mixture. Add egg and salt and pepper.
4. Heat oil in the pan, on medium to high heat, and place tablespoons of mixture in pan. Cook for 1–2 minutes on each side.
5. Serve with pesto crème fraîche (see page 93).

Makes 16 fritters

## SMOKED SALMON CARPACCIO WITH EXTRA VIRGIN OLIVE OIL AND LEMON

**Ingredients**

¼ cup extra virgin olive oil
1½ oz lemon juice
2 teaspoons small whole capers
12 oz thinly-sliced smoked salmon (allow 3–4 slices per person)
1 small red onion, finely chopped
1 tablespoon parsley, roughly chopped
black pepper, freshly ground
extra capers, for garnish

**Method**

1. To make dressing, combine oil, lemon juice, onion and capers in a bowl and whisk.
2. Arrange smoked salmon and onion on serving plates.
3. Drizzle the dressing over the smoked salmon, sprinkle with parsley and ground black pepper, and serve. Garnish with extra capers.

Serves 4

## CHAR-GRILLED VEGETABLES WITH PESTO

**Ingredients**

1 bell pepper, cut into pieces
1 eggplant, cut into slices
2 red onions, quartered
2 zucchini, sliced lengthwise
1 small sweet potato, thinly sliced

**Method**

1. Grease and heat a char-grill pan. Brush vegetable slices with a little olive oil and char-grill (until golden brown and vegetables are cooked).
2. Serve with pesto sauce or basil *aioli* (see recipes pages 92–93).

Serves 4

## ROAST PUMPKIN, POTATO AND ROSEMARY FRITTATA

**Ingredients**

12 oz butternut squash, peeled, seeded and diced into 1 inch pieces
8 oz potatoes, peeled and diced into 1 inch pieces
8 oz sweet potato, peeled and diced into 1 inch pieces
1 tablespoon olive oil
2 sprigs rosemary, roughly chopped
½ teaspoon sea salt
4 eggs
½ cup cream
½ cup milk
1 clove garlic, minced
½ cup Parmesan cheese, grated
salt and pepper to taste

**Method**

1. Preheat oven to 425°F.
2. Place squash, potato, sweet potato, oil, half the rosemary and sea salt in a baking dish, mix together, and bake for 20 minutes, or until just cooked.
3. Grease and line a 12-cup muffin pan with paper.
4. In a bowl, mix together eggs, cream, milk, garlic, cheese, rosemary, salt and pepper. Add squash, potato and sweet potato.
5. Pour into muffin pan and bake at 350°F for 30–35 minutes.

Makes 12

## BEEF CARPACCIO

### Ingredients

1 pound beef fillet, sliced into 1/4 inch slices
4 oz arugula, washed
1 tablespoon balsamic vinegar
1 1/2 oz extra virgin olive oil
pecorino cheese, shaved
black pepper, freshly ground
salt

### Method

1. Lightly oil a sheet of greaseproof paper and season lightly with salt and freshly ground black pepper.
2. Arrange 4 slices of beef on paper approximately 2 inches apart. Place another oiled piece of greaseproof paper on top, and gently beat the meat until it has spread out to at least twice its former size. Repeat with remaining meat slices.
3. Refrigerate until needed.
4. Place some arugula in the center of a plate and arrange the beef slices around it. Drizzle with some balsamic vinegar and olive oil.
5. Serve with shavings of pecorino cheese and black pepper.

Serves 6

## MARINATED CALAMARI WITH LEMON AND HERB DRESSING

**Ingredients**

2 pound calamari, cut into thin rings
3 oz lemon juice
3 cloves garlic, crushed
½ cup olive oil

*Dressing*

2½ oz lemon juice
4 oz olive oil
1½ tablespoon parsley, chopped
1 garlic clove, crushed
1 teaspoon Dijon mustard
salt and pepper
1 tablespoon olive oil

**Method**

1. Place lemon juice, garlic and oil in a bowl, add the calamari, and marinate for at least 3 hours. If time permits, marinate overnight.
2. To make dressing, place all ingredients in a bowl or jar and whisk well (until dressing thickens slightly).
3. Heat 1 tablespoon of oil in a pan, add the calamari, and cook for a few minutes until calamari are cooked through. Alternatively, the calamari can be cooked on a char-grill plate.
4. Serve calamari with lemon and herb dressing drizzled over.

Serves 4–6

## BUTTERFLIED SHRIMP WITH GARLIC, CHILI AND PARSLEY

### Ingredients

2 pounds , 8–12 count, raw shrimp, heads and shells removed, tails left on
2 tablespoons olive oil
1 tablespoon lemon juice
2 cloves garlic, crushed
2 red chilies, seeded and finely chopped
oil for frying
½ cup all-purpose flour
lemon, cut into wedges and 2 tablespoons parsley, chopped, to garnish

### Method

1. Cut shrimp down the back and remove vein.
2. Combine oil, lemon juice, garlic, chili and parsley in a bowl. Add shrimp, mix well, and leave to marinate for 2–3 hours.
3. Heat oil in a large pan, coat shrimp with flour, and cook quickly in oil for 2–3 minutes. Drain on paper towels.
4. Serve with lemon wedges and parsley.

Serves 6

## POTATO AND SPANISH ONION PIZZAS WITH CHILI OIL

**Ingredients**

1 quantity of pizza dough (see recipe page 93)
2 oz chili oil (see recipe page 94)
4 potatoes, thinly sliced
2 small red onions, thinly sliced
3 sprigs rosemary, chopped

**Method**

1. Preheat the oven to 500°F.
2. Dust a baking tray with flour. Dust bench with flour, take one piece of dough and press out with your hands to form a thick disc.
3. Roll-out dough in one direction, turn 90 degrees, and roll again in one direction, repeating this process until dough forms an 3 inch circle.
4. Place on a baking tray and brush with the chili oil, top with potato, onion and rosemary, and bake for 5–10 minutes, or until brown. Top with arugula before serving and drizzle with a little oil.

*Note:* Variations of toppings can be used: arugula and Parmesan; sun-dried tomatoes, fresh mozzarella and basil.

Makes 8 small pizzas

## MUSHROOMS WITH LEMON CREAM SAUCE

**Ingredients**

2 tablespoons butter
2 tablespoons olive oil
2 cloves garlic, minced
1 pound mushrooms, sliced ¾ inch thick
2 tablespoons lemon juice
½ cup cream
2 tablespoons chives, finely sliced
salt and freshly ground pepper
1 quantity of polenta (see recipe page 93)

**Method**

1. Heat the butter and oil in a skillet, add the garlic and cook for 2 minutes. Add the mushrooms and cook for 1–2 minutes on each side.
2. Add the lemon juice, cream, chives, salt and pepper and cook for 1 minute, until combined.
3. Serve with polenta.

Serves 8

## EGGPLANT ANTIPASTO

**Ingredients**

2 eggplants, cut into 1 inch slices
salt
olive oil
5 oz mozzarella cheese, sliced
1 tablespoon capers
2 gherkins, sliced lengthwise
2 tomatoes, sliced
12 slices leg ham or prosciutto, rolled
4 slices rye or whole wheat bread
4 lettuce leaves
4 tablespoons chutney or relish

**Method**

1. Sprinkle eggplant with salt and let stand for 15–20 minutes. Rinse under cold water and pat dry with paper towels.
2. Brush eggplant lightly with olive oil. Place under a preheated grill for 4–5 minutes each side or until cooked through.
3. Divide eggplant into four portions of three or four slices, overlapping in a shallow ovenproof dish. Top with mozzarella and grill for 4–5 minutes or until cheese melts.
4. Transfer eggplant to four plates. Top with capers and serve with an assortment of gherkins, tomatoes, ham, bread, lettuce and chutney.

Serves 4

# *soups*

# Bread, SOUP AND MINESTRONE

'Soup' is an umbrella term in Italian cooking covering *brodo di carne* (broth), *zuppa di pesce* (fish soup) and the many variations of *zuppa di verdura* (vegetable soup). Indeed, all soups are very satisfying and they are the perfect energy-booster on cold, winter days.

In Liguria, delicious pesto is added to the thickest vegetable soup immediately before it reaches the table, to make the famous *minestrone alla genovese*. In Tuscany, a dribble of golden olive oil is poured over each steaming dish. In the south of Italy, tomatoes and garlic are part of the basic cooking ingredients for vegetable soups. Rice or small shaped pasta can be added to soups, except, of course, to fish soup, which is at its very best when it is poured over thick slices of crusty bread.

*Cappelletti* (from Bologna), the smallest stuffed fresh pasta, can be added to *brodo di carne*. Soups take a long time to reach perfection and must be simmered gently to bring out the flavors of all ingredients. The final touch to a hearty soup (except, again, for fish soup) is Parmesan cheese, freshly grated and generously sprinkled over each dish.

## MINESTRONE

**Ingredients**

3 oz olive oil
1 medium onion, sliced
1 clove garlic, crushed
8 oz potatoes, peeled and chopped
5 oz carrots, thinly sliced
4 oz celery, thinly sliced
5 oz zucchini, sliced
4 cups beef bouillon
16 oz canned peeled tomatoes
rind from piece of Parmesan cheese
1 tablespoon parsley, chopped
16 oz cannellini beans, canned
salt and freshly ground black pepper

**Method**

1. Heat the oil in a saucepan, and cook the onion and garlic for 5 minutes (until onion is tender). Add the potatoes and cook for a further 5 minutes. Repeat with the carrots, celery and zucchini.
2. Add the beef bouillon, tomatoes and cheese rind, bring to a boil, and simmer covered, for 1 hour. If the soup becomes too thick, add more bouillon.
3. Add the chopped parsley and drained cannellini beans, and heat for a further 10 minutes.
4. To serve, remove the cheese crust, season with salt and black pepper, and serve with crusty bread.

Serves 6

## ROASTED TOMATO, RED BELL PEPPER AND BREAD SOUP

### Ingredients

2 pounds plum tomatoes, roasted
2 red bell peppers, roasted and roughly chopped
1 1/2 oz olive oil
3 cloves garlic, crushed
2 onions, finely chopped
2 teaspoons ground cumin
1 teaspoon coriander, ground
4 cups chicken bouillon
2 slices white bread, crusts removed and torn into pieces
1/2 oz balsamic vinegar
salt and freshly ground pepper to taste
Parmesan cheese, grated

### Method

1. Preheat the oven to 425°F.
2. Lightly oil a baking dish, place tomatoes and bell peppers in the dish and bake for 20 minutes, or until the skins have blistered. Set aside to cool, then remove skins and roughly chop.
3. Heat the oil in a saucepan, add the garlic and the onion, and cook for 5 minutes, or until soft. Add cumin and coriander, and cook for 1 minute, until well combined. Add tomatoes, bell peppers and bouillon to the saucepan, bring to a boil, and simmer for 30 minutes. Add bread, balsamic vinegar, salt and pepper, and cook for a further 5–10 minutes.
4. Serve with Parmesan cheese, if desired.

Serves 4

## POTATO AND LEEK SOUP WITH PANCETTA

**Ingredients**

2 tablespoons butter
5 oz pancetta, cut into strips
1 onion, chopped
1 pound potato, peeled and cut into chunks
3 cups chicken bouillon
1 large leek, washed and sliced
1 bay leaf
1/3 cup cream, optional
1 teaspoon nutmeg
salt and pepper
1/2 cup Parmesan cheese, grated

**Method**

1. Melt the butter in a large saucepan, add pancetta, and sauté for 5 minutes (until pancetta is crisp).
2. Add the onion and cook for a further 5 minutes (until onion is starting to soften), then add the potatoes and cook for 10 minutes (making sure the potatoes do not stick to the bottom of the saucepan).
3. Add the chicken bouillon, leek and bay leaf, and bring to a boil. Reduce the heat, and simmer for 45 minutes (or until potatoes are cooked). Remove the bay leaf, add the cream and nutmeg, and season with salt and pepper.
4. Stir through the grated Parmesan, and serve.

Serves 4–6

## MUSSEL SOUP IN A WHITE WINE AND ROASTED TOMATO SAUCE

**Ingredients**

3 pounds mussels
12 oz tomatoes
3 oz olive oil
4 cloves garlic, crushed
1 onion, chopped
4 oz white wine
14 oz canned tomatoes, peeled
1/4 cup tomato paste
4 oz fish bouillon, or water
2 tablespoons oregano, chopped
salt and pepper
crusty bread, for serving

**Method**

1. Wash mussels under water, scrub the shells with a scourer, and remove their beards. Discard any mussels that are open.
2. Place halved fresh tomatoes on a baking tray, drizzle with olive oil, sprinkle with salt, and roast in the oven for 20 minutes.
3. Heat the oil in a saucepan and sauté the garlic and the onion until soft. Add the white wine and cook for 2 minutes. Add the roasted tomatoes, can of tomatoes, tomato paste, bouillon (or water) and chopped oregano. Simmer for 5–10 minutes. Season with salt and pepper. Add mussels, cover, and cook for a further 5 minutes, until mussels have opened. Discard any that do not open.
4. Serve mussels with crusty Italian bread.

Serves 4–6

## SPINACH AND ARUGULA SOUP

**Ingredients**

2 tablespoons olive oil
2 cloves garlic, minced
1 medium onion, finely chopped
4 cups chicken bouillon
1 bunch spinach, roughly chopped
2 bunches arugula, roughly chopped
1/2 teaspoon nutmeg, ground
salt and pepper to taste
1/4 cup cream
1/2 baguette French bread
1 tablespoon olive oil

**Method**

1. Preheat the oven to 400°F.
2. Heat oil in a saucepan, add the garlic and the onion, and cook on low heat for 10 minutes (or until soft). Add the bouillon, bring to a boil, and add spinach, arugula, nutmeg, salt and pepper, and cook for 3 minutes.
3. Remove from heat and purée soup in a food processor (you may have to do this in two batches). Return the soup to the saucepan, add cream, and reheat.
4. Cut French bread into 8 slices, brush with olive oil, place on a baking tray, and bake for 5–10 minutes.
5. Serve soup with croûtons.

Serves 4

## SWEET POTATO AND ROSEMARY SOUP

### Ingredients

1½ oz olive oil
2 cloves garlic, crushed
1 medium onion, chopped
1 tablespoon rosemary, chopped
2 tablespoons sun-dried tomato pesto (see recipe page 93)
1 medium carrot, diced
1 large potato, diced
1½ pounds sweet potato, diced
4 cups chicken bouillon
freshly ground pepper and salt
2 tablespoons rosemary, chopped, extra

### Method

1. Heat oil in a saucepan, add the garlic, onion and rosemary, and cook on medium heat for 3–5 minutes, or until soft.
2. Add the tomato pesto and cook for 1 minute.
3. Add carrot, potato and sweet potato, and cook for a further 5 minutes. Add the chicken bouillon, and pepper and salt, bring to boil, reduce the heat and simmer (with the lid on) for 30–40 minutes, or until vegetables are soft.
4. Purée the soup in a food processor (you may have to do this in two batches), return the soup to pan, add the rosemary and heat through before serving. Add extra bouillon if soup is too thick.

Serves 4–6

## MIXED BEAN SOUP

**Ingredients**

3 oz dried red kidney beans
3 oz dried cannellini beans
2 tablespoons olive oil
3 oz bacon, chopped
1 onion, chopped
1 clove garlic, crushed
3 stalks celery, sliced
2 carrots, chopped
2 potatoes, chopped
6 cups chicken or vegetable bouillon
16 oz canned tomatoes, undrained and mashed
1/4 cabbage, finely shredded
2 oz small pasta shapes or rice
1 teaspoon dried mixed herbs
freshly ground black pepper
Parmesan cheese, grated

**Method**

1. Place red kidney and cannellini beans in a bowl. Cover with cold water and set aside to soak overnight. Drain.
2. Heat oil in a saucepan over medium heat, add bacon, onion and garlic and cook, stirring, for 5 minutes or until onion is tender. Add celery, carrots and potatoes and cook for 1 minute longer.
3. Stir in bouillon, tomatoes, cabbage, pasta or rice, red kidney and cannellini beans, herbs and black pepper to taste. Bring to a boil. Boil for 10 minutes, then reduce heat and simmer, stirring occasionally, for 1 hour or until beans are tender. Sprinkle with Parmesan cheese and serve.

*Note:* Extra vegetables of your choice may be added—it is a good way to use up vegetable leftovers.

Serves 4

# *pasta & rice*

# Ravioli to RISOTTO

Dried pasta and rice are sold in all Italian food shops, but Italian eating habits are divided between north and south. Fresh pasta dishes (such as cappellini and ravioli) and rice dishes are traditional in the north. In the south, rice is cooked for some special occasions and to make special dishes, but, as a main course, dried pasta is preferred.

The making of pasta can be traced back to a 4th century BC Etruscan tomb, where a stucco relief shows several kitchen utensils. However, despite such a long tradition, and contrary to popular belief, pasta became the 'people's food' only towards the end of the 18th century AD. Until that time, pasta was prepared in the kitchens of the rich and powerful, and then not even on a daily basis.

The selling of pasta started in Naples in about 1760 where several hundred shops and street-stalls sold bunches of dried spaghetti, and where improvised corner-stalls served cooked pasta—eaten in the street, al fresco.

In contrast to the well-documented history of pasta, mystery surrounds the appearance of rice in Italy. The earliest available document with references to rice is a letter written in 1475 by the Duke of Milan, Galeazzo Maria Sforza, to the Duke of Ferrara. The Milanese duke promised his counterpart in Ferrara a gift of several sacks of pearly rice from the Po Valley, the very same valley that is still producing rice today.

## CAPPELLINI WITH TOMATOES, GARLIC AND BASIL

**Ingredients**

1/2 cup olive oil
6 cloves garlic, thinly sliced
1 pound plum tomatoes, seeded and diced
1/3 cup basil, shredded
salt
black pepper, freshly ground
14 oz cappellini pasta

**Method**

1. Heat 1/4 cup of oil in a pan, add the garlic, and cook over medium heat until the garlic is slightly browned and golden.
2. Reduce the heat, and add tomatoes, basil, salt and pepper, and cook for 5 minutes (or until tomatoes are just heated through).
3. Cook the pasta in boiling salted water with remaining oil, until just cooked (*al dente*). Drain.
4. Serve the cooked pasta with tomato mixture.

Serves 4–6

## PENNE WITH TUNA, OLIVES AND ARTICHOKES

**Ingredients**

1 pound penne pasta
6 tablespoons olive oil
2 cloves garlic, minced
3 chilies, seeded and finely chopped
1 cup black olives, seeded
16 oz canned artichokes
2 tablespoons capers, finely chopped
16 oz canned tuna, drained
Parmesan cheese, shaved

**Method**

1. Cook the pasta in boiling salted water until just cooked (*al dente*). Drain, and rinse in cold water.
2. Heat 2 tablespoons of the oil in a pan, add the garlic and chili, and cook for 2–3 minutes.
3. Return the cooked pasta to the pan, add the remaining ingredients, and heat through.
4. Serve immediately with Parmesan cheese.

Serves 4–6

## RISOTTO MILANESE

**Ingredients**

4 cups chicken bouillon
2 tablespoons olive oil
1 onion, finely chopped
1 clove garlic, minced
2 cups arborio rice
1 cup white wine
½ cup pecorino cheese, grated
2 tablespoons parsley, finely chopped

**Method**

1. Heat the chicken bouillon in a saucepan, reduce the heat, and leave simmering.
2. Heat the oil in a heavy-based pan, add the onion and garlic, and cook, until soft.
3. Add rice, and stir until coated with the mixture, before adding the wine and cooking until wine has been absorbed, stirring continuously.
4. Add the chicken bouillon, one ladle at a time, stirring continuously, until liquid has been absorbed, before adding another ladle of bouillon. Continue adding the bouillon, one ladle at a time, until all the bouillon is used, and until the rice is cooked, but still firm to the bite. It may be necessary to add a little more liquid.
5. Stir in the cheese and parsley, serve immediately.

Serves 6

## FETTUCCINE WITH PESTO SAUCE

**Ingredients**

1½ cups basil leaves
¼ cup pine nuts, toasted
2 cloves garlic, roughly chopped
3 tablespoons Parmesan cheese, grated
3 tablespoons pecorino cheese, grated
½ cup olive oil
salt and freshly ground pepper to taste
14 oz fettuccine pasta
1 teaspoon salt
extra Parmesan, to garnish

**Method**

1. Place the basil, pine nuts, garlic, cheeses, oil, and salt and pepper in a food processor. Process until well combined.
2. Cook pasta in boiling salted water until just cooked (*al dente*). When pasta is cooked, drain in a colander, return to pan, and toss with pesto sauce.
3. Serve with extra Parmesan cheese.

Serves 6

## SPINACH AND RICOTTA CANNELLONI WITH TOMATO SAUCE

**Ingredients**

2 tablespoons olive oil
½ cup shallots
14 oz fresh ricotta
4 oz prosciutto
½ bunch English spinach, blanched and chopped
2 tablespoons thickened cream
pinch of nutmeg
salt and pepper to taste
16 cannelloni tubes

*Tomato sauce*

3 oz olive oil
2 cloves garlic, minced
2 medium onions, chopped
2 pounds plum tomatoes, peeled and seeded
2 teaspoon oregano leaves, roughly chopped
2 teaspoon rosemary leaves, roughly chopped
2 tablespoons balsamic vinegar
2 tablespoons tomato paste
salt and pepper to taste
2 tablespoons Romano cheese, grated

**Method**

1. Preheat the oven to 350°F.
2. Heat oil in a pan and sauté shallots for 3–5 minutes, until soft. In a bowl, mix together the ricotta, prosciutto, spinach, shallots, cream, nutmeg, salt and pepper. Fill cannelloni tubes with mixture. Set aside.
3. To make tomato sauce, heat oil in a saucepan, add the garlic and onion, and cook for 5 minutes or until soft. Add tomatoes, oregano, rosemary, balsamic vinegar, tomato paste, and salt and pepper, bring to boil, and leave to simmer with lid on for 30 minutes, or until it reaches a thick but runny consistency.
4. In a baking dish, spoon in a layer of tomato sauce, then a layer of cannelloni. Repeat the layers, covering with tomato sauce, and sprinkle top with cheese. Cover with foil and bake in oven for 30–40 minutes.

Serves 4

## RISOTTO WITH BABY SPINACH AND GORGONZOLA

### Ingredients

4 cups chicken bouillon
2 tablespoons olive oil
2 cloves garlic, crushed
1 onion, finely chopped
2 cups arborio rice
1/2 cup white wine
8 oz baby spinach
8 oz Gorgonzola cheese, in small pieces
salt and freshly ground pepper

### Method

1. Place bouillon in a saucepan and bring to a boil. Leave simmering.
2. Heat oil in a large saucepan, add garlic and onion, and cook for 5 minutes, or until soft. Add rice and stir until well coated.
3. Pour in wine, and cook until the liquid has been absorbed. Add the bouillon, one ladle at a time, stirring continuously, until liquid has been absorbed, before adding the next ladle of bouillon. Keep adding bouillon this way, and stirring, until all the bouillon is used, and until the rice is cooked, but still a little firm to bite.
4. Add the spinach, cheese, salt and pepper and stir. Cook until spinach is just wilted and cheese has melted.
5. Serve immediately.

Serves 6

## SMOKED SALMON RAVIOLI WITH LEMON DILL SAUCE

### Ingredients

4 oz smoked salmon pieces
1 egg white
1 ½ tablespoons cream
2 teaspoons fresh dill, roughly chopped
2–3 tablespoons cornstarch
32 wonton skins
1 teaspoon oil
2–3 cups ravioli pasta

*Lemon dill sauce*

1 tablespoon butter
1 tablespoon flour
¾ cup white wine
¾ cup thickened cream
½ lemon, juiced
2 tablespoons dill, roughly chopped
salt and freshly ground pepper

### Method

1. Place the salmon, 1 tablespoon of egg white, cream and dill in a food processor, and process until well combined, like a mousse.
2. Sprinkle the cornstarch on a bench and lay wonton skins in rows of four.
3. Brush every second skin around the edge with egg white. On alternate skins, place a teaspoon of mixture in the middle. Lie the other skin on top, gently pinch around mixture, so they look like pillows or rounds.
4. Half-fill a large saucepan with water and oil, bring to a boil, add 2–3 cups ravioli, and cook for 2–3 minutes. Set aside, and cover with plastic wrap.
5. To make the lemon dill sauce, melt the butter in a saucepan, add the flour, and cook for 1 minute. Add the wine, stir until smooth, and then add the cream and lemon juice. Bring to a boil, then reduce until sauce is a pouring consistency.
6. To serve, add the dill, salt and pepper to the sauce and pour over ravioli.

Serves 4

## SPAGHETTINI WITH BABY CLAMS, CHILI AND GARLIC

### Ingredients

14 oz spaghettini pasta
3 oz olive oil
4 cloves garlic, sliced
4 red chilies, finely chopped
2 cups tomatoes, finely diced
1 ½ pounds canned baby clams, or fresh if available
⅓ cup parsley, chopped
juice of 2 lemons
salt and freshly ground black pepper

### Method

1. Cook the spaghettini in boiling water with a little oil (until *al dente*). Run under cold water until cold, and set aside.
2. Heat half the oil on low and cook the garlic until it begins to change color. Add the chili and tomatoes, and cook for a few minutes.
3. Add the clams, parsley, lemon juice, remaining oil, spaghettini and a little of the water used to cook the clams, and heat through for a further 5 minutes. Season with salt and pepper.

***Note:*** If using fresh clams, wash under running water (scraping the shells with a sharp knife or scourer). Put them in a large pan with a little water over a gentle heat, until they open. Discard any that do not open.

Serves 4–6

## PAESANI WITH ARUGULA, HOT PANCETTA AND SUN-DRIED TOMATOES

**Ingredients**

1 pound paesani pasta
1 tablespoon extra virgin olive oil
2 cloves garlic, crushed
4 oz hot pancetta, roughly chopped
1 cup Italian tomato sauce
4 oz semi sun-dried tomatoes
1 bunch arugula, washed and drained
salt and freshly ground pepper
Parmesan cheese, shaved

**Method**

1. Cook pasta in boiling salted water until just cooked (*al dente*). Drain and set aside.
2. Heat oil in a saucepan, add garlic and pancetta, cook for 2 minutes, or until garlic is soft and flavors are well combined.
3. Add the pasta, tomato sauce, semi sun-dried tomatoes, arugula, and salt and freshly ground pepper to the pan, and heat through.
4. Serve with shavings of Parmesan cheese.

Serves 4

## LINGUINE WITH SHRIMP AND SCALLOPS IN A ROASTED TOMATO SAUCE

### Ingredients

1 pound linguine pasta
2 pounds tomatoes
olive oil, to drizzle over tomatoes
salt and pepper
3 oz olive oil, extra
8 oz scallops
8 oz raw shrimp, peeled
5 oz calamari, cut into rings
8 oz firm white fish pieces
3 garlic cloves, crushed
2 onions, diced
1 tablespoon tomato paste, optional
3 oz water
1/3 cup parsley, chopped
Parmesan cheese

### Method

1. Cook the linguine in salted boiling water (until *al dente*), and set aside.
2. To roast the tomatoes, preheat the oven to 350°F. Cut the tomatoes in half and place on a baking tray. Drizzle with olive oil, sprinkle with a little salt and pepper, and roast in the oven for 20–25 minutes.
3. Place in a food processor and process for a few seconds, do not over-process. The mixture should still have texture.
4. Heat half the oil in a pan, and sauté the scallops and the shrimp for 2 minutes until just cooked, and remove from the pan. Add calamari and cook for 2 minutes before removing from the pan. Adding a little more oil if needed, sauté the fish for a few minutes, until just cooked, then remove from the pan.
5. Heat the remaining oil, and sauté the garlic and onion for a few minutes (until cooked). Add the tomato mixture, tomato paste and water, and simmer for 10 minutes. Carefully add the seafood to the sauce, season with salt, pepper, and mix through the chopped parsley.
6. Serve linguine with the sauce and Parmesan cheese.

Serves 4

## MIXED MUSHROOM RISOTTO

**Ingredients**

2 tablespoons butter
1 pound mixed mushrooms (oyster, shiitake, enoki, brown), sliced
1 ½ oz olive oil
2 cloves garlic, minced
1 leek, finely sliced
4 cups chicken bouillon
2 cups arborio rice
½ cup white wine
rind of 1 lemon, finely grated
½ cup pecorino cheese, grated
½ cup Parmesan cheese, grated
2 tablespoons parsley, chopped

**Method**

1. In a pan, heat the butter, add the mushrooms, and cook for a few minutes. Remove from the heat and set aside.
2. Heat the oil in a large heavy-based saucepan, add the garlic and leek, and cook for 5–6 minutes. Meanwhile, place bouillon in a saucepan and simmer gently.
3. Add the rice and stir for 1 minute, to coat. Add the white wine, and cook until liquid is absorbed. Start adding the bouillon, one ladle at a time, stirring continuously, until liquid has been absorbed. Continue adding bouillon one ladle at a time until bouillon is used and rice is cooked, but still firm to bite.
4. Stir in mushrooms, lemon rind, cheese and parsley, serve immediately.

Serves 6–8

# *poultry & game*

# From capons TO QUAILS

Many Italian families still serve boiled capon as part of the traditional Christmas Eve meal, although the popularity of capon pre-dates the Christian era. Because of its delicate flesh, capon was a favorite of Imperial Rome and Renaissance Italy, along with other imported and local poultry. Peacock, a favorite in Renaissance dishes, has not maintained its popularity. It seems that the peacock was more satisfying to the eye than to the palate, and today's recipes have abandoned peacock in favor of turkey, which was brought from the Americas.

For a long time, chickens in Italy managed to live to a venerable age as they were kept mainly for laying eggs, and, eventually, for making chicken broth. Today, however, with recipes for free-range and commercially raised poultry, Italian cuisine includes innumerable recipes for birds and game of all sizes. Wild birds and game have always been considered to be more succulent than domesticated animals. During the Renaissance, private game-reserves were established within the estates of rich landlords. Of course, hunting on these reserves was at that time restricted to the landlord and his friends. Eventually, however, certain areas were opened up to everyone—perhaps in the hope of eliminating poachers.

Today, alongside commercially raised poultry, the eager Italian cook can also find commercially raised quail and rabbit.

## ROASTED CHICKEN WITH ROSEMARY, EXTRA VIRGIN OLIVE OIL AND LEMON JUICE

**Ingredients**

2 young chickens (each 1 pound, halved)

*Marinade*

1/4 cup extra virgin olive oil

2 tablespoons lemon juice

1 tablespoon rosemary, roughly chopped

1 clove garlic, crushed

black pepper, freshly ground

**Method**

1. Combine the marinade ingredients and whisk.
2. Place chickens in a large dish, pour the marinade over the birds and place in refrigerator for 3–4 hours.
3. Preheat the oven to 350°F.
4. Place chickens on a roasting rack, and roast in oven for 35–40 minutes, basting every 15 minutes until cooked. Serve with baked potatoes with rosemary (see recipe page 94).

Serves 4

## BUTTERFLIED QUAIL WITH LEMON AND SAGE LEAVES

### Ingredients

1½ oz olive oil
½ oz lemon juice
½ teaspoon lemon rind
1 clove garlic, crushed
freshly ground pepper
sea salt
1 tablespoon olive oil, extra
4 quails, butterflied
1 bunch sage leaves: 1 tablespoon chopped; the rest for garnish
¼ cup chicken bouillon

### Method

1. Preheat the oven to 350°F.
2. Combine the olive oil, lemon juice, lemon rind, garlic, pepper and salt in a bowl. Set aside.
3. Heat the extra oil in a large pan, add the quail and the chopped sage leaves, and brown quickly. Set aside in a baking dish.
4. To the pan, add oil, the lemon juice mixture and the chicken bouillon. Return to the heat, bring to a boil and simmer for 1 minute (to reduce liquid), stirring with a wooden spoon.
5. Pour the pan juices over the quail and bake in the oven for 20–25 minutes. Garnish with whole sage leaves.

Serves 4

## CHICKEN WITH RICOTTA, ARUGULA AND ROASTED RED BELL PEPPER

**Ingredients**

8 oz fresh ricotta

1 cup arugula, roughly chopped

¼ cup pine nuts, toasted

½ red bell pepper, roasted and finely chopped

freshly ground pepper and salt

4 chicken breasts, with skin on; each 7–8 oz

1 tablespoon butter

1 cup chicken bouillon

**Method**

1. Preheat the oven to 400°F.
2. Combine ricotta, arugula, pine nuts, bell pepper, and pepper and salt in a small bowl, and mix together until smooth.
3. Place 1–2 tablespoons of ricotta mixture under the skin of each chicken breast. Lightly grease a baking dish. Place chicken breasts in the dish, sprinkle with pepper and salt, place 1 teaspoon butter on each breast, pour bouillon around the chicken and bake for 20–25 minutes.
4. Serve chicken with pan juices and a arugula salad.

Serves 4

## CHICKEN WITH BASIL CREAM SAUCE

**Ingredients**

3 tablespoons flour
freshly ground pepper and salt
4 chicken breasts, each 7–8 oz
1 tablespoon olive oil
1 tablespoon butter

*Basil cream sauce*

1 tablespoon butter
2 cloves garlic, crushed
½ cup chicken bouillon
½ cup cream
¼ cup lemon juice
2 tablespoons basil, finely chopped
freshly ground pepper
sea salt

**Method**

1. Combine the flour, pepper and salt in a bowl and coat the chicken evenly with the flour, shaking off the excess.
2. Heat oil and butter in a pan, add the chicken, and cook over medium heat for 5–6 minutes each side. Remove from the pan and keep warm.
3. To make basil cream sauce, wipe out the pan, heat the butter, add the garlic, and cook for 2 minutes. Add chicken bouillon, cream and lemon juice, bring to boil, and reduce a little.
4. Just before serving, add the basil, season with pepper and salt, and serve the sauce with the chicken.

Serves 4

## PANCETTA-WRAPPED QUAIL WITH WILD MUSHROOM RISOTTO STUFFING

### Ingredients

*Risotto*

2 tablespoons olive oil
1 clove garlic, crushed
1 leek, finely diced
1 cup arborio rice
1 cup white wine
8 oz wild mushrooms
2 cups chicken bouillon
salt and black pepper

*Quails*

4 quails
1 cup chicken bouillon
4 pieces pancetta
8 sage leaves

### Method

1. Bring bouillon to boil in a saucepan.
2. Heat oil in a large heavy-based saucepan, add garlic and leek, and cook for 5–6 minutes, or until cooked. Add rice and stir for 1 minute, or until rice is coated. Add white wine, and cook until liquid is absorbed. Add mushrooms, and start adding the simmering bouillon, one ladle at a time, stirring well. When absorbed, keep adding one ladle at a time, until all bouillon is used and rice is cooked. Season with salt and black pepper.
3. Preheat oven to 400°F.
4. Fill each quail cavity with mushroom mixture, secure with a toothpick and place all birds in a baking pan. Wrap a piece of pancetta around each quail, top with a sage leave, and add half the bouillon and half the white wine to the pan. Roast in hot oven for 5 minutes, then reduce the oven to 350°F and roast for a further 20–25 minutes, or until quails are cooked. Add more bouillon during cooking if pan looks a little dry.
5. Remove from the oven and keep quails warm. Add the remaining bouillon and white wine to the pan. Simmer over heat for 5 minutes until sauce has thickened, scraping all the sediment with a wooden spoon.
6. Serve quails with pan juices spooned over.

Serves 4

## DUCK RAGOUT WITH PAPPARDELLE

### Ingredients

1½ pound duck breasts, cut into strips
8 oz pappardelle pasta
2 tablespoons olive oil
2 garlic cloves, crushed
1 onion, diced
1 pound tomatoes, peeled and chopped
5 oz chicken bouillon
5 oz black olives
10 fresh sage leaves
salt and pepper, to taste

### Method

1. Place the duck breasts in a saucepan, cover with water and boil for 5 minutes. Strain water, and remove the skins from the breasts. Cut into pieces, and set aside.
2. Cook the pappardelle in salted water, until *al dente*, and set aside.
3. Heat the oil and sauté the onion and garlic for a few minutes, until onion is soft. Add the duck pieces and sauté for 1 minute. Add the tomatoes and bouillon, and simmer for 5–10 minutes until the sauce thickens.
4. Just before serving, season with salt and pepper, add the olives and the sage leaves, and toss through the pappardelle.

Serves 4

## CHICKEN WITH PORCINI MUSHROOMS

### Ingredients

4 oz dried porcini mushrooms
½ cup boiling water
1 tablespoon olive oil
4–4½ pound chicken pieces, trimmed of fat
2 cloves garlic, crushed
1 onion, finely chopped
10 oz mushrooms, sliced
14 oz canned tomatoes, chopped
½ cup chicken bouillon
14 oz baby potatoes, washed and halved
4 sprigs each thyme and oregano, chopped
freshly ground pepper and salt

### Method

1. Place porcini mushrooms in a small bowl, pour boiling water over mushrooms, let stand for 30 minutes. Drain, and reserve liquid. Chop the mushrooms roughly.
2. Heat the oil in a pan, and add the chicken pieces in 2 batches. Brown on both sides for a few minutes. Remove chicken from the pan, and set aside. Add the garlic and onion to the pan, and cook a further few minutes, until soft.
3. Return chicken to pan, add the mushrooms and their liquid, and then add all other ingredients.
4. Bring to the boil, reduce the heat, and simmer on a low heat for 40–50 minutes or until chicken is tender. Adjust the seasoning to taste.

Serves 4–6

# *meat*

# From lamb shanks TO OSSO BUCCO

Italian cuisine has an extraordinary number of different ways of cooking meat. These vary from the time-consuming *bollito misto* (mixed boiled meats) to the fast and finger-licking *saltimbocca alla romana*; from the different regional versions of tripe dishes to that typically Milanese dish, osso buco; from the traditional Sunday roast to delicate meatballs.

Regional differences, of course, are to be found in all meat dishes. Veal and beef dishes reflect the more generous pasture of the north, while lamb and kid reflect the dry and sunny regions of the south. Pork dishes have no boundaries, but there are regional cooking habits that mirror more closely the climatic differences and gastronomic habits of Italians.

All recipes are full of inventiveness. Herbs and spices are used to bring out and enhance the flavor of the meat, and absolutely no part of the animal is wasted. According to gastronomic folklore, when the city of Modena was under siege in 1511, the Modenese people (who were short of casings) resorted to the use of pig's foot—and thus was born the *zampone* sausage.

## VEAL WITH MUSHROOMS AND OREGANO CREAM SAUCE

**Ingredients**

4 veal escalopes (each 4 oz)
1 tablespoon olive oil
1 tablespoon butter
12 oz button mushrooms, sliced
2 teaspoons oregano leaves, roughly chopped
1 tablespoon butter, extra
1 tablespoon lemon juice
$\frac{1}{4}$ cup cream

**Method**

1. Pound veal escalopes (if they are a little thick) between sheets of plastic wrap. With a knife, cut the sides, so they don't curl up when cooking.
2. Heat the oil and butter in a pan, add the veal pieces and brown quickly, 1–2 minutes each side. Remove from the pan.
3. Add the mushrooms, oregano and extra butter to the pan, and cook for 2 minutes, or until mushrooms are soft. Add the lemon juice and cream, and cook until well combined.
4. Return the veal to the pan, and cook for 2–3 minutes, or until sauce thickens.
5. Serve veal with extra sauce alongside in sauce boat.

Serves 4

# RACK OF VEAL WITH THYME ON ROASTED GARLIC MASHED POTATOES

## Ingredients

1½ pounds potatoes, peeled, chopped
½ cup olive oil
1 tablespoon capers, chopped
2 tablespoons roasted garlic, puréed (see recipe page 93)
salt
black pepper, freshly ground
2 tablespoons olive oil
2 pound (8 points) rack of veal
2 tablespoons thyme leaves, chopped
10 oz white wine
10 oz chicken bouillon

## Method

1. Preheat the oven to 350°F.
2. Boil the potatoes until soft. Drain, then mash or purée, and add olive oil, chopped capers and 1 tablespoon roasted garlic purée. Mix well, season with salt and pepper to taste, and set aside until ready to serve.
3. Heat 2 tablespoons of olive oil in a pan, and brown the veal on both sides until well sealed. This will take approximately 5 minutes. Remove the veal from the pan, and place on a rack in a baking dish. Rub veal with 1 tablespoon of roasted garlic purée and 1 tablespoon of thyme leaves, season with salt and pepper, and add half the wine and bouillon to the baking dish.
4. Roast in the oven for 20 minutes, or until veal is cooked to your liking. Wrap in foil and let rest for 10 minutes.
5. Add remaining bouillon, wine and thyme to the pan juices and cook over medium heat for 5 minutes, until the liquid has reduced by a third.
6. Serve veal on a bed of mashed potatoes with pan juices and sage leaves.

Serves 4

## VEAL SALTIMBOCCA

### Ingredients

4 veal escalopes, each 4 oz
2–3 tablespoons butter
8 oz mozzarella, sliced into 8 rounds
8 slices prosciutto
bunch sage
2 teaspoons sage, roughly chopped
½ cup white wine
¼ cup chicken bouillon

### Method

1. Using a meat mallet, pound the veal until thin.
2. Heat the butter in a pan, add the veal, and brown quickly on both sides. Remove from pan, top each with 2 slices mozzarella, 2 slices prosciutto and 2–3 sage leaves. Secure together with toothpicks.
3. Under a hot grill, grill veal for approximately 2 minutes, until cheese has just started to melt. Set aside.
4. Reheat butter, add the sage and cook for 1 minute. Add the white wine and reduce the sauce slightly.
5. Pour the sauce over the veal, and serve immediately.

Serves 4

## VEAL ESCALOPES WITH MOZZARELLA, EGGPLANT AND ROASTED TOMATOES

**Ingredients**

2 tablespoons butter

4 veal escalopes, each 3–5 oz, pounded flat

7 oz mozzarella cheese (1/4 inch-slices)

2 medium eggplants, 1/4 inch slices, char-grilled

1 1/2 oz olive oil

8 plum tomatoes, halved and roasted

1 cup chicken bouillon

1 tablespoon fresh basil leaves

**Method**

1. Preheat the char-grill.
2. Heat the butter in a pan, add the veal, and cook for 2–3 minutes on each side. Remove from the heat.
3. Place 2 slices of cheese on top of each piece of veal, and place under a hot grill for 2–3 minutes, or until cheese has melted. Cut each veal piece in half, and on each half place a slice of eggplant and 2 tomato halves on top. Repeat the layering for other pieces of veal.
4. Heat the remaining pan juices, add chicken bouillon and basil, bring to a boil, and then simmer for 2 minutes.
5. To serve, pour the pan juices over the veal, and serve immediately.

Serves 4

## LAMB CUTLETS WITH OLIVES AND ROSEMARY

**Ingredients**

1 tablespoon olive oil
2 cloves garlic, minced
8–12 lamb cutlets, depending on size
⅔ cup white wine
2 tablespoons tomato paste
⅔ cup beef bouillon
2 sprigs rosemary, roughly chopped
⅓ cup black olives
black pepper, freshly ground, to taste

**Method**

1. Preheat oven to 350°F.
2. Heat the oil in a large pan, add garlic and lamb cutlets, and brown on medium heat for 2–3 minutes on each side.
3. Add wine and cook for 2 minutes. Mix the tomato paste with the beef bouillon and add to the lamb cutlets. Add the rosemary, black olives and pepper.
4. Transfer lamb to a casserole dish and bake for 30–40 minutes.

Serves 4

## CHAR-GRILLED LAMB WITH MINT PESTO AND CREAMY POTATOES

**Ingredients**

1 pound potatoes, sliced thinly
salt and freshly ground pepper
1 garlic clove, crushed
1 teaspoon nutmeg
1 tablespoon all-purpose flour
1/3 cup Parmesan cheese, grated
1 cup cream
2 tablespoons Parmesan cheese, grated; extra
salt and freshly ground black pepper

*Mint pesto*

1 cup mint leaves
1/2 cup parsley leaves
2 cloves garlic
1/2 cup pine nuts, toasted
3 tablespoons Parmesan cheese, grated
3 tablespoons pecorino cheese, grated
1/3 cup olive oil
4 lamb backstraps, each 1 pound
salt and freshly ground black pepper

**Method**

1. Preheat oven to 450°F.
2. Lightly grease an ovenproof dish with butter, and arrange the potato slices in overlapping rows in the dish, seasoning with salt and pepper, garlic and nutmeg, in between each layer.
3. Mix the flour and Parmesan cheese into the cream, and pour over the potatoes.
4. Sprinkle with extra Parmesan cheese, and bake in the oven for 40–45 minutes, or until potatoes are cooked.
5. To make pesto, place the mint, parsley, garlic, pine nuts and cheeses in the bowl of a food processor and process until finely chopped. Add the olive oil in a steady stream, with processor still running. Season with salt and pepper, and set aside.
6. Preheat char-grill plate, or pan, and grease lightly with a little oil. Season lamb with extra salt and pepper to taste. Char-grill the lamb on both sides, or approximately 5–10 minutes or until done to your liking.
7. Serve the lamb, sliced diagonally, on a bed of creamy potatoes with the mint pesto.

Serves 4–6

## LAMB SHANKS WITH ROOT VEGETABLES

### Ingredients

1½ oz olive oil
2 parsnips, peeled, and cut into large chunks
1 medium sweet potato, peeled, and cut into large chunks
1 rutabage, peeled, and cut into large chunks
1 bunch scallions, trimmed
1½ oz olive oil, extra
2 cloves garlic, crushed
4 lamb shanks
1 cup beef bouillon
¼ cup water
½ cup red wine
1 tablespoon tomato paste
2 sprigs rosemary, chopped
bouquet garni (see recipe page 82)
freshly ground pepper and salt

### Method

1. Heat 1 tablespoon oil in a large heavy-based saucepan, add root vegetables, and cook quickly until brown. Set aside on a plate. Add the extra oil to the pan, and brown the garlic and shanks for a few minutes.
2. To the pan, add the bouillon, water, red wine, tomato paste, rosemary, bouquet garni and pepper and salt. Bring to a boil, reduce the heat, and leave to simmer, with the lid on, for 20 minutes.
3. Return vegetables to the pan, and continue to cook for another 30 minutes, until vegetables and lamb are cooked.
4. Before serving, remove the bouquet garni and season to taste.

Serves 4

## LOIN OF LAMB WITH ROSEMARY, GARLIC AND SUN-DRIED TOMATOES

**Ingredients**

2 lamb loins each weighing 13–14 oz
1 ½ oz olive oil
1 clove garlic, crushed
5 oz semi-sun-dried tomatoes, sliced
4 sprigs rosemary
freshly ground pepper and salt
string, for tying lamb

*Rosemary jus*

1 cup beef bouillon
2 teaspoons balsamic vinegar
2 teaspoons sugar
1 tablespoon rosemary, chopped

**Method**

1. Preheat the oven to 350°F.
2. Place lamb on a board, skin-side down, brush inside with oil, and sprinkle with garlic.
3. Add half the sun-dried tomatoes, place 2 sprigs of rosemary inside each loin of lamb, and season with pepper and salt.
4. Tie up lamb with string, place on a roasting rack, roast for 30 minutes, or until lamb is cooked to your liking. Leave to rest for 10 minutes, covered.
5. To make rosemary jus, in a small saucepan place bouillon, vinegar, sugar and rosemary. Bring to a boil, leave to simmer, and reduce for 5 minutes.
6. Serve sliced lamb with rosemary jus poured over.

Serves 6

## SEARED BEEF WITH MUSHROOMS, GARLIC AND BASIL POLENTA

### Ingredients

2 oz porcini mushrooms, dried
$^1/_4$ cup olive oil
3 pounds rump or fillet steak, cut into 6
1 onion, chopped
2 garlic cloves, crushed
12 oz shiitake/button mushrooms, mixed
$^1/_4$ cup red wine
1 cup beef bouillon
2 tablespoons parsley, chopped
salt and pepper
parsley, chopped; extra
1 quantity of basil and garlic baked polenta (see recipe page 93)

### Method

1. Soak the porcini mushrooms in boiling water for 20 minutes. Drain and chop. Set aside.
2. Heat the oil in a shallow pan, and cook the beef for a few minutes on each side. Remove from pan. Sauté the onion and garlic for a few minutes, then add all mushrooms and cook over high heat, until they are soft.
3. Add the wine and bouillon, bring to boil, and then simmer for 10 minutes. Remove from the heat, add parsley, and season with salt and pepper.
4. Serve the beef with mushrooms and polenta, and sprinkle with extra chopped parsley.

Serves 6

## OSSO BUCO

**Ingredients**

2 pounds veal shanks
2 tablespoons olive oil
1–2 tablespoons flour, seasoned
1 clove garlic, minced
1 onion, finely chopped
1 carrot, finely diced
2 celery stalks, finely diced
½ cup white wine
4 plum tomatoes, peeled and chopped
1 cup beef bouillon
2 tablespoons tomato paste
1 tablespoon basil, finely chopped
1 tablespoon parsley, finely chopped
salt and pepper to taste

**Method**

1. Place shanks on a board, and cut edges across, to stop from turning up. Heat oil in a large pan.
2. Coat shanks with seasoned flour and brown quickly in pan for 2–3 minutes each side. Remove from the pan and keep warm.
3. Add the garlic, onion, carrot and celery to the pan and cook for 5–8 minutes, or until soft. Add wine, and cook until evaporated. Add the tomatoes, bouillon and tomato paste, and return the shanks to the pan.
4. Bring to a boil, and add the herbs, salt and pepper. Reduce the heat, then cover and simmer for 1–1½ hours, or until the meat starts to come away from the bone.

Serves 4

## ROLLED ROAST PORK WITH APRICOT STUFFING

### Ingredients

3 pound foreloin pork roast
freshly ground black pepper to taste
1 teaspoon olive oil
1 cup white wine

*Apricot stuffing*

2 cups fresh breadcrumbs
½ cup shallots, chopped
¾ cup dried apricots, chopped
1 tablespoon lemon juice
1 tablespoon dried parsley flakes
salt and freshly ground black pepper to taste
1 egg, lightly beaten
½ cup water
2 teaspoons all-purpose flour, optional
lemon juice
white string, for tying pork

### Method

1. Preheat the oven to 350°F.
2. With a long sharp knife, slit along the length of the foreloin, making an incision just past the center.
3. Combine stuffing ingredients together, mix well. Place stuffing along the incision packing in well. Close the slit, secure with two skewers, then tie roast at intervals with string. Remove the skewers.
4. Sprinkle roast with pepper and brush with a little oil.
5. Place roast in roasting pan and add white wine.
6. Place roast in preheated oven for approximately 75 minutes. Turn roast halfway through cooking time, baste with pan juices. Baste twice more during second half of cooking time.
7. Test if cooked by piercing pork with a skewer: if juices run clear, roast is cooked.
8. Remove to a platter, cover with foil, and let stand 10 minutes.
9. Skim fat from the pan juices, add ½ cup water and deglaze pan. If desired, gravy may be thickened with 2 teaspoons of flour blended with a little water. Add salt and pepper and a little lemon juice.
10. Remove string and slice roast. Serve immediately with gravy and vegetables.

Serves 6–8

## ROAST LOIN OF PORK WITH MUSHROOMS AND PANCETTA

### Ingredients

1½ oz olive oil
1 medium leek, washed and finely sliced
4 oz mushrooms, chopped
2 oz pancetta, chopped
¼ cup parsley, chopped
freshly ground pepper and salt
2 pound loin of pork
1½ oz sun-dried tomato paste
1 cup veal bouillon
white string, for tying pork

### Method

1. Preheat the oven to 350°F.
2. Heat oil in a pan, add the leek, and cook for 3–5 minutes, or until soft. Add mushrooms, pancetta, parsley, pepper and salt, and cook for a further 3 minutes. Set aside to cool.
3. Cut pork down middle, and open out. Place mushroom mixture down the center of the meat, roll up and tie with the string at 1 inch intervals.
4. Rub sun-dried tomato paste over the pork, place on a roasting rack, and bake in oven for 50–60 minutes, or until tender. Cover in foil, and rest for 10 minutes.
5. Heat the pan juices over the stove, and add the veal bouillon. Scraping the pan with a wooden spoon, bring the bouillon to a boil, and reduce for 5 minutes.
6. Serve pork in slices with the pan juices.

Serves 4–6

# *seafood*

# From swordfish TO SNAPPER

The sea has always been a rich source of food. For those Italians living along the coast, the sea has been very generous with a variety of fish—from the very large swordfish to the smallest mollusk. The pristine lakes and rivers of Italy have also been generous with their bounty. The noble sturgeon from the Po River has been, since the Middle Ages, a much sought-after delicacy. The trout has been dubbed the 'queen of the lakes', while the hybrid common eel is at home in both salt and fresh waters.

Italian culinary inventiveness has even developed precious regional dishes for the dried cod that was first imported during the Middle Ages, not only to supplement the diet of those living in the more mountainous areas of the peninsula, but also as a cheaper alternative to expensive fresh fish during periods of religious fasting.

Larger fish, such as tuna, are sold as thick, juicy steaks. Smaller fish, such as the red mullet and the silver-blue sea bass, are cooked whole, and great care is taken to retain their natural color. The smaller fish, anchovies and sardines, are fried, broiled, baked or stuffed, and are served as appetizers or as a main course. They may also be preserved in a variety of ways with added herbs, spices, salt, balsamic vinegar and oil. Similar culinary techniques are used for the shellfish and for the smallest fish of all, the *bianchetti* (literally 'little white ones') which are very tiny, translucent fish. All in all—a seduction for the eye, and a true feast for the palate!

## BLUE-EYED COD WITH BASIL AIOLI

**Ingredients**

1 clove garlic, minced
2 tablespoons olive oil
1 tablespoon lemon juice
4 blue-eyed cod cutlets
1 quantity of basil *aioli* (see recipe page 92)
1 quantity of Parmesan potatoes (see recipe page 94)

**Method**

1. Combine the garlic, olive oil and lemon juice in a dish, and marinate the fish cutlets for 1 hour.
2. Grease a char-grill, or skillet, and grill fish for 3 minutes on each side.
3. Serve with basil *aioli* and Parmesan potatoes.

Serves 4

## PAN-FRIED SARDINES WITH MIXED HERBS

**Ingredients**

⅓ cup all-purpose flour

3 tablespoons mixed herbs: parsley, basil, oregano and marjoram, roughly chopped

½ teaspoon coarse black pepper

pinch sea salt

3 pounds sardine fillets

¼ cup olive oil

2 lemons, cut into wedges

**Method**

1. On a large plate, combine flour, herbs, pepper and salt.
2. Coat sardine fillets with flour mixture, pressing mixture firmly onto fish.
3. Heat oil in a large skillet, add sardines 4 at a time, and cook for 1–2 minutes each side, or until they are crisp and lightly browned.
4. Serve with lemon wedges and a green leaf salad.

Serves 4

## SWORDFISH STEAKS WITH TOMATO SALSA

**Ingredients**

$^1/_4$ cup pesto sauce (see recipe page 93)

1 tablespoon olive oil

4 swordfish steaks, each 7–8 oz

extra oil, for char-grill

*Salsa*

2 plum tomatoes, finely chopped

1 small red onion, finely chopped

1 teaspoon coarse black pepper

2 tablespoons basil, chopped

1 $^1/_2$ oz extra virgin olive oil

$^1/_2$ oz lemon juice

**Method**

1. Combine pesto and olive oil.
2. Brush fish with pesto and set aside.
3. Heat char-grill and cook fish 2–3 minutes on each side.
4. Combine all salsa ingredients in a small bowl, and mix well.
5. Serve the fish with salsa over the top.

Serves 4

## SALMON CUTLETS WITH DILL HOLLANDAISE SAUCE

### Ingredients

1½ oz extra virgin olive oil
1 tablespoon lemon juice
¼ teaspoon coarse black pepper
4 salmon cutlets, each 7–8 oz
extra oil for char-grill
1 bunch asparagus, for serving

*Dill hollandaise sauce*

3 oz white wine vinegar
freshly ground pepper
¼ cup water
4 egg yolks
8 oz unsalted butter, melted
1½ oz lemon juice
3 tablespoons fresh dill, chopped
extra freshly ground pepper and salt

### Method

1. Combine oil, lemon juice and pepper in a large ceramic dish. Add salmon cutlets and leave to marinate for 3–4 hours.
2. To make the dill hollandaise sauce, in a small saucepan mix vinegar, pepper and water. Bring to a boil, then reduce until 1 tablespoon of the liquid is left.
3. Place egg yolks and vinegar mixture in a food processor, and process for 1 minute. With the motor still running, gradually add the hot melted butter, and process until thick.
4. Add lemon juice, dill, and salt and pepper to taste, and keep warm.
5. Lightly oil and heat a char-grill pan, or preheat a grill. Cook salmon cutlets for 2–3 minutes each side, until done to your liking.

*Note:* Grilling may take a little longer.

6. Dribble dill hollandaise sauce over salmon.
7. Trim asparagus and blanch in a bowl of boiling water for 2–3 minutes.
8. Serve fish with hollandaise sauce and asparagus on the side.

Serves 4

## SNAPPER FILLETS WITH WHITE WINE AND PARSLEY

**Ingredients**

½ cup all-purpose flour
1 teaspoon coarsely ground pepper
¼ teaspoon sea salt
4 snapper fillets, each 8 oz
2 tablespoons olive oil
2 oz butter
2 cloves garlic, crushed
½ cup white wine
2 tablespoons parsley, finely chopped

**Method**

1. Combine the flour, pepper and salt in a dish, and coat the fish fillets evenly with flour, shaking off excess.
2. Heat the oil in a skillet, add the fish, and cook over medium heat for 5–6 minutes on each side, depending on thickness of fish. Set fish aside on a plate, and keep warm.
3. Wipe out the skillet, then melt butter, add garlic, and cook for 2 minutes. Add the white wine and simmer, until the sauce reduces.
4. Just before serving, add chopped parsley to the sauce and serve with the fish.

Serves 4

# salads

# Cool and CRUNCHY

The most appreciated and upmarket salad is the Roman *misticanza*, a mixture of wild greens that includes arugula, different kinds of wild chicory, *radicchio*, dandelion, borage and mint, all subtly and simply sprinkled with salt, vinegar and olive oil. This love of *misticanza* is testimony to what was once *de rigueur*, when the content of vegetable dishes relied upon what was growing in the wild, and upon what was available in any particular season. And where the biting winter froze the ground, Italian inventiveness turned to legumes—the 'cooked' salad replaced the fresh vegetable salad. With the cultivation of what were once 'wild greens', with the arrival of refrigeration and with the introduction of frozen foods, wintry chicory and summery tomatoes can share the same table.

The success of a salad depends on a perfectly balanced dressing and perfect timing. To avoid sad-looking, limp lettuce leaves and watery slices of tomato, the dressing must be added to the salad just before serving. Salt, oil and balsamic vinegar are fundamental, and herbs can add that extra tantalizing tang. But remember to never drown salad in dressing!

Shellfish can also make delicious salads to be served as appetizers or as light summer meals, while thin wedges of cold meats, strips of prosciutto and thick shavings of different cheeses (all judiciously added to fresh or cooked vegetables) definitely create exotic combinations of flavors and colors.

## BABY SPINACH, TOASTED PINE NUT AND AVOCADO SALAD

**Ingredients**

3 oz *coppa* ham, sliced
8 oz baby spinach
2 oz pine nuts, toasted
1 avocado, sliced
1/4 cup olive oil
2 tablespoons balsamic vinegar
1/4 cup pecorino shavings
sea salt
freshly ground black pepper

**Method**

1. Place the slices of *coppa* under a broiler, and broil until crispy. Place spinach, *coppa*, pine nuts and avocado in a bowl.
2. Mix together the oil and balsamic vinegar, pour the dressing over the salad, and then toss through the pecorino shavings.
3. Season with salt and pepper and serve.

Serves 4–6

## TOMATO, FRESH MOZZARELLA AND BASIL SALAD WITH BALSAMIC DRESSING

**Ingredients**

1 pound plum tomatoes, sliced thickly
8 oz fresh mozzarella, sliced
½ cup fresh basil leaves, shredded
extra virgin olive oil
balsamic vinegar
salt and freshly ground black pepper
crusty bread, for serving

**Method**

1. Arrange tomatoes, cheese and basil leaves on individual plates.
2. Drizzle with extra virgin olive oil and balsamic vinegar, and sprinkle with sea salt and freshly ground black pepper.
3. Serve with crusty bread.

Serves 4–6

## GREEN BEANS WITH PROSCIUTTO, PARMESAN, EXTRA VIRGIN OLIVE OIL AND VINEGAR

**Ingredients**

6 quail eggs
8 oz French green beans, blanched
2 oz prosciutto, sliced
Parmesan cheese, shaved
black pepper, freshly ground
sea salt

*Dressing*

2 tablespoons extra virgin olive oil
1 tablespoon white wine vinegar

**Method**

1. Place quail eggs in a small saucepan of cold water, bring to a boil, and boil for 3 minutes. Rinse under cold water until eggs are cool, then peel and cut in half.
2. Combine the beans, prosciutto, quail eggs and Parmesan cheese in a bowl. Sprinkle with the black pepper and sea-salt flakes. Drizzle dressing over the dish, and serve.

Serves 4

## EGGPLANT, BELL PEPPER, TOMATO AND FRESH MOZZARELLA WITH BALSAMIC DRESSING

**Ingredients**

¼ cup olive oil
2 large eggplants, each 12 oz, sliced into 8 slices each ½–¾ inch thick
1 red bell pepper, quartered, seeded, roasted and finely sliced
4 plum tomatoes, sliced into ⅓ inch slices, and roasted
black pepper, freshly ground
4 fresh mozzarella, sliced; 3 slices per serving
basil leaves, to garnish
crusty Italian bread, for serving

*Balsamic dressing*
¼ cup olive oil
2 tablespoons balsamic vinegar
sea salt and freshly ground black pepper

**Method**

1. Preheat the oven to 300°F.
2. Heat a char-grill pan, brush lightly with oil. Brush eggplant slices with oil and char-grill, 2–3 minutes each side. Place bell pepper under a broiler, and cook until skin is black.
3. Brush tomato slices with oil, sprinkle with pepper, place on a lightly oiled baking-tray, and roast in a slow oven for 20–30 minutes.
4. On a serving plate, place 2 slices of eggplant, top with 3 strips of bell pepper, 3 slices tomatoes, 3 slices cheese, and 2 strips red bell pepper. Garnish with basil leaves.
5. Combine the dressing ingredients. Drizzle balsamic dressing over dish, and a good grinding of sea salt and black pepper just before serving. Serve with crusty Italian bread.

Serves 4

## ITALIAN SAUSAGE WITH ZUCCHINI AND MEZUMA LEAVES

**Ingredients**

2/3 oz olive oil
2 medium zucchini, cut into 1/2 inch slices
12 oz Italian sausages (5–6 sausages)
1 thin French baguette, cut in 1 inch slices
1 1/2 oz olive oil, extra
2 bunches *mezuma* leaves, washed
1/4 cup basil leaves, shredded
4 oz semi-sun-dried tomatoes
1/4 cup Parmesan, grated

*Dressing*

1/4 cup olive oil
1 1/2 oz lemon juice
freshly ground pepper and salt

**Method**

1. Lightly brush a char-grill pan with oil and heat. Char-grill zucchini slices, 2–3 minutes each side, then remove and set aside.
2. Add the sausages and cook for 6–8 minutes, turning frequently, then remove from the grill and set aside to cool. Slice sausages into 1 inch slices.
3. Brush slices of bread with oil, and cook on char-grill for 2–3 minutes each side. Combine *mezuma* leaves, basil, sausages, zucchini, sun-dried tomatoes and Parmesan in a large bowl.
4. To make the dressing, mix together oil, lemon juice, salt and pepper, and whisk. Drizzle dressing over salad before serving.

Serves 4–6

## SALAD OF ROASTED TOMATOES AND BELL PEPPERS

**Ingredients**

*Semi-roasted tomatoes*

1 tablespoon olive oil
1 teaspoon oregano, chopped
sprinkling of sugar and pepper
2 plum tomatoes, cut into quarters

*Salad*

1/2 bunch arugula
1/2 red bell pepper, roasted
1/4 cup pine nuts, roasted
2 eggs, hard-boiled and quartered
1/4 cup scallions, sliced

*Dressing*

1/4 cup olive oil
1 tablespoon balsamic vinegar
2 teaspoons sesame oil
1/2 teaspoon sugar

**Method**

1. To make semi-roasted tomatoes, combine the olive oil, oregano, sugar and pepper together, and brush over tomatoes.
2. Place on a baking dish and bake at 250°F for 1 hour.
3. Place all salad ingredients in a bowl.
4. Mix the dressing ingredients together, and pour over the salad before serving.

Serves 4

## CAESAR SALAD WITH BABY COS, CRISPY PROSCIUTTO AND PECORINO

**Ingredients**

*Dressing*

2 egg yolks
1 tablespoon Dijon mustard
2 garlic cloves, crushed
4 oz white wine vinegar
2 anchovy fillets
1 tablespoon Worcestershire sauce
juice of 1 lime
1/4 cup parsley, chopped
1/2 cup olive oil
1/3 cup Parmesan, grated
black pepper, freshly ground

*Salad*

1 Turkish bread, cut into 1/2 inch slices
1 clove garlic
1 1/2 oz olive oil
8 slices prosciutto
2 baby Romaine lettuces
12 anchovy fillets
Parmesan cheese, shaved

**Method**

1. To make the dressing, place the egg yolks, mustard, garlic, vinegar, anchovies, Worcestershire sauce, lime juice and parsley in the bowl of a food processor and blend.
2. Add the oil in a steady stream with the motor still running, until all the oil is used, and mixture is thick. Mix in Parmesan cheese and season with ground black pepper.
3. To make salad, first preheat oven to 350°F. Place Turkish bread, garlic and olive oil in a bowl, and mix. Transfer the slices to a baking tray and bake in oven until golden and crisp. Set aside.
4. Place the prosciutto on a grill and grill until crisp, then break into pieces.
5. Wash and separate leaves of baby cos, and place in 4 individual bowls. Divide the prosciutto, bread and anchovies between bowls.
6. Pour the dressing and Parmesan shavings over each, and serve.

Serves 4

# desserts

# Delicious DOLCI

Italian palates indiscriminately and passionately love sweets, whether they are home made or are bought from the *pasticceria* (pastry shop), which provides more elaborate and refined types of cakes, tartlets, pastries, cream puffs, cassatas, tiramisù—the list could go on. Desserts, however, are not part of everyday Italian meals, although fresh fruit and cheeses are usually served at the end of a meal. In fact, the Italian language does not even have a word for the concept embodied in the term 'dessert'. Italians have a general-purpose word: *dolci*—sweets. *Dolci* are part of Sunday rituals, religious festivities, special occasions and special regional feast days. If one puts all these 'special' days together, sweets are, indeed, an integral part of Italian eating habits! Delicious sweets are accessible at any time of the day in all the *pasticcerie* and coffee bars around Italy—indulge yourself!

## PASSION FRUIT ZABAGLIONE WITH FRESH BERRIES

**Ingredients**

5 egg yolks
½ cup superfine sugar
½ cup sweet white wine
3 oz passion fruit pulp
4 oz blueberries
5 oz raspberries
5 oz strawberries

**Method**

1. Combine egg yolks and sugar in a heatproof bowl, and beat until thick and pale. Beat through the sweet wine, and place the bowl over a saucepan of simmering water. Continue to beat for 15 minutes, or until the mixture is very thick, not allowing the bowl to overheat too much. The mixture is ready when it forms soft mounds.
2. Remove the bowl from the heat, and continue beating for a further 5 minutes, or until the mixture has cooled. Fold through the passion fruit pulp, and serve with the fresh berries.

*Note:* To make vanilla zabaglione, omit the passion fruit pulp and add seeds from 1 vanilla pod by splitting the pod down the middle and scraping out the seeds.

Serves 4–6

## FRANGELICO CHOCOLATE CAKE WITH RASPBERRY SAUCE

**Ingredients**

7 oz dark chocolate, chopped
4 oz butter
5 eggs, separated
½ cup superfine sugar
⅓ cup all-purpose flour, sifted
½ teaspoon baking soda
½ cup hazelnuts, ground
2 oz Frangelico liqueur

*Raspberry sauce*

8 oz raspberries
2 tablespoons confectioner's sugar
1 tablespoon lemon juice

**Method**

1. Preheat oven to 375°F.
2. Melt chocolate and butter over hot water, remove from heat, and stir in egg yolks, sugar, flour, baking soda, hazelnuts and Frangelico. Beat egg whites until soft peaks form.
3. Fold lightly into chocolate mixture and pour into a greased and lined round 8 inch cake tin and bake for 40–45 minutes, or until cake shrinks slightly from sides of tin.
4. To make raspberry sauce, place raspberries, confectioner's sugar and lemon juice in a food processor, and blend until smooth. Strain, and add a little water if mixture is too thick.
5. Serve cake, cut into wedges, with raspberry sauce and cream.

Serves 8

## FIG PUDDINGS WITH BUTTERSCOTCH SAUCE

### Ingredients

8 oz dried figs, chopped
1 cup water
2 teaspoons baking soda
2 eggs
2 oz butter
¾ cup superfine sugar
1 cup all-purpose flour
1 vanilla bean
1 teaspoon vanilla extract

*Butterscotch sauce*

1 cup brown sugar
⅔ oz cream
1 oz unsalted butter
cream or ice cream, for serving

### Method

1. Preheat oven to 375°F.
2. Place the figs, water and baking soda in a saucepan, and cook for about 20 minutes, or until mixture has reached a jelly-consistency.
3. Pour the fig mixture into a bowl, and beat in the remaining ingredients. Split the vanilla bean down middle, scrape out the seeds, and add them to the mixture.
4. Pour mixture into individual ramekins or timbale-molds, and bake in the oven for 25 minutes.
5. To make butterscotch sauce, combine all the ingredients in a saucepan, and stir over low heat until dissolved.
6. Serve the individual puddings with the sauce, and cream or ice cream.

Serves 6

## RICOTTA FRITTERS WITH ORANGE SAUCE (photograph page 155)

### Ingredients

*Sauce*

1 cup orange juice, strained
⅓ cup superfine sugar
2 tablespoons butter
1½ oz cream
1 tablespoon Triple Sec or Cointreau

*Fritters*

1 cup oil, for frying
8 oz fresh ricotta, mashed
¼ cup all-purpose flour, sifted
2½ tablespoons superfine sugar
2 eggs
1 tablespoon orange zest

*For serving*

2 tablespoons confectioner's sugar
1 orange, segmented

### Method

1. In a small saucepan, combine the orange juice, sugar, butter, cream and Triple Sec. Heat until butter has melted and bring to a boil.
2. Reduce the heat, and simmer until sauce thickens.
3. Heat oil in a large frypan. Place all ingredients for fritters in a large mixing bowl, and mix together until well combined.
4. Place 1 tablespoon of mixture in the hot oil, and cook 3–4 at a time, for 1–2 minutes, turning over to cook on both sides. Take out with a slotted spoon, and drain on paper towels.
5. To serve the fritters, pour over orange sauce and dust with confectioner's sugar. Garnish with orange segments.

Serves 4

# SPANISH
## food

# the land AND ITS PEOPLE

| | |
|---|---|
| Status | Constitutional Monarchy |
| Area | 250 000 sq mi |
| Population | 38 000 000 |
| Language | Castilian Spanish |
| Religion | 97 percent Roman Catholic; 3 percent other, including Protestant, Muslim and Jewish |
| Currency | Euro |
| National Day | October 23 |

## HISTORY

In ancient times, the Iberian Peninsula was inhabited by cave dwellers who left behind extraordinary art, such as the paintings found at Altamira, which date back about 17,000 years. Civilization on the peninsula has been recorded as far back as 7,000 BC. Various peoples migrated to the area over the centuries. Rome began to exercise its influence around 218 BC, and Spain was a Roman province from 19 BC until it was overrun by Germanic tribes in the late 5th century. By the early 5th century, the Visigoths had established a powerful kingdom that survived until the Moors invaded from North Africa in 711 AD.

Muslim power reached its peak in the 10th century, but was increasingly opposed by Christian feudal kingdoms that emerged in the north. Granada was the last Muslim city to fall to the Christians in 1492.

The rule of King Ferdinand V and Queen Isabella I, with the approval of the Roman Catholic Church, established the Spanish Inquisition in 1478 to ensure purity of faith and to police the sincerity of those Muslims and Jews who had chosen Baptism into the Christian faith in preference to expulsion. The Inquisition was later used to resist the Protestant Reformation and to secure the Roman Catholic faith.

In 1516, the Spanish crown passed to Charles of Habsburg, who had already inherited parts of Italy, the Netherlands and Burgundy from his father. In 1519, Charles was elected Holy Roman Emperor. By the time Charles abdicated in 1556, Spain was the world's dominant power. The reign of Charles' son, Philip II, brought further conquests, including that of Portugal, but during the later part of his rule, the Spanish empire was in decline. In 1588, the Spanish Armada was defeated by the English. In 1640, Portugal regained its independence. By the end of the *Thirty Years' War* in 1648, Spain had lost to France its European territory and dominance and it was forced to recognize Dutch independence. More territories were lost during the War of the Spanish Succession (1701–14) and during the Napoleonic Wars the Bourbons were overthrown and did not regain the crown until 1875. In 1898, Spain lost its war with the United States (and also the lost Philippines—which had been named after Philip II).

Spain was neutral in WWI (1914–18), a period that marked the growth of Republicanism. In 1931, after elections had produced a Republican majority, King Alfonso XIII abdicated. A civil war broke out in 1936 between the Nationalists (led by General Francisco Franco and supported by Fascists in Germany and Italy) and the Republicans (supported by the USSR). After a brutal war, in which some 750,000 people were killed, the Republicans surrendered in 1939. Franco assumed complete control of the government and ruled as a dictator until 1975. When Franco died in 1975, Juan Carlos de Borbón y Borbón became King Juan Carlos I.

The following year, a political reform law was passed, and in 1977 the first free elections in

four decades were held. They were won by the Union of the Democratic cos (UCD). In 1981, an attempted coup failed, thanks largely to the intervention of the king. In the 1982 elections, the UCD was defeated by the Spanish Socialist Worker's Party (PSOE) led by Felipe Gonzáles Marquez. Support for the PSOE, however, has been on the decline in recent years. In the 1989 elections, it won only half the seats in the Congress of Deputies and four years later it won even fewer seats, although it remained the largest party.

## GEOGRAPHY

Spain spreads over a quarter of a million square miles, making it the third largest nation in Europe (after Russia and France). Only Switzerland comprises a more elevated average altitude—in fact, one Spanish peak tops 11,000 feet. Contrasting with this is Spain's abundant sand along 2,400 miles of coastline.

Spain is 550 miles wide by 400 miles long, wider at the top and pointed at the bottom (the part that juts into the sea to reach for Gibraltar). A mere 7 miles of sea separates Morocco from Spain. The country is tied to Europe by a 300 mile northern isthmus consisting of the towering Pyrenees. Spain separates into three horizontal climatic regions.

The central part, an immense dusty plateau half a mile above sea level, is arid. This *meseta* comprises La Mancha, where locals describe the climate as nine months of winter followed by three of hell. South of La Mancha, a line of Sierra mountains seals the cold from Andalucía, preserving a warm Mediterranean climate.

Galicia, in Spain's northwestern corner, is hilly, misty, green, and cut by precipitous deep inlets from the sea, rather like Norwegian fjords. Moving east, Asturias, Cantabria, and the Basque provinces present the same green and moist appearance and temperatures as Galicia, but the terrain here is sedimentary rock instead of granite.

Navarra is mountainous in the northeast, hilly in the northwest and descends into cereal plains in the south. Vineyards cover the southeast near Ribera. The Pyrenees run through the north of Aragon, then descend to the basin of the Ebro River. Shut off from the tempering influence of the sea, olives are grown in Southern Aragon. The Pyrenees continue across to the northwestern corner of Spain, there renamed the Cantabrian Mountains, completing a mountain barrier that seals off the north of Spain. Rain clouds are held by these mountains to make the north green and wet.

# the land AND ITS PEOPLE

Catalonia is host to the scenic and rocky north coast of Costa Brava, turning later into golden sand in the southern Costa Dorada.

New Castile lies east, with Extremadura to its west. Valencia hugs the coast east of New Castile and above Murcia. The Meseta begins in Old Castile and León. To its east lies La Rioja, the great wine region of Spain. New Castile's Madrid is located almost exactly at the geographic center of the country. In New Castile's southern half is La Mancha. Extremadura is strewn with boulders and is home to more sheep than humans. Andalucia is home to the Sierra Nevada (Snow Mountains), capped all year in white. To the west, the Guadalquivir River breaks the mountains to form a wide basin that steams in summer.

## ARTS AND CULTURE

Spain's oldest art does not suffer from comparison with the best work the country ever produced. The finest Paleolithic paintings in the world adorn the ceilings of the cave of Altamira.

The *mesquita* (mosque) in Córdoba has no parallel in the world. And at the 14th century Alhambra in Granada, nature is brought inside with stalactite ceilings that convey the sense of a starry sky; outside are gardens and pools. As the Reconquest advanced, some Moors found themselves behind the lines in Christian territory. Prizing the Moorish skills, the Christians engaged them, originating a style known as Mudéjar-Islamic art, to serve Christian ends.

Throughout the time of the Reconquest, religious feeling was intense in Christian Spain. In the 8th century, bones believed to be those of St. James were found at Santiago de Compostela and the area became the holiest Catholic site outside the Holy Land and Rome. By the 11th century, one of the world's great churches had been built there. The cathedral's splendid 18th century baroque front belies the majesty of its Romanesque interior—a towering barrel ceiling with enormous ribs supported by colossal columns.

The Spanish built one breathtaking Gothic church on the French model: the cathedral at Leon. By the 13th century, however, they had modified the original style to create a new version, wider in plan and lightened more by ornate decoration than by the light of windows. The cathedrals at Burgos and Toledo are masterpieces of this Spanish Gothic style.

15th century Isabeline buildings added a trace of lacy decoration to otherwise bare walls, the prime example of which is the sumptuous entrance to the Colegio San Gregorio in Valladolid. A century later, the Isabeline effect evolved into the plateresque—the word means 'like silverwork'—intricate, chiseled, curving and precious. The plateresque refers mainly to appliqué decoration; it serves no structural function, but is a retreat from Gothic design.

The plateresque was still at its height at the beginning of the 16th century, but then Felipe II reacted against its decorative excesses by originating a new style. El Escorial, outside Madrid, was the start. When the designer Juan Bautista de Toledo died four years into the project, he was replaced by the genius of Spanish architect, Juan de Herrera, who followed no known style, only his feeling of what was right.

Herrera's originality died with him, to be replaced by a return to the ornate. The baroque excess of the 17th century holds its own fascination, as the Spanish version, called Churrigueresque (after the Churriguera family) exuberantly demonstrates. The original business of the Churrigueras was designing altars—the altarpiece in the Convento de San Esteban in Salamanca shows their extravagant work.

In the 18th century, when Bourbon rule began in Spain, Felipe V built a 'mini-Versailles' near Segovia to remind him of his home in France. The palace at La Granja is sumptuous, the gardens grand. Succeeding sovereigns built extensively in Madrid, favoring architects of a classical, Italian inclination. One of the best was Juan de Villanueva, who designed the Museo del Prado.

## PAINTING

Romanesque and Gothic painting in Spain can best be appreciated in the superb collection of the Museu d'Art de Catalunya in Barcelona. Often captivating and always deeply expressive of the artist's religious feeling, early Spanish painting is remarkable for the quantity of blood it portrayed. Perhaps the wars of the Reconquest spilled into Spanish art; perhaps Spain's particularly primitive, strict version of Roman Catholicism affected its artists; or perhaps that facet of the Spanish character that finds excitement in the elaborate and bloody ritual of the bullfight expressed itself in its art.

The most prolific, versatile, and influential modern artist was surely Pablo Ruiz Picasso (1881–1973). Picasso, who lived in French exile most of his life, belongs to the world as much as to Spain. Still, the Museu Picasso in Barcelona, Spain displays a good collection of his art, stronger in early paintings than in later works. It is interesting to see the first realistic works of the teenager Picasso, and some favorite pieces from his Rose and Blue Periods.

Picasso's most dramatic, and many would say, his finest work, the tormented *Guernica*, was finally returned to Spain from the United States and is displayed in Spain's new museum of modern art, the Centro de Arte Reina Sofía in Madrid.

Spain does better in collecting the works of another native son, the Catalan Joan Miró (1893–1983). The Fundacío Miró in Barcelona presents the breadth of his work, from painting to sculpture to prints and fabrics, in a most appropriate building designed by Joseph Sert. Salvador Dalí (1904–89), the great surrealist, has a worthy surreal gallery in the Museo-Teatro of his home town of Figueres, northeast of Barcelona.

# Spanish FOOD

## FOOD AND DRINK

There is enormous variety in regional Spanish specialties. Since the nation is chiefly agricultural, chefs have a field day in the marketplace. Through swift transport systems, fish reaches interior towns on the same day it is netted. Beef, once scorned for its toughness, is now tender and flavorful. Salads and fresh vegetables are safe to eat wherever you go.

Roast lamb (*cordero asado*) and roast suckling pig (*cochinillo*) are generally the finest meats. Spanish hams, such as those from Jabugo, Trevelez and Teruel, deserve worldwide admiration. Poultry is delicious, especially when grilled on an open fire.

There are all kinds of exquisite fruits in Spain, including the world's best oranges (in winter only). Spanish honey can have the fragrance of rosemary, marjoram or orange blossoms. You'll also find nougat, marzipan and many other types of confectionery.

The better types of cheese include the Tetilla (soft and greasy), Cabrales (fermented and piquant), Burgos (all cream) and Manchego. If you try the Manchego, which has been molded in matting and preserved in oil, your

SPICED OLIVES, PAGE 174

SPANISH FISH SOUP WITH SAFFRON, PAGE 183

friends might avoid you for a couple of days afterward, but it's worth the gamble!

Sherry, the national wine, is available in seven major types, some with a number of sub-classifications. Like port in neighboring Portugal, sherry is always bottled blended rather than 'straight'. Call it *jerez* (pronounced 'hair-eth') if you want to please the bartender. Through the revolving *solera* system of mixing, old and new vintages are combined to produce a product that is always standard. Manzanillas and finos are examples of extremely dry sherry; now many are served chilled to soften the bite. San Patricio, when it's very cold, is very nice, but some Spaniards shudder at the thought of cooling sherries. Tío Pepe ('Uncle Joe' in Spanish) has a good reputation and is sold to international markets. Long life (or any similar Oloroso blend) is old, soft and golden, with just enough dryness and richness of body to give pleasure to those who pucker up with the drier varieties.

Spanish red table wines are perhaps the most underrated of any in Europe. Countless gallons flow over the border each year to be sold as 'French' wines in France and elsewhere. Most of these reds resemble burgundies rather than Bordeaux in their heaviness and fullness; the whites, not as fine, are often very sweet. The other extreme is the type with little body, but which can be pleasantly refreshing. Some of the rosés (such as Marqués de Riscal or Senorío de Sarria) are commendably dry and crisp.

The word *cava* on labels of Spanish sparkling wine means that it has rested in lodges (French style) and is of superior quality. Viña Pomal and Federico Paternina remain superior rubies in their *reserva* class. Many *reserva* and *gran reserva* types have deteriorated. Aside from NPU, the sparkling wine range from sweet to cloying to extremely cloying.

During summer, sample the cooling, refreshing wine punch called sangría. Choose your own base (red, white, or sparkling wine); it will be served in a pitcher with orange slices, lemon slices, soda water and sugar, but you often also get a tiny glass of cognac for flavor. Available anywhere at any mealtime, sangría is light, delicate and delicious.

Fundador is by far the leading cognac because it's the only truly dry brandy on the local market. Spaniards enjoy Carlos I, González Byass Lepanto, Larios 1866 and similar distillates, but these can be rich and heavy. The lighter brands are Fundador, Soberano, '103', Terry and about a dozen more.

Any big bar stocks at least 30 or 40 varieties of liqueurs. The prices are so low (because the liqueurs are made under license in Spain) that you should ask only for the original, not the cheaper copies with phonetic names such as Perry Herrink, Quandro and Shardroos.

All leading brands of beer on the Continent are now imported, and 40 breweries have spread over 25 of Spain's provinces. San Miguel has taken the lead among domestic labels.

## EATING OUT

Spanish meal hours call for heroic belt-tightening and self-discipline. Breakfast is generally as early or late as you choose. Lunch is from about 2–3.30pm—so it might be 4.30pm before you stagger away from the table for your siesta.

Dinner usually starts at about 9.30pm at the earliest, which means the dessert and demitasse arrive after midnight.

Scan the menu in restaurants for the words *servicio incluído*, which means your bill already includes tips. If so, a small additional gratuity is sufficient, say 5 percent, whichever is greater. Otherwise, 15 percent is a normal tip for the underpaid waiters in Spanish restaurants. In elegant restaurants, where a captain orchestrates the meal and a sommelier presents the wine, the captain should receive 5 percent, the sommelier 10 percent and the server 15 percent.

BEEF BRAISED IN RIOJA, PAGE 206

# tapas

# Appetizers or TAPAS

The *tapas* tradition is the delightful Spanish custom of gathering before lunch or again before dinner for a glass of wine or beer and sampling appetizers.

*Tapas* will be found in even the smallest bar or the tiniest village in Spain. The choice in such places will typically be limited to cured ham and cheese, unless there is someone particularly inventive in the kitchen. But it is in the big regional centers of Madrid, Barcelona, Santiago de Compostela, Sevilla and Málaga where *tapas* often become inspired and are of an overwhelming variety. In one bar in Madrid, one sees nothing but armies of mushrooms sizzling on the grill. Another has nothing but grilled shrimp served with a robust house wine, or spicy snails, or grilled red peppers or smoked fish.

The word *tapa*, meaning cover or lid, is thought to have originally referred to the complimentary plate of appetizers that many *tascas* (bars) would place on top of one's wineglass—like a 'cover'. Anything, however, served in small portions can be considered a *tapa*. A quail, for example, is a *tapa* when only one is served.

*Tapas* and first course dishes are often interchangeable, therefore whatever is included in this section of the book may precede a main course.

## SALTED ALMONDS

**Ingredients**

1 tablespoon egg white, lightly beaten
½ teaspoon coarse sea salt
1 cup whole almonds in their skins

**Method**

1. Preheat the oven to 350°F. Spread almonds on a baking sheet and roast for about 20 minutes, until nutty and golden.
2. Combine egg white and salt with almonds and shake well to coat
3. Tip out onto the baking sheet, give a shake to separate the nuts, then put back into the oven for 5 minutes, until nuts have dried. Leave until cold, then store in an airtight container until ready to serve.

Serves 2–4

## MARINATED SARDINES

### Ingredients

1½ pounds fresh sardines
2 onions, sliced into thin rings
1 carrot, thinly sliced
1 tablespoon parsley, chopped
½ cup white wine vinegar
½ cup water
¼ teaspoon ground cinnamon
1 bay leaf
6 peppercorns
½ teaspoon dried thyme
½ teaspoon salt
2 tablespoons olive oil

### Method

1. Preheat oven to 350°F. Prepare fish: cut off fins and remove backbone. Leave head and tail intact. Wipe over with damp kitchen paper. Arrange fish in a shallow ovenproof dish and cover with onion rings, carrots and parsley.
2. Add remaining ingredients, cover with lid or foil and bake for 25 minutes.
3. Allow to cool completely before serving as tapas.

Serves 6

## SCALLOPS BAKED WITH CURED HAM

**Ingredients**

2 tablespoons olive oil
1 pound scallops, in half shell
salt and freshly ground black pepper
½ cup onion, minced
1 clove garlic, minced
¼ cup cured ham such as proscuitto, minced
3 tablespoons dry white wine
½ cup breadcrumbs
1 tablespoon parsley, minced
1 teaspoon lemon juice

**Method**

1. Heat 1 tablespoon oil in a large skillet and sauté the scallops over high heat for 1 minute. Divide scallops among the shells and sprinkle with salt and pepper.
2. Add onion and garlic and a little more oil, if necessary, to the skillet. Cover and cook over low heat for 15 minutes. Add ham and sauté for 1 minute. Stir in the wine and let it cook off. Spoon mixture over scallops.
3. Preheat the oven to 450°F. In a small bowl, combine breadcrumbs, parsley, lemon juice and remaining oil. Sprinkle over scallops. Place shells on baking sheet and bake 10 minutes. If necessary, put under the grill to brown the top crumbs.

Serves 2–4

## BELL PEPPER AND ONION TART

**Ingredients**

2 cups all-purpose flour
salt and pepper
1 teaspoon active dry yeast
2/3 cup warm milk
1 egg yolk
4 tablespoons olive oil
1 pound Spanish onions, halved and sliced
4 red bell peppers, sliced
4 yellow bell peppers, sliced
1/2 cup fresh thyme, oregano and parsley sprigs
16–20 canned anchovy fillets, drained

**Method**

1. Sift flour and salt into a bowl. Stir in yeast.
2. Sir milk into egg yolk, then slowly pour into flour, stirring constantly. Beat 5–10 minutes, or until dough comes cleanly away from the bowl.
3. Turn dough onto a lightly floured surface and knead until smooth and elastic. Form into a ball, place in an oiled bowl, cover and leave in a warm place for about 1 hour until doubled in size.
4. Meanwhile, in a skillet, heat 3 tablespoons of oil. Add onions, bell pepper and herbs and cook over medium heat, stirring occasionally for 20–25 minutes or until vegetables are soft, but not browned. Add a few tablespoons of water if necessary to prevent browning. Season with salt and pepper and set aside.
5. Preheat oven to 475°F. On a lightly floured surface, punch down and flatten dough. Roll out to a 12 inch circle. Carefully transfer to an oiled baking sheet. Turn up edge to make a rim. Prick well with a fork.
6. Spread vegetable mixture over dough, arrange anchovy fillets on top, drizzle with remaining oil and bake for 25–30 minutes, or until the dough is well risen, crisp and golden. Serve warm.

Serves 6

## MOORISH PICKLED ANCHOVIES

**Ingredients**

2 pounds fresh anchovies, sardines or smelts
6–8 tablespoons olive oil
⅓ cup all-purpose flour
salt and freshly ground black pepper
6 garlic cloves, finely chopped
small pinch of saffron strands
1 teaspoon cumin seeds
1 teaspoon ground ginger
1 cup red wine vinegar
4 bay leaves
1 lemon, thinly sliced

**Method**

1. Cut off fish heads, and remove the innards. Slit fish down the belly as far as the tail, and rinse the insides under a tap. Put each fish down on a board, black back upwards, and press a thumb firmly down on the back bone of the fish. This opens the fish out like a book and makes it easy to remove the backbone and tail.
2. Heat 4 tablespoons of oil in a large frying-pan. Dust the fish with seasoned flour on a baking tray and fry. Put fish in oil, skin side down and turn after 1–2 minutes. Remove fish from oil and place on paper towels to drain. Take the pan off the heat between batches and add more oil as necessary.
3. Fry garlic in remaining oil, then place in a mortar or a small herb (or coffee) mill. Add saffron, cumin seeds, ginger and a pinch of salt and work to a paste. Work in vinegar. Arrange fish in an earthenware dish, skin up. The dish can be shallow if you are planning to serve them within 24 hours, but should be smaller and deeper if you want to keep the fish.
4. Mix 1 cup of water into the spice mixture and pour over fish. Add more vinegar and water to cover fish completely if you are planning to keep them. Lay bay leaves and very thinly sliced lemon over the top. Refrigerate for half a day before eating. They can be served straight from the dish and should be eaten within a week.

Serves 8

## POTATO OMELETTE

### Ingredients

2 pounds potatoes, peeled

1 small onion, peeled (optional)

1 cup olive oil

5 eggs, beaten

salt

### Method

1. Wash and dry potatoes, then cut into thin slices. If you are using onion, dice it finely.
2. Heat oil in a skillet, add potatoes and onion, season and cover. Fry gently, moving the skillet so that vegetables don't stick. Once potatoes are cooked (take care they don't become crisp) break them up a bit and remove from the skillet with a slotted spoon. Add to the beaten eggs. Stir potatoes around until they are well covered with egg. Add salt to taste.
3. Remove most of the oil from the skillet, leaving about 1 tablespoon, and reheat. You will need a plate with a slightly larger diameter than the skillet. Return egg and potato mixture to the skillet and cook for a few minutes until one side is golden.
4. Next, and this is slightly tricky, slip the omelette out onto your plate, cooked-side down, and then slip it back into the skillet, cooked-side up. Cook until firm.
5. Your omelette should be about 1 ½ inches thick. If you are using it for tapas, then cut it into squares.

Serves 6–8

## SPICED OLIVES (below)

**Ingredients**

1 pound green or ripe olives
1 fresh oregano sprig
1 fresh thyme sprig
1 teaspoon fresh rosemary, finely chopped
2 bay leaves
1 teaspoon fennel seeds, bruised
1 teaspoon cumin seeds, finely crushed
1 fresh red chili, seeded and chopped
4 cloves garlic, crushed
olive oil

**Method**

1. Using a small sharp knife, make a lengthwise slit through to pit of each olive. Put olives into a bowl. Stir in oregano, thyme, rosemary, bay leaves, fennel seeds, cumin seeds, chili and garlic.
2. Pack olive mixture into a jar with a tight fitting lid. Add enough oil to cover olives, seal and leave for at least 3 days, shaking jar occasionally, before using.

Makes 6 servings

## MARINATED TUNA

**Ingredients**

8 oz canned yellowfin tuna, with its oil
2 teaspoons vinegar
2 teaspoons onion, minced
1 teaspoon capers, chopped if they are large
2 teaspoons parsley, minced
salt
freshly ground pepper

**Method**

1. Place tuna in a bowl and flake with a fork. Stir in remaining ingredients and refrigerate overnight.
2. Use this tuna as it is, served on a salad plate, spread it on bread, combine with mayonnaise or use it as a filling for an omelette.

Makes 1 ½ cups

## PORK BALLS

### Ingredients

8 oz ground pork loin
7 tablespoons parsley, minced
2 cloves garlic, minced
1 tablespoon onion, minced
3 tablespoons breadcrumbs
2 eggs, lightly beaten
salt
freshly ground pepper
all-purpose flour for dusting
oil for frying

*Aioli sauce*

4 cloves garlic, peeled and minced
1 teaspoon salt
1 cup olive oil

### Method

1. Combine pork, parsley, garlic, onion, breadcrumbs, 1 of the eggs, salt and pepper. Form into 1 inch balls and roll in flour.
2. Heat oil, at least ½ inch deep, to smoking point. Dip the meatballs in remaining beaten egg and place directly in hot oil. Lower the flame and fry slowly until well browned on both sides and cooked through.
3. To make the sauce, crush garlic in a mortar with salt until it becomes a pulp, then gradually beat in oil. The result should be like a pale, thick mayonnaise. A milder version is made exactly like mayonnaise: simply crush garlic with lemon juice and egg yolk and then add the salt and oil. Makes 1 cup.

Makes 20 small meatballs

## MUSHROOMS STUFFED WITH CRAB AND WALNUTS

**Ingredients**

50 button mushrooms

*Vinaigrette*

¼ cup red wine vinegar
salt and freshly ground pepper, to taste
¾ cup olive oil
12 oz canned crab meat, flaked
⅓ cup mayonnaise
⅓ cup scallion, finely chopped
⅓ cup parsley, finely chopped
1 cup walnuts, finely chopped
salt and pepper

**Method**

1. Remove stems from mushrooms and discard. Wipe mushroom caps with a damp cloth.
2. To make vinaigrette, in a small bowl combine vinegar, salt and pepper. Whisk in oil and let stand 5 minutes. Whisk again, then taste and adjust seasoning. Brush the inside of each mushroom with vinaigrette.
3. Combine crab meat, mayonnaise, scallion, parsley and walnuts. Mix well, and season to taste with salt and freshly ground black pepper.
4. Place a heaping teaspoon into each mushroom cap. Refrigerate until ready to serve.

Makes 50

## HOT OYSTERS AND LEEKS

**Ingredients**

20–24 large oysters on the half shell
coarse sea salt
1 oz butter
1 small leek, washed and finely sliced
salt and pepper
pinch of sugar
squeeze of lemon juice
½ cup dry white wine
pinch of saffron threads or curry powder
½ cup cream
1 egg yolk

**Method**

1. Remove oysters from their shells and keep chilled. Wash the shells and arrange 4 individual gratin dishes on a bed of coarse sea salt to keep shells level.
2. Melt butter in a pan and toss leek in the hot butter. Season with salt, freshly ground pepper and sugar, cover tightly and cook gently until tender. Season with lemon juice.
3. Boil wine with the saffron or curry powder over moderate heat until reduced by half. In a small bowl, combine cream with egg yolk and whisk. Whisk into the hot wine mixture and return to gentle heat, if necessary, to thicken slightly, whisking all the time. Do not let it boil. Add salt and white pepper to taste and remove from heat.
4. Arrange cooked leeks in the oyster shells. and place oysters on top. Coat each oyster with sauce and place under a preheated hot grill for a minute or so to glaze. Serve immediately.

Serves 4

## DEEP-FRIED CRAB BALLS

**Ingredients**

1 pound crab meat, flaked
1/4 cup butter, softened
1 tablespoon Dijon mustard
1/8 teaspoon Tabasco sauce
2 egg yolks
1/2 cup fresh breadcrumbs
salt
all-purpose flour
oil for deep-frying

*Tartar sauce*

1 cup mayonnaise
1 teaspoon onion, finely chopped
1 teaspoon parsley, finely chopped
1 teaspoon basil, finely chopped
1 teaspoon gherkins, finely chopped
1 teaspoon green olives, finely chopped
1 teaspoon Dijon mustard
salt and pepper

**Method**

1. To make sauce, combine all ingredients in a bowl and refrigerate until ready to use.
2. Combine crab meat, butter, mustard, Tabasco, egg yolks and breadcrumbs in a bowl. Mix well, add salt to taste. Cover and refrigerate until firm.
3. Shape into balls the size of a small walnut and return to refrigerator for 30 minutes. Roll balls in flour and deep-fry in hot oil until golden. Drain on paper towels. Serve with tartar sauce.

Makes about 36

## FRIED VONGOLE (below)

### Ingredients

2 eggs, lightly beaten
salt and pepper
2 cups dry breadcrumbs
1 tablespoon dry mixed herbs
2 pounds clams, cleaned and steamed
oil for deep-frying
3 tablespoons tartar sauce (see page 178)

### Method

1. Place eggs in a bowl and season with a little salt and pepper.
2. Combine breadcrumbs and herbs in a separate bowl.
3. Dip clams in egg mixture, then roll in breadcrumbs.
4. Deep-fry clams in hot oil until golden brown.
5. Drain on paper towels and serve immediately with tartar sauce.

Serves 4

## ANCHOVY, CHICKEN AND TOMATO CANAPE

### Ingredients

10 slices French-style bread, 2 inches thick
mayonnaise
20 anchovy fillets
2 roasted red peppers
4 tablespoons tomato sauce
cayenne pepper to taste
4 tablespoons boiled chicken, finely chopped
chopped parsley, for garnish

### Method

1. Toast bread slices in a 450°F oven for 5 minutes. Spread them with mayonnaise. Cut anchovy fillets in pieces and arrange them on top of the toast. Spread on another layer of mayonnaise and cover with a piece of pepper the size of the toast. Mix tomato sauce with cayenne. Spread 1 teaspoon of tomato sauce on each canapé, sprinkle with chicken and garnish with parsley.

Makes 10 pieces

## SPANISH MARINATED MUSSELS

### Ingredients

1 pound mussels
1 onion, chopped
2 sticks celery, chopped
2 cloves garlic, chopped
1 cup white wine or water
pepper
1 tablespoon butter
parsley, for garnish
1 hard-boiled egg (white only), chopped finely
2 tablespoons baby capers
2 tablespoons fresh aromatic herbs (thyme, rosemary, marjoram), chopped
2 vine-ripened tomatoes, finely chopped
5 oz Spanish virgin olive oil
1 tablespoon Dijon mustard
1 oz old sherry vinegar
1 tablespoon fresh basil, roughly chopped
salt

### Method

1. Place mussels, onion, celery, garlic and water (or white wine) in a large saucepan.
2. Cook over medium heat until mussels have opened. Stir frequently to ensure mussels cook evenly.
3. Add pepper to taste. Stir in butter and parsley just before serving.
4. Combine remaining ingredients together and marinate in the refrigerator for 2 hours.
5. Serve with salad or as tapas with glass of wine.

Serves 4

# *soups*

# Spanish SOUPS

In evaluating Spanish soups, it soon becomes evident that there could be a division between those soups light enough for first courses and those that most of us would consider meals-in-a-pot.

Traditionally, Spanish soups were of the robust variety, providing inexpensive eating that was filling and nutritious. Such soups utilize cheap and easily obtainable ingredients from each region of Spain. Like so many other eating habits that began for economic reasons, the Spanish still continue their love of soups.

The best Spanish soups are the hearty peasant variety. Rarely will you find a soup mellowed with cream and butter. Even the most worldly city-dwellers, when given a choice, will invariably choose a soup that reminds them of their family roots, and the most exclusive Spanish restaurants will usually present a selection of regional, down-to-earth Spanish soups.

There are, nevertheless, a limited number of Spanish soups that fall into a 'first course' category, most notably, the consommés, some garlic soups, and several of the simpler fish soups. Also included in this category are the ever popular cold summer soups; when temperatures rise, even a Spaniard with the most robust appetite will prefer the refreshing icy *gazpacho*.

In the final analysis, there are Spanish soups to satisfy all tastes. Try the light, as well as the hearty, but take care to select the type of soup that best suits the season and best complements your menu plans.

## RICE, BEAN AND GREENS SOUP

**Ingredients**

8 oz large dried white beans
8 cups water
12 oz collard greens or Swiss chard, thick stems removed (weigh after trimming), coarsely chopped
½ teaspoon paprika
few strands of saffron
1 turnip, scraped and thinly sliced
7 cups chicken broth, preferably home made
salt
1 cup rice, preferably short-grain

**Method**

1. Place beans and water in a large pot, bring to a boil and simmer, covered, for 1 hour.
2. Add greens, paprika, saffron, turnip, chicken broth and salt.
3. Cook for 30 minutes more, or until beans are almost tender.
4. Add rice, cover, and cook for 20 minutes, until rice is done. Add more liquid if necessary—the soup should be thick, but there should also be some broth.

Serves 6

## SPANISH FISH SOUP WITH SAFFRON

### Ingredients

2 tablespoons olive oil
2 large carrots, finely chopped
3 leeks, finely sliced and well washed
1 red bell pepper, chopped
1 green bell pepper, chopped
1 tablespoon Spanish paprika
large pinch of saffron threads
2 cups white wine
3 cups fish bouillon
14 oz firm white fish fillets
14 oz shrimp, shelled and deveined
14 oz baby calamari or squid
2 tablespoons parsley, chopped
1 lemon, cut into wedges

### Method

1. Heat olive oil in a large saucepan. Add carrots, leeks and bell peppers and sauté until softened (about 10 minutes). Add paprika and saffron, and continue to cook for a few minutes more.
2. Add wine and bouillon and bring to a boil, simmering for 15 minutes.
3. Add diced fish, shelled shrimp and squid and simmer for a further 5 minutes.
4. Garnish with some chopped parsley and a squeeze of lemon.

Serves 4

## ALMOND SOUP

**Ingredients**

7 oz almonds
1 clove garlic, peeled
1 tablespoon parsley, finely chopped
8 slices stale bread, preferably brown bread
1/3 cup olive oil
1 teaspoon ground cumin
1/2 teaspoon saffron
4 cups good chicken bouillon
1 cup milk
salt and pepper

**Method**

1. Fry almonds, garlic, parsley and 4 slices of bread in about 4 tablespoons of oil. When golden, put the contents of the pan in a food processor and purée with cumin, saffron and a little bouillon. Put in a saucepan, pour in remaining bouillon and milk, season with salt and pepper, and bring to a boil. Lower the heat and cook slowly for about 15 minutes.
2. Meanwhile, fry remaining bread slices in remaining olive oil until crisp and golden.
3. Bring the soup to a boil again and add 4 slices of fried bread. Cover, remove from the stove and leave for 5 minutes before serving.

Serves 4

## GAZPACHO

### Ingredients

2 slices of stale bread (optional)
4 pounds tomatoes, washed and roughly chopped
1 cucumber, peeled and chopped
1 green pepper, seeded and chopped
1 small onion, peeled and chopped
2 cloves garlic, peeled and chopped
5 tablespoons olive oil
1–2 tablespoons good wine vinegar, to taste
1 teaspoon cumin seeds or cumin powder

### Method

1. Soak bread (if using) in a little water, and squeeze it out before using. (The bread helps to thicken the soup and give it a nice consistency.)
2. Blend all vegetables and garlic in a food processor, and push through a sieve into a bowl. Use the processor again to beat bread, oil and vinegar together. Add some of the tomatoes, the cumin seeds and salt to taste. Add a little water and mix into the bowl with the soup. Add a few ice cubes and leave to become cold. You can add more water if necessary.

***Note:*** Traditionally, this soup was made by crushing the ingredients with a mortar and pestle and then adding cold water. Gazpacho should be served in wooden bowls and eaten with a wooden spoon. Make large quantities of gazpacho as it keeps well—but it won't last long, as you are bound to keep sipping it!

Serves 6–8

## ICED TOMATO SOUP

**Ingredients**

3 slices bread, crusts removed
2 pounds tomatoes, skinned, seeded and chopped, or 28 oz canned peeled tomato pieces, chopped
1 cucumber, peeled, seeded and chopped
½ cup onions, chopped
2 cloves garlic, crushed
½ green bell pepper, seeded and chopped
1 teaspoon salt
1 teaspoon ground cumin
2 tablespoons olive oil
2 tablespoons wine vinegar
2–3 cups iced water

*To garnish*

1 red or green bell pepper, diced
1 small cucumber, diced
1 onion, finely chopped
2 hard-boiled eggs, chopped
croûtons

**Method**

1. Place all ingredients, except water, into a large bowl and allow to stand for 30 minutes to soften bread and blend flavors.
2. Purée one third of the mixture at a time in an electric blender or food processor. Pour back into a bowl and thin down to desired consistency with iced water.
3. Cover and chill well. Adjust seasoning to taste. Serve in chilled bowls or in a large bowl over ice.
4. Place garnish ingredients in separate bowls and allow each diner to add garnish to their own soup.

Serves 8

## SPANISH PEA SOUP

### Ingredients

2 cups dried green split peas
3 cups water
1 tablespoon olive oil
1 tablespoon Spanish paprika
2 onions, chopped
1 clove garlic, minced
1 green bell pepper, chopped
1 medium carrot, thinly sliced
3 medium red potatoes, peeled and diced
8 cups chicken or vegetable bouillon
salt and pepper to taste
2 ears fresh corn
½ bunch chives, chopped
low-fat yogurt to garnish (optional)

### Method

1. Rinse peas thoroughly. Place them in a large pot, cover with water and bring to a boil. Simmer for 2 minutes then remove from the heat, cover and let stand for 1 hour.

2. Meanwhile, heat oil in a large saucepan and add paprika, onion and garlic, and sauté for 5 minutes until the mixture is fragrant and onions have softened. Add green bell pepper, carrot and potato. Toss the vegetables thoroughly with the onion and paprika mixture until well coated, then continue to cook for 10 minutes, stirring continually.

3. Add bouillon, peas, and salt and pepper to taste then simmer, uncovered, for 2–3 hours or until peas are very tender.

4. Cut kernels off corn cobs. Reserve ½ cup of corn and add the remainder to the soup and simmer for 2 minutes. Purée the soup until thick and smooth then serve with a few scattered corn kernels and some chopped chives. Garnish each plate with a teaspoon of low-fat yogurt if desired.

Serves 4

## GARLIC SOUP

**Ingredients**

7 cups chicken broth

2 beef bones

1 head garlic, separated into cloves, unpeeled, plus 8 cloves, peeled and chopped

4 parsley sprigs

salt and freshly ground pepper

2½ – 3 tablespoons olive oil

¼ pound cured ham, such as prosciutto, sliced ¼ inch thick and diced

1 tablespoon paprika

½ teaspoon ground cumin

8 bread slices, 2 inches thick, from a French baguette

4 large eggs (optional)

**Method**

1. In a large saucepan, combine broth, bones, garlic head, parsley, and salt and pepper. Bring to a boil, reduce heat to medium and simmer, uncovered, for 30 minutes. Strain into another saucepan.
2. Meanwhile, heat 1 tablespoon oil in a medium skillet and sauté chopped garlic over medium heat until lightly golden. Add ham and cook for 1 minute. Stir in paprika and cumin and remove immediately from heat. Add the garlic mixture to the soup and simmer.
3. Preheat the oven to 350°F. Arrange bread slices on a baking sheet and brush lightly with oil on both sides. Bake, turning once, until golden on both sides (about 5 minutes).
4. Place the toasted bread in a soup tureen and pour in the hot soup. If adding eggs, use a heatproof tureen, slide eggs into the soup, and bake at 450°F until set (about 3–4 minutes).

Serves 4

# vegetables & salads

# Vegetables and SALADS

Spain's summers tend to be long and very warm, and perhaps for this reason, Spaniards are inordinately fond of foods bathed in cooling vinaigrettes. Visit any restaurant in Spain and you will probably find just two salads listed on the menu: a simple lettuce and tomato combination and the more complex *ensalada mixta*, which may have tuna, asparagus, onion, egg and olives. The tomatoes are sweet and vine ripened, and the lettuce a flavorful cos. However, it would be wrong to say that this is the extent of the Spanish salad repertoire, for delicious bean, vegetable, rice and seafood salads abound.

Vegetables, on the other hand, are not generally the most popular foods in Spain. In fact, many Spaniards seem to have an absolute aversion to anything green. But some of Spain's most popular dishes include a combination of eggs, sweet peppers, tomatoes, eggplants, red peppers and artichokes.

Potatoes, however, are in a class by themselves. Ever since they were introduced from South America in the sixteenth century, potatoes have been a staple of the Spanish diet. A main-course dish without its fried potatoes would appear naked in Spanish eyes.

The historic lack of fresh water in many areas of Spain means that vegetables are rarely boiled, but rather quick fried or slowly sautéed in oil until tender. Vegetables are also combined in casseroles.

## CHICKEN AND AVOCADO SALAD

**Ingredients**

3½ cups chicken strips, cooked
1 small head lettuce, shredded
1 large red onion, thinly sliced
½ cup olive oil
¼ cup red wine vinegar
salt and pepper
lettuce leaves
2 oranges, peeled and sliced
2 avocados, peeled and sliced
1 bunch radishes, sliced

**Method**

1. Place chicken, lettuce and onion in a bowl. Thoroughly combine oil and vinegar. Season to taste with salt and pepper. Pour over salad, toss gently, then arrange chicken on lettuce leaves. Garnish with orange, avocado and radish slices.

Serves 6

## SPINACH WITH RAISINS AND PINE NUTS (below)

### Ingredients

3 tablespoons seeded raisins
1 bunch English spinach
2 tablespoons olive oil
2 tablespoons pine nuts
1 medium onion, finely chopped
1 clove garlic, crushed
salt and freshly ground black pepper

### Method

1. Soak raisins in cold water for 15 minutes. Drain well.
2. Cut off roots from spinach, just above the pink tip, and wash in 3 changes of water. Shake off excess water and place in a large saucepan. Cover and cook over medium heat until spinach has just wilted. Remove to a colander to cool and drain. Chop spinach roughly.
3. In a large skillet, heat 1 tablespoon of oil, add pine nuts and cook, stirring, until golden. Remove with a slotted spoon. Add remaining tablespoon of oil, onion and garlic, and cook over moderate heat until onion is soft, but not colored.
4. Add spinach, drained raisins, salt and pepper, and toss gently to heat through. Sprinkle pine nuts over. Serve hot as a side dish.

Serves 4

## FAVA BEANS WITH HAM

### Ingredients

2 tablespoons olive oil
4 large green onions, finely chopped
1 red bell pepper, seeded and diced
2 oz ham, diced
2½ cups shelled fava beans
¾ cup dry white wine
salt and black pepper
fresh herbs, chopped, to garnish

### Method

1. In a saucepan, heat oil, add green onions, bell pepper and ham and cook for 3 minutes.
2. Stir in beans and cook for 1 minute. Add enough wine to cover, bring to a boil, then cover pan and simmer for about 20 minutes or until beans are tender.
3. Uncover and boil off excess liquid. Add salt, if necessary, and black pepper. Cool slightly before serving. Garnish with chopped herbs.

Makes 4 servings

## CAULIFLOWER SAUTEED IN GARLIC (below)

### Ingredients

1 medium cauliflower

2 cloves garlic, peeled and sliced

4 oz olive oil

salt and white pepper

1 teaspoon parsley, chopped

### Method

1. Boil cauliflower in lightly salted water, being careful not to overcook it. Drain off water and break cauliflower into florets. Dry cauliflower with a clean towel.
2. Heat garlic in oil. Sauté cauliflower in oil and garlic until golden. Season with salt and pepper and sprinkle with parsley.

Serves 4

## SPANISH VEGETABLE STEW

### Ingredients

3 pounds zucchini

2 large onion, peeled and diced

1 clove garlic, peeled and diced

1 pound green bell peppers, seeded and chopped

2 pounds tomatoes, skinned, seeded and chopped

6 tablespoons olive oil

salt and pepper

sugar

### Method

1. Prepare the vegetables first. In Spain, zucchini are peeled, but if they are the small variety leave the skins on as they are tastier. Dice them fairly large.
2. Heat oil gently in a large casserole dish. Cook the onion, garlic and bell pepper until onion is transparent. Add tomatoes and cook for another 5 minutes, stirring all the time with a wooden spoon. Add zucchini and stir in well. Season with salt and pepper, and add a pinch of sugar.
3. Cook over low heat with the lid on for about 20 minutes, stirring occasionally, until the vegetables are cooked (not overcooked). If it is too liquid, remove the lid, turn up the heat and cook for a few minutes so that the surplus juice evaporates.

Serves 6

## ARTICHOKES BRAISED IN WHITE WINE

### Ingredients

6 artichokes

$\frac{1}{4}$ cup olive oil

1 small onion, peeled and finely chopped

2 cloves garlic, peeled and finely sliced

7 oz white wine or dry sherry

salt

freshly grated nutmeg

### Method

1. Remove stalks and outer leaves from artichokes and wash well. Cut each one into pieces. Heat oil in a casserole dish and gently sauté onion and garlic for about 4 minutes. Add artichokes and wine, and season with salt and nutmeg. Cook gently until done (20–40 minutes, depending on size and type). Test by pulling a leaf; if done it will come away easily. If the liquid reduces too much you can add a little water.

Serves 4

## SPANISH RICE

### Ingredients

3 cups cooked rice

3 tablespoons olive oil

1 medium onion, finely diced

1 tablespoon garlic, finely minced

1 small green pepper, finely diced

1 small red pepper, finely diced

2 ripe tomatoes, peeled, seeded and diced

salt and pepper, to taste

### Method

1. Cook rice according to the instructions on the package and keep warm. Heat oil over medium heat in a large skillet and add onions. Cook, stirring, for about 5 minutes. Add garlic and cook for another minute. Add the peppers and tomatoes, cover and cook for about 5 minutes. Add rice, stir to combine, replace the cover and cook for another minute or so. Season with salt and pepper and serve immediately.

Serves 4

## FRIED POTATOES (below)

**Ingredients**

1½ tablespoons butter

3 tablespoons olive oil

4 potatoes, peeled and sliced ⅜ inch thick

salt and pepper

chopped parsley

**Method**

1. Heat butter and oil together in a large pan. Fry potatoes until tender and browned on both sides. Drain on paper towels. Place on serving plate, sprinkle with salt, pepper and chopped parsley.

Serves 4

## CUCUMBER, TOMATO AND BELL PEPPER SALAD

**Ingredients**

1 cucumber, peeled and cut in 1 inch cubes

2 tomatoes, cut in eighths, then halved

1 green bell pepper, in 1 inch pieces

1 small onion, chopped

6 tablespoons olive oil

3 tablespoons red wine vinegar

½ teaspoon sugar

salt

freshly ground pepper

**Method**

1. Combine all ingredients. Refrigerate for at least 30 minutes before serving.

Serves 4–6

## SPANISH CARROT AND PRAWN SALAD

### Ingredients

1½ pounds carrots
4 cloves garlic
1 tablespoon fresh rosemary
¼ cup virgin olive oil
1 teaspoon ground cumin
2 teaspoons mild paprika
3 tablespoons white wine vinegar
salt and freshly ground pepper to taste
1 pound large peeled, cooked shrimp (tail on)
¼ cup chopped Italian parsley
low-fat yogurt, to garnish (optional)

### Method

1. Peel and trim carrots, then slice on the diagonal into ¼ inch slices. Bring a large pot of salted water to a boil and add sliced carrots. Boil vigorously for 3–4 minutes or until almost crisp-tender then drain.
2. Meanwhile, peel garlic and pound in a mortar and pestle with fresh rosemary until the two are finely ground and fragrant. Alternatively, finely chop garlic and rosemary together.
3. Heat a tablespoon of oil in a small skillet and add garlic and rosemary mixture, cumin and paprika and sauté for 1–2 minutes until very fragrant. Remove from heat and whisk in remaining olive oil and white wine vinegar. Add salt and pepper to taste.
4. Toss carrot slices and cooked shrimp with the warm garlic and rosemary dressing, making sure that all the ingredients are well coated. Garnish with fresh parsley and yogurt, if using.
5. Chill for at least 4 hours then serve cool or at room temperature. Serve with plenty of crusty bread if desired.

Serves 4

## ASPARAGUS WITH EGG

**Ingredients**

1 1/2 pounds fresh asparagus spears
1 hard-boiled egg, finely chopped
1/3 cup olive oil
1 clove garlic
3/4 cup fresh, coarse breadcrumbs
2 tablespoons fresh parsley, chopped
kitchen string

**Method**

1. Using a small sharp knife, cut off woody part at end of asparagus stems. Working from tip to bottom, scrape off scales from stems. Tie stems into 4 bundles with kitchen string.
2. In a deep saucepan, bring 2 inches of water to a boil. Add asparagus bundles, tips pointing upward. Cover pan with a lid or dome of foil and simmer for 8–10 minutes or until asparagus is just tender. Remove asparagus and untie bundles. Drain asparagus on a thick pad of paper towels. Arrange on a warm serving plate, sprinkle egg over stems, cover and keep warm.
3. Meanwhile, heat oil in a skillet. Add garlic and fry until lightly browned. Discard garlic. Stir breadcrumbs into pan and cook 5–7 minutes, stirring, until crisp and golden. Remove from heat and stir in parsley, then pour it over the asparagus, leaving tips uncovered. Serve immediately.

Serves 4

# *meat*

# Succulent and TENDER MEAT

Those who love Spanish roasts are very specific in their requirements: for the best, the beast must be less than one month old. The cut of lamb must be the forequarter. The meat must be prepared in an earthenware dish in a wood-fired oven. The ultimate test comes in cutting: if the roast is top quality, it can be cut with the edge of a plate!

Because of the gastronomic love for young animals and the roasting tradition, Spaniards prefer their meats simply prepared—roasted, grilled or quick-fried. It is the best way to prepare meats of this calibre, and could hardly be improved by the addition of sauces and garnishes. Of course, such young animals are hard to find here, so recipes have been chosen that translate well with older meat.

Although simply prepared meats are most common, each Spanish region does have its specialties, which are either stews, meats in combination with peppers, or sausage and chopped-meat dishes.

Speciality meats, particularly tripe or kidneys, are popular all over Spain and appear in many regional variations, such as kidneys in sherry sauce.

No matter what the preparation, the general accompaniment to meat is fried potatoes. Rice rarely appears as a side dish. Since there is no rice to blend with the sauce, meats with sauces are usually served in their own individual casserole dishes with no accompaniment. Spaniards rely on their first course to provide them with vegetables and use bread to absorb the sauces.

## KIDNEYS IN SHERRY

**Ingredients**

1 pound lamb kidneys
3 tablespoons olive oil
2 cloves garlic, chopped
2 cups mushrooms, chopped
2 oz serrano ham, sliced
salt and pepper
6–8 tablespoons dry sherry
fresh parsley to garnish

**Method**

1. With a sharp knife, remove skin from outside of kidneys. Cut each kidney in half lengthwise, then snip out and discard cores. Quarter kidneys, and set aside.
2. In a skillet, heat oil and add garlic and cook for 2–3 minutes. Stir in mushrooms and ham and fry until liquid from mushrooms has evaporated.
3. Stir kidneys into skillet and fry for 2–3 minutes, stirring frequently, so kidneys are lightly browned on outside and still pink in center. Add seasoning and sherry and boil, stirring occasionally, until sherry has almost evaporated. Garnish with parsley and serve hot.

Serves 4

## FILLET STEAK WITH MUSHROOMS

**Ingredients**

8 oz mushrooms, washed and thinly sliced
olive oil
butter
salt and black pepper
4 slices of thinly sliced white bread
4 x 5 oz fillets of beef
2 oz ham, diced
1 truffle, sliced or cut into small pieces
1 chicken liver, cut into small pieces
1 tablespoon tomato purée
1 small glass of dry sherry

**Method**

1. In a skillet, sauté sliced mushrooms in some oil and butter, adding a pinch of salt and some black pepper. Set aside. In the same skillet, fry bread on both sides until golden, place onto serving dishes and keep hot. In the same skillet, fry fillets of beef, adding seasoning if desired, then place on top of the slices of bread. In the oil that is left over, toss pieces of ham, truffle and liver. Stir well and add tomato purée and sherry, leaving to heat through for 1 minute.
2. To serve, pour sauce over fillets and dish mushrooms on the side. Serve very hot.

Serves 4

## PORK IN WALNUT SAUCE

**Ingredients**

3 pounds lean pork (any joint will do)
coarse salt
1 tablespoon butter
freshly grated nutmeg
freshly ground black pepper
1 tablespoon brandy
4 cups milk
5 oz shelled walnuts, scalded and peeled if desired
3 apples (optional)
butter
lemon juice
ground cinnamon

**Method**

1. Sprinkle pork with salt and leave for 1 hour. Preheat oven to 400°F.
2. Rub meat with butter, and season with nutmeg and pepper. Brown on all sides in a skillet, then flame with the brandy. Place meat on a low rack (or upturned plate) in a fairly deep dish that will hold meat snugly. Cover with milk and cook in the oven for 1½ hours. (You can also cook it on top of the stove over a low flame if you prefer.) After about 1 hour add walnuts. Adjust the seasoning. You can add more milk if necessary.
3. When meat is cooked, remove it, slice it and serve the sauce separately. Mashed potato is the best accompaniment. Baked apple slices also go well. Just slice apples and bake them with a little butter, salt, a few drops of lemon juice and a pinch of cinnamon.

Serves 6

## LAMB WITH LEMON AND GARLIC

**Ingredients**

3 tablespoons olive oil
2 pounds lean, boneless lamb, cut into 1 inch pieces
1 Spanish onion, finely chopped
3 cloves garlic, crushed
1 tablespoon paprika
3 tablespoons fresh parsley, finely chopped
3 tablespoons fresh lemon juice
salt and pepper
3 tablespoons dry white wine (optional)

**Method**

1. In a large heavy-based skillet, heat oil. Add lamb and cook, stirring occasionally, until lightly browned. Do this in batches so the pieces are not crowded. Using a slotted spoon, transfer meat to a plate or bowl and reserve.
2. Add onion to skillet and cook for 5 minutes, stirring occasionally, until softened. Stir in garlic and cook for 2 minutes, then stir in paprika. When well blended, add lamb (and any juices on plate or in bowl), parsley, lemon juice, salt and pepper. Cover tightly and cook over very low heat 1¼–1½ hours, shaking pan occasionally, until lamb is very tender. If necessary, add wine or 3 tablespoons of water.

Makes 3–6 servings

## LAMB CHOPS WITH GARLIC MAYONNAISE

**Ingredients**

6 tablespoons olive oil
2 garlic cloves, minced
2 tablespoons parsley, minced
1 tablespoon fresh thyme, chopped or ½ teaspoon dried
1½ tablespoons lemon juice
12 lamb rib chops, each 1 inch thick
salt and freshly ground pepper

*Quick garlic mayonnaise*

¾ cup mayonnaise
1 tablespoon extra-virgin olive oil
4 cloves garlic, mashed through a garlic press
1 tablespoon lemon juice

**Method**

1. In a shallow bowl, mix together oil, minced garlic, parsley, thyme and lemon juice. Add chops and coat well. Cover and refrigerate for at least 2 hours.
2. To make the mayonnaise, whisk all the ingredients together in a small bowl.
3. Transfer to a serving bowl.
4. Drain chops, reserving marinade. Cook chops under a preheated broiler or over a hot charcoal fire until browned and cooked to your taste. Baste occasionally with marinade. Season with salt and pepper. Serve with the mayonnaise.

Serves 4

## STUFFED BELL PEPPERS

### Ingredients

8 medium mixed bell peppers

*Sauce*

1 onion, peeled and finely chopped
1 carrot, peeled and chopped
3 tablespoons olive oil
1 tablespoon tomato purée
1 teaspoon parsley, chopped
1 tablespoon all-purpose flour
5 oz white wine
4 oz water
salt and pepper

*Stuffing*

4 tablespoons olive oil
1 onion, peeled and finely chopped
1 clove garlic, peeled and finely chopped
2 teaspoons parsley, chopped
8 oz ground meat (beef, lamb or pork)
2½ oz fresh breadcrumbs, soaked in a little milk
salt and pepper

### Method

1. For the sauce, gently fry onion and carrot in oil. Add tomato purée, parsley and flour. Stir well and cook for 1 minute then add white wine, cold water and some salt and pepper. Bring to a boil, reduce heat, cover and cook slowly while you prepare the stuffing.
2. To make the stuffing, heat oil in a skillet then add onion, garlic and parsley and sauté for a few minutes. Add meat, stir through and cook for a few minutes. Add squeezed-dry breadcrumbs, season with some salt and pepper, and cook for another 4 minutes, stirring continuously.
3. Preheat the oven to 375°F. Stuff bell peppers with mixture and put them in an overproof dish. Sieve the sauce or purée it in a food processor. Pour into the dish and cook in oven for 30 minutes.

Serves 4

## BOILED BEEF AND VEGETABLES, MADRID-STYLE

### Ingredients

$1\frac{1}{2}$ cups dried chickpeas
12 cups water
1 pound beef chuck steak
1 pound large chicken thighs
4 oz salt pork or bacon
4 oz cured ham, such as prosciutto, in a thick slice
1 beef bone
salt and freshly ground pepper
4 oz chorizo sausage, or other mild or breakfast sausage
1 large carrot
2 large whole garlic cloves plus 1 clove, minced
1 turnip, halved
1 large leek, well washed
1 small whole onion plus 3 tablespoons onion, chopped
2 parsley sprigs
few threads of saffron
6 small red potatoes, skin on
2 tablespoons olive oil
1 small green cabbage, coarsely chopped
3 oz very thin noodles

### Method

1. Cover chickpeas with cold water and soak overnight.
2. In a large soup pot, combine water, beef, chicken, salt pork, ham, beef bone and salt and pepper. Bring to a boil, cover and simmer for $1\frac{1}{2}$ hours. Let cool. Refrigerate overnight if you wish to remove the fat that solidifies.
3. Drain and rinse chickpeas. Add to soup pot (preferably in a string bag to keep them together) with chorizo, carrot, whole garlic, turnip, leek, whole onion, parsley and saffron. Bring to a boil, cover and simmer for 2 hours or until chickpeas are almost tender. Add potatoes and cook for 30 minutes more. Taste for salt.
4. Meanwhile, prepare cabbage. Heat oil in a large skillet and sauté minced garlic and chopped onion over medium-high heat until onion is wilted. Add cabbage, season with salt and pepper, and stir-fry for 5 minutes. Cover, lower the heat, and cook for 5 minutes more. Cook noodles in a separate pan of boiling salted water until just done. Drain.
5. To serve, strain the broth, returning enough of it to the pot to keep the remaining ingredients moist. Combine broth with noodles and serve as a first course.
6. Cut meats and vegetables into serving pieces. Arrange with cabbage on 1 or 2 large platters with the chickpeas heaped in the center.

Serves 6

## BEAN STEW WITH CHORIZO

### Ingredients

1 pound dried white beans
5 cups water
4 oz chorizo sausage or other mild sausage
4 oz salt pork or slab bacon, cut in 1 inch cubes
1 small onion, chopped
4 cloves garlic
2 tablespoons parsley, minced
1 bay leaf
freshly ground pepper
¼ teaspoon ground cumin
1 tablespoon olive oil
1 teaspoon paprika
salt

### Method

1. Cover beans with cold water and soak overnight. Drain and rinse.
2. In a large soup pot, combine beans with water, chorizo, salt pork, onion, garlic, parsley, bay leaf, pepper and cumin. In a small cup, mix together oil and paprika until smooth then stir into the pot. Bring to a boil, cover and simmer 2 hours, or until beans are tender. Add salt to taste. Turn off the heat and let stew stand 20 minutes to thicken, then reheat. Serve in soup bowls. Add a piece of chorizo and salt pork to each serving.

Serves 4–6

## BEEF BRAISED IN RIOJA

### Ingredients

3 tablespoons olive oil
1½ pound stewing beef, trimmed of fat and cut into 2 inch chunks
6 shallots, finely chopped
2 cloves garlic, crushed
2 sticks celery, thickly sliced
12 oz mushrooms, thickly sliced
½ teaspoon ground allspice
½ bottle full-bodied red wine
1 cup tomato purée
2 sprigs fresh thyme
salt and black pepper

### Method

1. Preheat the oven to 350°F. Heat oil in a flameproof casserole dish or large saucepan and fry meat over high heat, stirring, for 5–10 minutes or until browned. Remove from the pan. Add shallots, garlic and celery to pan and cook, stirring, for 3–4 minutes, until lightly browned.
2. Add mushrooms and cook for 1 minute or until softened. Stir in allspice, wine, tomato purée and 1 sprig of thyme, and season with salt and pepper. Return meat to the dish or pan and bring to a simmer.
3. Cover and cook in the oven or over low heat on the stove for 1½ –2 hours, until beef is tender. Season again if necessary, then serve garnished with remaining thyme.

Serves 4

# poultry & game

# Rabbit, partridge AND CHICKEN

Game birds have a wider appeal in Spain than chicken. They are widely available and can be bought at everyday prices. The reason for the abundance of game is twofold. Spain's topography and climate are ideal for the proliferation of game—most of the country is mountainous with sufficient forests to harbor large game animals such as deer, bear, wild boar and wild goat, and there are millions of acres of low mountain brushland, ideal breeding grounds for pheasants, partridge, quail and rabbits. There are also vast expanses of marshlands in the south and east that ducks and geese call home.

Such abundance means that game—especially partridge, quail and rabbit—is an everyday item on Spanish restaurant menus. Game is almost as common as chicken. However, chicken should not be looked down upon—chickens are often still bred on small farms in Spain where they have the run of the grounds and eat whatever their pecking encounters. These conditions produce chickens that have less fat and much more flavor and texture that what we are used to.

*Aves y caza*, poultry and game, will appear on restaurant menus in limited, but delicious, preparations. Chicken is usually roasted or *al ajillo* (fried with garlic), quail is roasted and partridge and pheasant is usually stewed in red or white wine sauce.

But visit some of the new regionally oriented restaurants, and it becomes apparent that in the field of poultry and game, Spanish cuisine shines. Unusual combinations of grapes, grape leaves, pears, raisins, figs, olives, eggplant, pine nuts, almonds, chorizo, chocolate, shrimp and lobster all enter into Spanish poultry and game recipes.

## TURKEY STUFFED WITH DRIED FRUIT AND NUTS

### Ingredients

1 turkey, approximately 8–10 pounds
salt and pepper
butter and dripping for roasting

*Stuffing*

8 oz sausage meat
butter
1 oz onions, chopped
4 oz raisins
5 oz prunes, stoned and chopped
5 oz dates, stoned and chopped
5 oz dried apricots or peaches, chopped
5 oz dried figs, chopped
2 oz almonds
2 oz pine nuts
4 oz brandy or port

### Method

1. Make the stuffing first. Fry sausage meat gently in a little butter with onion. Add the dried fruit, nuts, pine nuts, seasoning and brandy or port. Mix well then stuff the turkey.
2. Preheat the oven to 425°F. Season turkey well, then cover the breast generously with butter so that it doesn't get dry. Cover breast with foil. Roast for 30 minutes, then turn the oven down to 325°F. Roast for a further 3–3½ hours, basting occasionally. (Re-cover with the foil each time.) Remove foil about 30 minutes before the end of this time and turn the oven up to 400°F so that the breast browns nicely. Baste frequently. Test to see that the bird is cooked by piercing the thickest part of the leg with a skewer; if pink juices run out the turkey must be cooked for a little longer.
3. Carve the turkey and serve surrounded with stuffing.

*Note:* You can also make this dish with a capon or large chicken; adjust the proportion of stuffing and the cooking times accordingly.

Serves 6–8

## SPANISH CHICKEN WITH CHORIZO

### Ingredients

8 chicken joints, such as thighs and drumsticks
2 tablespoons olive oil
1 onion, sliced
2 cloves garlic, crushed
1 red and 1 yellow bell pepper, seeded and sliced
2 teaspoons paprika
¼ cup dry sherry or dry vermouth
14 oz canned chopped tomatoes
1 bay leaf
1 strip orange rind, pared with a vegetable peeler
3 oz chorizo, sliced
2 oz pitted black olives
salt and black pepper

### Method

1. Place chicken joints in a large, non-stick frying-pan and fry, without oil, for 5–8 minutes, turning occasionally, until golden. Remove chicken and set aside, then pour away any fat from the pan.
2. Add oil to the pan and fry onion, garlic and bell pepper for 3–4 minutes until softened. Return chicken to the pan with the paprika, sherry or vermouth, tomatoes, bay leaf and orange rind. Bring to a boil then simmer, covered, over low heat for 35–40 minutes, stirring occasionally, until chicken is cooked through.
3. Add chorizo and olives and simmer for a further 5 minutes to heat through, then season with salt and pepper.
4. Serve 2 joints with chorizo and pan ingredients onto 4 plates.

Serves 4

## CHICKEN WITH SAFFRON RICE AND PEAS

**Ingredients**

3 pound chicken, cut into 6–8 serving pieces
freshly ground black pepper
2 tablespoons oil
4 oz salt pork, finely diced
2 Spanish onions, sliced
1 teaspoon garlic, finely chopped
$2\frac{1}{2}$ teaspoons paprika
1 medium-sized tomato, finely chopped
$1\frac{1}{4}$ cups uncooked rice
5 oz fresh or frozen peas
3 cups boiling water
$\frac{1}{8}$ teaspoon ground saffron or 1 teaspoon turmeric
2 tablespoons parsley, finely chopped

**Method**

1. Pat chicken pieces dry with paper towels and sprinkle with a few grindings of pepper.
2. Heat oil over moderate heat in a heavy-based saucepan. Add diced salt pork and cook, stirring, until brown and crisp. Remove pork with a slotted spoon and drain on paper towels.
3. Add chicken to fat in pan and brown evenly on all sides. Set chicken aside.
4. Pour off all but a little fat from the pan. Stir in onions and garlic and cook for about 5 minutes, until onions are soft and transparent. Stir in paprika, then tomatoes and bring to a boil, stirring frequently. Cook briskly, uncovered, for about 5 minutes until most of liquid in pan has evaporated.
5. Return chicken and pork to the pan. Add rice, peas, boiling water and saffron or turmeric and stir well to combine. Bring quickly to a boil and reduce heat to low. Cover and simmer for 20–30 minutes until chicken and rice are tender and all liquid is absorbed. Taste and adjust seasoning. Sprinkle with parsley and serve.

Serves 6

## CHICKEN IN PUREED ONION AND WINE SAUCE

**Ingredients**

2 tablespoons olive oil
1 medium onion, chopped
1 clove garlic, peeled
3 pound chicken, cut into serving pieces
coarse salt
freshly ground pepper
3 tablespoons parsley, minced
pinch saffron
$\frac{1}{2}$ cup dry white wine
$\frac{1}{2}$ cup chicken bouillon
$\frac{1}{4}$ teaspoon thyme
1 bay leaf

**Method**

1. Heat oil in a shallow casserole. Sauté onion and garlic until onion has wilted. Transfer onion and garlic to a food processor or blender. Season chicken pieces with salt and pepper. Brown chicken in the casserole, adding more oil if necessary.
2. Meanwhile, add 2 tablespoons of parsley, saffron, salt and pepper to onion and garlic and blend well. Gradually pour in wine and chicken bouillon and beat until smooth. Strain sauce over chicken pieces. Sprinkle with thyme, add bay leaf, then cover and cook over a low flame for 30 minutes, adding more chicken broth or water if the sauce becomes too thick. Sprinkle with remaining tablespoon of parsley and serve.

Serves 4

## RABBIT IN ZUCCHINI AND TOMATO SAUCE (below)

**Ingredients**

4 tablespoons olive oil
1$\frac{3}{4}$ pound rabbit, cut into bite-size pieces
2 medium onions, sliced
1 small red bell pepper, seeded and finely chopped
1 medium zucchini, finely sliced
8 medium tomatoes, skinned and chopped
salt and pepper

**Method**

1. In a large skillet, heat oil and brown the rabbit pieces. Transfer rabbit to a casserole dish and set aside. In the same pan, sauté onion. When onion begins to turn golden, stir in chopped bell pepper and zucchini and fry for about 5 minutes. Add chopped tomato and cook for a further 5 minutes. Pour tomato mixture over rabbit pieces, seasoning as desired, then cover and cook slowly for approximately 1–2 hours or until cooked to your liking. Serve very hot.

Serves 4

## CHICKEN IN GARLIC SAUCE

(opposite)

### Ingredients

3 pounds chicken, cut into small serving pieces (split the breast and cut in half again, cut each thigh in half)
salt
5 tablespoons olive oil
6 cloves garlic, chopped, plus 1 extra clove, minced
1 tablespoon parsley, minced
2 tablespoons dry white wine

### Method

1. Sprinkle chicken with salt. Heat oil in a shallow flameproof casserole and brown chicken over medium-high heat on all sides. Add chopped garlic, reduce heat to medium and cook, stirring occasionally, for 30 minutes. Stir in minced garlic, parsley and wine. Cover and cook for 15 minutes more, or until chicken is done and the juices run clear when the thigh is pricked with a fork.

Serves 4

## CHICKEN WITH RED BELL PEPPER

### Ingredients

3 pound chicken, cut into serving pieces
coarse salt
2 tablespoons olive oil
1 clove garlic, minced
1 onion, chopped
2 tablespoons cured ham, diced
2 red bell peppers, seeded and cut into strips
1 tomato, skinned and chopped
freshly ground pepper

### Method

1. Sprinkle chicken pieces with salt. Heat oil in a large, shallow casserole. Brown chicken well on all sides. Add garlic and onion and sauté until the onion has wilted. Stir in ham, bell pepper, tomato, pepper and more salt if necessary. Cover and cook for 30 minutes. Uncover and continue cooking for 20 minutes more (most of the liquid should evaporate, leaving only a small amount of sauce). A green salad and a light red wine are appropriate accompaniments.

Serves 4

## BRAISED RABBIT WITH CHOCOLATE

### Ingredients

2 oz lard
4 oz salt pork, finely diced
1 rabbit (3 pound) cut into 8 serving pieces
salt and pepper
12 small pickling onions, peeled
1½ teaspoons all-purpose flour
½ cup dry red wine
½ cup water
1 bay leaf, crumbled
1½ tablespoons parsley, finely chopped
¼ teaspoon thyme
¼ cup blanched almonds
¼ cup pine nuts
1½ teaspoons unsweetened cooking chocolate, finely grated

### Method

1. Heat lard in a heavy-based saucepan and add diced pork. Cook over moderate heat, stirring frequently, until pork is crisp and browned. Remove from the pan with a slotted spoon and drain on paper towels.
2. Pat rabbit pieces dry with paper towels and season with salt and pepper. Add half the rabbit to fat in the pan and brown on all sides. Remove from the pan to a heated serving plate and repeat with remaining pieces of rabbit. Remove.
3. Add onions to the pan and brown. Remove with a slotted spoon and place with rabbit.
4. Pour all but a little fat from the pan and stir in flour. Cook for 1 minute until flour has browned slightly. Pour in wine and water and bring to a boil over high heat, scraping in any brown particles clinging to the bottom and sides of the pan. Add bay leaf, parsley, thyme, diced pork and rabbit. Reduce heat to low, cover tightly and simmer for 30 minutes.
5. Grind almonds and pine nuts in a blender or nut grinder. Mix with grated chocolate and add to casserole with reserved onions. Stir thoroughly and cover again. Simmer for 30 minutes longer, until rabbit is tender. Taste and adjust seasoning. Place in serving dish and serve immediately.

Serves 6

## DUCK WITH OLIVES AND SHERRY (opposite)

**Ingredients**

½ cup large Spanish green olives, sliced or chopped
5 pound duck as much fat removed as possible
salt and freshly ground pepper
1 tablespoon olive oil
1 medium onion, finely chopped
2 carrots, finely chopped
3 cloves garlic, minced
¾ cup chicken bouillon
¼ cup dry sherry or white wine
¼ teaspoon dried thyme
1 tablespoon parsley, minced

**Method**

1. Put olives in a small bowl, cover with warm water and set aside.
2. Preheat the oven to 350°F. Sprinkle duck inside and out with salt and pepper. Truss duck, place it in a roasting pan and prick it all over with a fork. Roast for 1 hour.
3. Meanwhile, heat oil in a shallow flameproof casserole and sauté onion, carrots and garlic over medium-high heat until onion has wilted.
4. Cut duck into serving pieces, removing the backbone and rib cage and discarding them. Transfer the pieces to the casserole. Pour off the fat in the roasting pan and deglaze the pan with chicken bouillon, scraping up any particles stuck to the bottom. Strain the liquid into the casserole.
5. Drain olives and add to the casserole along with sherry, thyme, parsley and salt and pepper. Bring to a boil on top of the stove, then cover and cook in the oven for 1 hour.

Serves 4

## PARTRIDGE BRAISED WITH VEGETABLES AND WINE

**Ingredients**

4 x 12 oz partridge or squabs
1½ pounds pickling onions, peeled
2 tablespoons olive oil
3 pieces thick bacon, diced
2 cloves garlic, sliced
2 carrots, sliced
½ cup white wine
1 cup water
1 tablespoon tomato paste
2 cloves
2 bay leaves
2 inch long cinnamon stick
salt and pepper to taste
1 pound canned small potatoes, drained
½ cup frozen peas

**Method**

1. Wash partridges or squabs and pat dry with paper towels.
2. Peel pickling onions and cross-cut root end to prevent popping. If onions are difficult to peel, plunge into boiling water for 2 minutes then drain and rub off skins.
3. Heat oil in a large heavy-based saucepan. Brown and sear each bird all over then transfer to a dish. Add bacon, garlic and onions, and sauté until onions have colored slightly. Return birds to saucepan. Add remaining ingredients except potatoes and peas. Bring to simmering point, cover and simmer slowly for 30 minutes. Check during cooking and add a little extra water if necessary.
4. Add potatoes and peas. Simmer for 15 minutes more. Sauce should be reduced and slightly thick on completion of cooking. Transfer to serving platter and serve accompanied with a side salad and crusty bread.

Serves 4

## POUSSINS WITH ALMONDS AND PINE NUTS

**Ingredients**

4 small chickens
salt and freshly ground black pepper
olive oil to brush
4 small lemon wedges
4 bay leaves
2 tablespoons olive oil
1 medium onion, thinly sliced
3 cloves garlic, crushed
1 pound tomatoes, skinned, seeded and roughly chopped
½ cup red wine
2 tablespoons sun-dried tomato purée
1 green chili, seeded and thinly sliced
1 medium red bell pepper, cut into thin strips
1 small green bell pepper, cut into thin strips
3 tablespoons blanched almonds, chopped
1 tablespoon pine nuts
12 pitted black olives
2 tablespoons golden raisins

**Method**

1. Preheat the oven to 375°F. Rub chickens with salt and pepper, inside and out. Brush the skins with olive oil and stuff a lemon wedge and bay leaf inside each one. Roast for about 45 minutes, until tender.
2. Meanwhile, heat olive oil in a large frying-pan, and sauté onion and garlic until translucent. Add tomatoes and fry lightly for a further 2 minutes. Add all remaining ingredients and simmer for 20–25 minutes, until sauce has thickened and tomatoes are soft.
3. Place chickens in a serving dish and spoon the sauce over. Serve with remaining sauce in a jug.

Serves 4

# seafood

# Sensational SEAFOOD

Spain is definitely a fish-lover's paradise. Blessed with the longest coastline in Europe and facing the Mediterranean Sea, the fertile Bay of Biscay, and the Atlantic Ocean, Spain has an overwhelming variety of fish, from huge open-water species, such as tuna, to the tiny coastal *chanquette*, no bigger than a thumbnail.

On the central plains and mountainous interior areas of Spain, seafood is less commonly eaten. Dried cold- and freshwater fish, especially trout, are more likely to be eaten.

Although the variety of seafood in Spain is tremendous, and to the casual visitor quite overwhelming, the real key to the popularity of Spanish fish is freshness. Day-old, or frozen fish or shellfish, is not tolerated. Boats arrive at ports up and down the coast daily. The fish are bought within minutes of unloading, and in many areas, cooked and sold on the spot.

When fish is fresh, Spaniards like to eat it unaccompanied by extra ingredients. Fish is usually simply prepared, even in restaurants—baked, grilled or fried. Spanish regional cooking is most inventive with fish, combining it with locally available ingredients.

If you really want to sample Spain's shellfish at its best, there is nothing quite like sitting at a beachside café, leisurely tackling a tray of unshelled crustaceans. Such shellfish delights include scallops, clams and shrimp.

## FRIED SQUID

**Ingredients**

4 oz prepared squid, cut into rings
2 tablespoons seasoned all-purpose flour
1 egg
2 tablespoons milk
olive oil for frying
sea salt
lemon wedges, to serve

**Method**

1. Toss squid rings in seasoned flour in a bowl. Whisk egg and milk together in a separate bowl. Heat oil in a heavy-based frying-pan.
2. Tip out the floured squid rings, one at a time, into the egg mixture, shaking off any excess liquid. Place into the hot oil, in batches if necessary, and fry for 2–3 minutes on each side until golden.
3. Drain the fried squid on paper towels, then sprinkle with salt. Move to a small warm plate and serve with lemon wedges.

Serves 4

## BAKED SEA BREAM

### Ingredients

1 whole sea bream, about 3 pounds, gutted
salt
1 onion, peeled and sliced
2 tomatoes, washed and sliced
1 lemon, washed and sliced
sprig of parsley
⅔ cup olive oil
4 medium potatoes, peeled and thinly sliced

### Method

1. Preheat the oven to 400°F. Wash fish then sprinkle with salt inside and out. Put fish in a large, oval ovenproof dish. Cut 2 slices of the onion in half and fit them into one of the gills of the fish. Do the same with 2 slices of tomato and lemon. Put some lemon and parsley inside the fish and a round of lemon in the eye. Pour oil over fish. Arrange potato slices around the dish and any remaining slices of onion and tomato. Season and put in the oven.
2. Bake for about 20–25 minutes. If fish is large, cover the top with a piece of foil for about 15 minutes of the cooking time. Baste occasionally. If you are not going to serve immediately, turn off the oven before the fish has finished cooking and leave it. It will be done, but not overcooked.

Serves 4

## JUMBO SHRIMP IN SHERRY

**Ingredients**

12 raw jumbo shrimp, peeled
2 tablespoons olive oil
2 tablespoons sherry
few drops of Tabasco sauce
salt and freshly ground black pepper

**Method**

1. Make a superficial cut down the back of each prawn, then pull out and discard the dark intestinal tract.
2. Heat oil in a frying-pan and stir-fry shrimp for 2–3 minutes until pink. Add sherry and season with Tabasco sauce, salt and pepper. Tip into a dish and serve immediately.

Serves 4

## SHELLFISH STEW (opposite)

**Ingredients**

1 1/2 pounds live lobster or 2 frozen lobster tails
6 tablespoons olive oil
1 pound shrimp, shelled
1 pound fresh cod, monkfish or other firm-fleshed fish steak
8 oz whole small squid, cleaned
1 small onion, chopped
1 red bell pepper, chopped
3 cloves garlic, minced
3 medium tomatoes, peeled, seeded and chopped
1/4 teaspoon saffron threads
2 tablespoons parsley, minced
1 bay leaf
1/2 teaspoon dried thyme
1/4 teaspoon red bell pepper flakes
3/4 cup dry white wine
1/4 cup lemon juice
salt and freshly ground pepper
12 very small clams, thoroughly scrubbed
12 mussels, scrubbed and beards removed

**Method**

1. As close as possible to the time you are going to cook the lobster, have the fishmonger cut off the claws and tail and break the lobster into serving size pieces. If using frozen lobster, cut the tails into serving size pieces.
2. Heat oil in a large, shallow flameproof casserole and quickly sauté lobster over high heat for 3 minutes. Remove to a platter and set aside.
3. Sauté shrimp and fish over high heat for 1 minute and remove to platter.
4. Add squid to the casserole and sauté 1 minute. Add onion, bell pepper and garlic and sauté over medium heat until onion has wilted. Stir in tomatoes, saffron, 1 tablespoon of parsley, bay leaf, thyme and crushed pepper and sauté for 2 minutes. Stir in wine, lemon juice and salt and pepper and cook, uncovered, for 10 minutes. Add reserved seafood, cover and simmer for 10 minutes longer.
5. In a covered skillet, steam clams and mussels with 2 cups water over high heat. As clams open, remove them and add to casserole. Cut fish into pieces. Serve the stew in the casserole.

Serves 6

## SPANISH RICE WITH SQUID, SCAMPI AND SHRIMP

**Ingredients**

3 tablespoons olive oil
1 medium onion, finely chopped
2 fresh squid, cleaned and finely chopped
1 large ripe tomato, skinned and chopped
10 oz short-grain rice
3 cups water
pinch of saffron threads
salt and ground pepper, to taste
8–16 fresh or thawed frozen scampi
1 pound raw jumbo shrimp

**Method**

1. In a large, heavy, deep frying-pan heat oil and gently fry onion and squid for about 5 minutes. Add tomato and cook for a further 5 minutes.
2. Add rice and stir through for 1–2 minutes. Bring water to a boil with saffron, salt and ground pepper and pour over rice.
3. Add shellfish. The scampi may be left whole or halved and the shrimp shelled whole or left unshelled.
4. Simmer over gentle heat until rice is cooked. The rice should not be stirred at all during the cooking so that the shellfish sits on top. Serve from the pan.

Serves 4

## SPANISH-STYLE FISH CUTLETS

### Ingredients

4 grouper or sea bass cutlets
olive oil
1 tablespoon dried parsley flakes
3 teaspoons garlic, freshly crushed
1 oz almonds, slivered
1 tablespoon shallots, chopped
½ teaspoon ground paprika
½ teaspoon lemon rind, grated
14 oz canned tomatoes, drained and roughly chopped

### Method

1. Preheat oven to 350°F.
2. Arrange fish in a shallow ovenproof dish that has been lightly brushed with olive oil. Brush the top of each cutlet with olive oil.
3. Combine parsley, garlic, almonds, shallots, paprika, lemon rind and 1½ tablespoons olive oil. Spoon over fish and press down well.
4. Bake fish in a moderate oven for 10 minutes.
5. Pour tomatoes around fish and cook for a further 10 minutes or until fish is cooked.
6. Serve a piece of fish with tomato sauce added to each.

Serves 4

## SEAFOOD PAELLA (opposite)

**Ingredients**

1 tablespoon olive oil
2 onions, chopped
2 cloves garlic, crushed
1 tablespoon fresh thyme leaves, chopped
2 teaspoons lemon rind, finely grated
4 ripe tomatoes, chopped
4 cups chicken or fish bouillon
2½ cups short-grain white rice
pinch of saffron threads, soaked in 2 cups water
12 oz fresh or frozen peas
2 red bell peppers, chopped
2 pounds mussels, scrubbed and beards removed
1 pound firm white fish fillets, chopped
12 oz peeled uncooked shrimp
7 oz scallops
3 calamari tubes, sliced
1 tablespoon fresh parsley, chopped

**Method**

1. Preheat barbecue to medium heat. Place a large paella pan or skillet on barbecue, add oil and heat. Add onions, garlic, thyme leaves and lemon rind and cook for 3 minutes or until onion is soft.
2. Add tomatoes and cook, stirring, for 4 minutes. Add rice and cook, stirring, for 4 minutes longer or until rice is translucent. Stir in saffron mixture and bouillon and bring to a simmer. Simmer, stirring occasionally, for 30 minutes or until rice has absorbed almost all of the liquid.
3. Stir in peas, red bell pepper and mussels and cook for 2 minutes. Add fish, shrimp and scallops and cook, stirring, for 2–3 minutes. Stir in calamari and parsley and cook, stirring, for 1–2 minutes longer or until seafood is cooked.

Serves 8

## POTATOES WITH CLAMS

**Ingredients**

8 oz small clams
salt
¼ cup white wine
¼ cup olive oil
1 medium onion, peeled and diced
2 medium tomatoes, skinned, seeded and chopped
2 pounds potatoes, peeled and cut into chunks
5 cups water
1 clove garlic, peeled and roughly chopped
1 teaspoon parsley, chopped
4–5 threads of saffron

**Method**

1. Wash clams well in cold water with some salt. Change the water a couple of times. Put clams in a saucepan and barely cover with cold water. Add wine and a teaspoon of salt. Bring to a boil and as soon as clams open, remove from the heat. Strain off the liquid and keep. Remove clams from their shells and place in the liquid. Set aside.
2. Heat oil in a skillet and sauté onion until transparent, then add tomatoes and continue to sauté for another 5 minutes. Transfer to a large saucepan, add potatoes, cover with 5 cups of water and bring to a boil.
3. Meanwhile, crush garlic with parsley, saffron and a little salt. Add a tablespoon of the liquid from the clams, mix well and stir into potatoes with the rest of clam liquid (keep clams to one side). Cover and simmer for 30 minutes or until potatoes are done. Heat clams through in the soup just before serving.
4. You can thicken the liquid by puréeing a potato or two and adding to the saucepan. If, you find you have too little liquid, you can always add more hot water when the potatoes are cooking.

Serves 4

## PAELLA VALENCIA

**Ingredients**

4–6 chicken thighs
salt and freshly ground black pepper, to taste
½ teaspoon paprika
3 tablespoons oil, for frying
1½ cups water
1 cup dry white wine
1 bay leaf
4 oz Spanish sausage (chorizo) or peppery salami, sliced diagonally
8 oz calamari, cleaned, rinsed and cut into rings
2 green bell pepper halved, seeded and cut into lengthwise strips
4 fresh tomatoes (or canned), peeled, seeded and chopped
1 medium onion, finely chopped
pinch saffron threads
¾ cup long-grain rice
1 pound medium large raw shrimp
12 oz fresh mussels, scrubbed, cleaned and beards removed

**Method**

1. Season chicken thighs with salt, freshly ground pepper and paprika. Heat oil in a heavy-based skillet and cook chicken until golden brown on both sides. Reduce heat and cover chicken with water, white wine and bay leaf and simmer for 15 minutes. Remove chicken and keep liquid bouillon for later.
2. To the same skillet, add Spanish sausage and cook for 4 minutes. Then add calamari, bell pepper, tomato, onion and saffron, and gently stir. Cover and cook over gentle heat, stirring occasionally, for 10 minutes. Sprinkle rice over cooked vegetables in pan and pour 1½ cups of liquid bouillon over. Bring to a boil, reduce heat, cover and simmer for 20 minutes, stirring occasionally.
3. Place shrimp, chicken and mussels on top of rice mix. Check rice and add more liquid bouillon if required. Cover and cook over gentle heat until rice is tender and shrimp and mussels are cooked. Discard any mussels that have not opened. Serve from pan at the table. Serve with lemon or lime wedges and fresh bread.

Serves 6

## GARLIC SHRIMP

### Ingredients

2 pounds shrimp

4 cloves garlic, crushed

1 small fresh chili, seeded and chopped

¼ cup olive oil

juice of 2 lemons

black pepper

lemon wedges to garnish

### Method

1. Place shrimp in a shallow dish. If you prefer them shelled, remove heads and shell, leaving tails intact.
2. Combine garlic, chili, oil, lemon juice and pepper. Pour over shrimp and leave to stand for 20 minutes. Cook over medium heat for about 3 minutes on each side, according to size, just until shrimp turn pink.
3. Place into individual serving dishes or onto a large platter. Pour juices from pan over shrimp. Garnish with lemon and serve immediately.

Serves 4–6

## SEARED TUNA WITH ROASTED PLUM TOMATOES

**Ingredients**

1 clove garlic, finely chopped
finely grated rind and juice of 1 lime
5 tablespoons olive oil, plus extra for greasing
3 tablespoons fresh rosemary, chopped
4 tuna steaks, about 5 oz each and 1 inch thick
6 plum tomatoes, halved lengthwise
1 red onion, halved and thinly sliced lengthwise
salt and black pepper

**Method**

1. In a large dish, mix together the garlic, lime rind, half the lime juice, 2 tablespoons of oil and 1 tablespoon of rosemary. Add tuna and turn to coat evenly. Cover and place in the refrigerator for 30 minutes.
2. Preheat the oven to 425°F. Place tomatoes and onion in a shallow ovenproof dish with remaining rosemary. Drizzle with remaining oil and season. Roast in the oven for 15–20 minutes, until tender and lightly browned.
3. Lightly oil a ridged cast-iron grill pan or large skillet and heat over medium-high heat. Add tuna and cook for 4–5 minutes, turning once, until golden. Serve with tomatoes and onion, sprinkle with remaining lime juice and salt and pepper to taste.

Serves 4

# desserts

# Delicious DESSERTS

Nowhere in Spanish cuisine is the Moorish influence more pronounced than in dessert making. Almonds, egg yolks and honey have been the mainstays of most Spanish confections since the Arabs left their culinary and cultural marks on Spain many centuries ago.

When considering Spanish desserts, certain characteristics come to mind: ground almonds are used in abundance and often replace flour in cake baking; baking powder is rarely used; and beaten egg whites are invariably the leavening agent in cakes. Milk desserts are often spiced with cinnamon and lemon peel rather than vanilla, and anisette liqueur is frequently used.

Pastries are commonly coated with honey, the sweetener preferred over sugar. The heavy use of egg yolks also characterises Spanish dessert making, especially in the preparation of custards and candies. Fried desserts are perhaps the most popular sweets in Spain, consisting of little more that flour and water.

Until now your only familiarity with Spanish desserts may have been flan, and enjoying this world-famous custard is a delightful and refreshing way to end a meal. However, this section will provide other exciting and unusual alternatives.

## SANTIAGO ALMOND TART

**Ingredients**

4 large eggs
¾ cup sugar
1 zest of lemon, grated
1 teaspoon ground cinnamon
7 oz ground almonds
2 oz butter
a little all-purpose flour
⅓ cup confectioner's sugar

**Method**

1. Heat the oven to 300°F.
2. In a bowl, beat eggs, sugar, lemon zest and cinnamon until thick and creamy. Carefully stir in ground almonds. Take a smooth, round baking tin or mold, grease well with butter and dust with flour. Pour in the mixture and bake for about 30 minutes. Leave to cool before removing from the mold and placing on a round serving plate. Dust with confectioner's sugar.

Serves 4

## SWEET BREAD (TORRIJAS) (below)

### Ingredients

1 loaf of spongy or soft white bread, preferably round in shape
½ cup sugar (use more or less depending on your taste)
4 cups milk
6 eggs
olive oil for frying
1 cup sugar, for dusting
4 oz ground cinnamon, for dusting

### Method

1. Cut bread into slices about 1 inch thick.
2. Mix sugar and milk and dip slices of bread into mixture. Leave bread until it is well soaked. Put slices on a rack or in a colander to drain any surplus liquid.
3. Beat eggs well and coat soaked bread on all sides. Heat oil, which shouldn't be excessively hot, and fry bread slices until they are golden on all sides. Remove, drain and sprinkle with sugar and cinnamon and serve immediately. *Torrijas* can be eaten hot or cold, but they are much better freshly made.

Serves at least 6

## LIGHT-AS-THE-WIND FRITTERS

### Ingredients

½ cup water
½ cup milk
5 tablespoons pure olive oil, plus additional oil for deep-frying
¼ teaspoon salt
¼ teaspoon grated lemon zest
1 cup all-purpose flour
4 large eggs
confectioner's sugar for dusting

### Method

1. In a saucepan, bring water, milk, 5 tablespoons oil, salt and lemon zest to a boil. Add flour all at once, lower the heat and stir vigorously with a wooden spoon until dough leaves the sides of the pan and forms a smooth ball. Cook, turning the dough frequently, for 2–3 minutes. Remove from heat and cool slightly.
2. In a food processor, process dough for 20 seconds. Add eggs and process for 30 seconds.
3. Heat about 1 inch of oil in a large skillet or electric frying-pan to 375°F. Drop teaspoons of dough into hot oil. The dough should puff, forming fritters and become golden and hollow inside. Using a slotted spoon, remove fritters and drain on paper towels. Allow to cool then dust with sugar.

Serves 8–10

## RICE PUDDING (above)

**Ingredients**

20 cups milk
4 oz butter
1 pound Spanish short-grain rice
1 teaspoon salt
2 cinnamon sticks
1 pound sugar
ground cinnamon

**Method**

1. Bring the milk to a boil in two or more saucepans. Let it cool.
2. Put the butter in a very large saucepan (not aluminium) over gentle heat. When it starts to soften, brush the butter up the sides, then add the boiled cooked milk, rice, salt and cinnamon sticks. Bring to a boil and then lower the heat and cook gently, stirring frequently with a wooden spoon until it is done; about 2 hours.
3. Just before your rice is ready, stir in the sugar. Leave the pudding to rest for about 10 minutes before serving sprinkled with cinnamon.

Serves 6

## CHOCOLATE MOUSSE VALENCIA

**Ingredients**

2 tablespoons sugar
4 eggs, separated
1 tablespoon all-purpose flour
1/4 cup milk
2 tablespoons butter
grated rind and juice of 1 orange
8 oz dark chocolate, broken in pieces
1/4 cup cream, whipped
toasted flaked almonds

**Method**

1. In a heatproof bowl, mix together sugar, egg yolks, flour and milk. Place over a saucepan of simmering water and stir continuously until mixture thickens. Add butter a little at a time while stirring.
2. Add orange rind and juice and slowly stir in chocolate. Continue stirring until chocolate has melted and mixture is smooth. Remove from heat and cool a little.
3. Whisk egg whites until stiff and fold into the chocolate mixture. Pour into dessert glasses and chill. Garnish with whipped cream and sprinkle with flaked almonds.

Serves 4

## FRUIT GRATIN (below)

**Ingredients**

8 egg yolks
1 cup sugar
3 cups single cream
1 teaspoon kirsch liqueur
1 cup heavy cream
2 pounds mixed fresh fruit, cut into pieces and any stones removed

**Method**

1. Beat egg yolks with sugar. Heat single cream in a saucepan to boiling point then stir into the egg and sugar mixture. Return it all to the saucepan and stir until mixture boils. Flavor with kirsch. Pour cream over fruit and place under the grill for a few seconds.

Serves 8

## ALMOND AND MARMALADE PUFF PASTRY STRIPS

**Ingredients**

8 oz puff pastry
¾ cup quince marmalade or other fruit preserve, such as apricot
⅓ cup sliced almonds
confectioner's sugar, for dusting

**Method**

1. Roll pastry out to ½ inch thick . Cut into 4 inch x ⅛ inch strips.
2. Return to the oven for about 5 minutes more, until the pastries are golden. Remove and cool slightly.
3. Arrange the almonds in overlapping rows along the length of the pastry. When cool, dust with confectioner's sugar.

Serves 4

## CARAMEL CUSTARD

**Ingredients**

½ cup, plus 6 tablespoons sugar
2 tablespoons water
3 whole eggs
2 egg yolks
2½ cups milk
⅛ teaspoon salt
¼ teaspoon lemon zest, grated
whipped cream (optional)

**Method**

1. To caramelize sugar, in a small heavy saucepan, heat ½ cup sugar with water over medium heat, stirring constantly, until the syrup turns golden in color (the sugar will crystallize before it liquifies). Immediately pour the syrup into 6 individual custard cups.
2. Preheat the oven to 350°F. Whisk whole eggs and egg yolks in a large bowl until uniform in color. Whisk in the milk, remaining sugar, salt and lemon zest. Divide the mixture among the prepared cups. Place cups in a baking pan and add enough hot water to come halfway up the sides of the cups. Bake for about 45 minutes, or until a knife inserted in the custard comes out clean. Remove cups from pan and let cool. Cover and refrigerate until chilled.
3. Run a knife around the edge of each cup and unmold the flan, spooning the caramelized sugar over it. Serve with whipped cream, if desired.

Serves 6

# GREEK
food

# the land AND ITS PEOPLE

| | |
|---|---|
| Status | Republic |
| Area | 82 012 sq mi |
| Population | 10 120 000 |
| Language | Greek |
| Religion | Orthodox 83% |
| Currency | Euro |
| National Day | 25 March |

people

## ZESTY AND COLD

'Come for your lunch,' cried the Greek village woman to her husband one stifling summer mealtime, just after she had removed their repast from a searing stove. 'Your food is getting hot.'

The significance of hot food and Greece may be lost on those readers who have never been to the Hellenic Republic, but those visitors to Greece who have objected to taverna tucker being served lukewarm at lunch (or cold in the evening), will encounter no such difficult temperature problems after preparing a tasty dish from this book. Home cooks can present fine Greek fare at any temperature they desire. If in Greece you find restaurant choices too cool for your liking, two words will remedy it: '*Zesty, parakalo*' ('Hot, please'). It's unlikely to be microwaved, but more likely to be gently reheated in the oven, or on a hotplate. However, cooks who prefer to prepare their meals early should not despair: many Greek dishes respond well to the microwave.

## GREEK CUISINE, ANCIENT THEN STOLEN

Although Greek cuisine may be less revered throughout the world than French or Chinese cuisine, it is the world's most ancient, and possibly its healthiest. Greece has one of the lowest incidences of heart disease in the world. This can perhaps be attributed to a relaxed lifestyle, to a sunny Mediterranean climate (which may be the reason food tends to be served lukewarm), and to natural ingredients (including pure olive oil, fresh vegetables and herbs, juicy citrus fruits, fish, meats low in fat and calories, and dairy products from goats and sheep). The Greeks also drink lots of water whenever they drink coffee and spirits.

Archaeologists and historians confirm that in the Archaic Period before the Golden Age of Greece, about 25 centuries ago, Greek cooks experimented with vegetables, herbs and meats at a time when other European civilizations knew only how to roast meat over a fire. Aphdonites, one of seven great cooks who were regarded as the seven wise men of Greece at that time, created the sausage. His contemporaries made innovative sauces. Following Rome's conquest of Greece, Greek chefs were taken to Italy where food preparation was at that time still primitive. They influenced its cuisine forever. The ultimate status symbol in a rich Roman household was a Greek cook. Much later, during the Turkish domination of Greece, the Turks took Greek recipes and claimed them as their own. So, erroneously, some people think that Turkish and Greek cuisines are synonymous. The Ionian island of Corfu was the only Greek island not to be conquered by Turkey. Corfiot recipes were influenced by the Spanish and Italians who took, and later brought back, the ancient Greek traditions. In this section, you can discover the varied and still developing art of Greek food.

When entertaining, give atmosphere to your dining room with traditional folk, bouzouki or rembetika music. Rembetika is somewhat like the American blues and has been wonderfully adapted by one of Greece's most loved contemporary composers, Mikis Theodorakis, who composed Zorba the Greek.

## THE GREEK PEOPLE

The Greek people are possibly the most passionate on the planet—passionate about everything. Even the least educated person living on a remote Greek island will know the mythology, history, traditions, music, politics and produce of their country and will likely be obsessed by Greek cuisine.

The Greeks are physically expressive and often use their hands in gesture. Whether stressed or contemplative, the men play with *koboloi* (worry beads) as they sit in their favorite *kafenion* (coffee house), lingering over the thick coffee (often called Turkish coffee by outsiders because the Turks also adopted the brew). On the table, placed beside the coffee, these men will often have a glass of clear water, and later in the day, an ouzo, the aniseed-flavored spirit that is diluted with water and thereupon turns cloudy. The Cretans and Greeks living close to Turkey are more likely to choose raki as their tipple. Alcohol is always accompanied by *mezethes* (an appetizer). This may be bread with feta cheese, tomato and olives, or perhaps a few whitebait (small fish). Water is served separately with any alcohol. Maybe this is why one rarely sees a Greek in a drunken state.

## XENIA, STRANGER AND FRIEND

The Greeks are gregarious and hospitable. Their word *xenia* means both 'stranger' and 'friend'.

Welcoming a guest into the home in the traditional way, a wife living in a small community or village will present a sweet or a fruit preserve to be eaten with a spoon from her best small dish. After eating the sweet, and drinking an accompanying glass of water, the visitor will be offered ouzo (or perhaps brandy) and/or coffee.

Affluent Greeks in big cities also exude hospitality. Although busy, they will offer visitors (at least) coffee, and perhaps a meal. The best way to show gratitude for a meal is with flowers. Every Greek has a garden, if only on a tiny apartment patio, and flowers are loved. They reflect the colorful and generous, personalities of the Greeks who are proud of their heritage and traditions, no matter what their personal status in society may be.

# daily food in GREECE

## NOT A HEARTY STARTER

If you're a fan of big breakfasts (bacon and eggs), forget Greek breakfasts, because the Greeks don't take breakfast all that seriously. Life in the Hellenic Republic begins at the crack of dawn, but millions of people begin work having consumed only Greek coffee or instant coffee, or perhaps warm milk with a cake or dunked rusk. Some city workers eat breakfast on the run—a traditional ring of bread encrusted with sesame seeds, or a corn cob bought from a street vendor. Later in the day, especially in winter, these same busy people will rush home, pausing only to buy hot chestnuts from a seller roasting them over coals in a battered tin drum.

Tourists looking for a breakfast in the style of Greek cuisine may enjoy sheep's milk yogurt topped with honey. Most Greeks prefer this as a dessert with a main meal, but tourists can obtain it for a breakfast treat if they so desire.

Before lunch, innumerable tiny cups of thick coffee may be drunk, or, in summer, frappé, surely the world's best version of iced coffee.

## LUNCH—THE BIG DEAL MEAL

Shopping is completed early and food choices are based on freshness. The Athens' food market is a cornucopia of stalls and specialty shops displaying gleaming produce, including meat, fish, cheese and mountains of grains. Aromatic smells, shouting hawkers, debating customers and sellers assail the senses. Supermarkets are increasing in number, but nothing beats a city market or a small, sociable village market (these may not be open daily) to which the self-sufficient villagers bring their surplus food for sale.

In a city restaurant, more than a dozen traditional dishes, pre-cooked and kept warm in pots or bains-marie, are offered. These are served with crusty bread, for which one pays extra. Vegetables or salads come separately and are often shared at table. Other little places specialize in grilled and vertically spit-roasted meats, including *kokoretsi* (offal-stuffed lamb entrails). These meats come with fried potatoes and salad. Small family restaurants may only offer about four dishes, but as everywhere, the guest is welcomed to visit the kitchen to choose which looks most appetizing, or for first hand advice when language difficulties have defeated attempts to master the menu.

When possible, families lunch at home. Food is wholesome, but choices are fewer. Lunch may include soup, a main course, plus vegetables and/or salad, bread and dessert (usually fruit). A more lavish lunch may include appetizers. These may be savory pies (spinach or cheese) in filo pastry, seafood (such as squid, mussels, pickled octopus or little fish) or stuffed vine leaves.

When guests come to lunch, a huge array of appetizers, main dishes, salads, fruit and cheese is presented, almost all at once. No wonder that the Greeks, like other Mediterranean people, need to siesta afterwards! Activity, including work, resumes at about 5pm.

## TIME TO EAT AGAIN—DINNER

The evening meal can begin as late as 8pm, and many tavernas remain open until 1am. In some, diners can still be lingering at 5am. The fare is similar to lunch, but metropolitan tavernas may offer grills and also provide music. From morning to early evening, sustenance can be sought at a *galaktopoleia* (a milk shop) serving dairy products, pastries and tea and coffee. A *zaharoplasteia* (a sweet shop) offers cookies, cakes, chocolates and beverages, including bottled alcohol.

The *kafenion*, a haven for men to talk, play cards and backgammon, drink coffee or take ouzo with *mezethes*, is usually closed during siesta. Greek women are more tolerated at *kafenia* now; they can thank foreign female tourists for paving the way.

The *ouzeri* obviously serves ouzo. But *mezethes* are becoming increasingly more creative and many *ouzeri* offer evening meals featuring regional dishes, including omelettes for people who do not wish a heavy dinner. And so to bed, late, unless, after an evening out, an *ouzeri* supper is sought. It could comprise soup, fish (with garlic sauce), salad, stuffed eggs, feta, olives and anchovies with water and wine. City *ouzeri* present recorded or live music, and they are fashionable with the young.

Generally, the best meals in Greece are enjoyed in private homes. These recipes by Stephanie Souvlis will enable eager cooks to duplicate these meals.

## THE VILLAGES

Stroll into a Greek village square. Your nose will indicate that much of life revolves around the preparation of food.

If it's a remote village with only one weekly market day, it's likely you'll be in a community where many houses do not have ovens. The smell of yeasty bread, risen in the home kitchen but speedily dispatched to the village by housewives, will be all-pervading from the local bakery. The baker may preside over the goldening of most of the loaves in the village. By the time bartering in the market for fruit and vegetables, live poultry, eggs, fresh and home-pickled olives is done, the bread will almost be ready. Before the bread is fully baked, there is time to pop into a *kafenion*-cum-general-store for supplies such as tinned milk, rusks and non-food requirements; time to duck into the cavernous shop that sells local pottery casserole dishes, pots, pans and coffee pots; time to peruse the butcher's meats; time to gossip in the street or *kafenion*; and time to greet everyone warmly before the bread is baked. Then it is taken home proudly, perhaps along with a dish of moussaka or pastitcio which needed browning in the baker's oven, and was dropped off in the morning with the family bread.

# daily life in GREECE

## TIME FOR CELEBRATION

Easter is the pre-eminent festival in Greece. After the Lenten fast and the midnight church service to welcome the resurrected Christ, *mayiritsa* or *mageiritsa* (Easter soup) is savored. Some non-Greeks are daunted by this thick combination of offal, onions, garlic, dill, rice, egg and lemon sauce, but it is marvellous. To accompany it, bread containing red-dyed, hardboiled eggs is broken before Sunday church, and after church a feast is enjoyed: a spit-roasted lamb. Special Easter cakes, breads and cookies (known generally as *koulouria*) are prepared for the guests, recipes varying from region to region. Almond cookies are made for Easter and other very special occasions.

Whole suckling pig, cooked in the same marinade used to baste Easter lamb (oil, lemon juice, oregano, salt and pepper), is an essential part of the village feast on 15 August, Assumption Day. Only in village homes will one be offered chipura (made from grape skins), the Greek equivalent of Irish poteen (which is derived from potatoes). To a foreigner, it may taste very strong. Gasp, but be polite. Feel privileged during the toast: '*Chronia polla!*' ('Long life!).

## THE CITIES

Village traditions are not forgotten in the cities, but the cities, like the villages, are dependent on available produce. For example, a *lagos stifado* (stewed hare) may be a premium-priced dish in Athens because supplies are few, whereas, in the countryside, during the shooting season, people enjoy hare for the price of a few shotgun pellets. No one off the island can taste the tomatoes of Santorini—there aren't enough to export from the island. Blood-red and very thick, they are served without additives or artificial color.

## A MELLOW MELDING

Athens is a melting pot: it absorbs as many styles of Hellenic cuisine as possible. Cuisine in Athens is also marked by foreign influences, such as the fast food chains of today, and the dominant aggressors of the past. Few recipes acknowledge Athens as their source. Her chefs try to recreate as many regional variations as possible, variations derived from both the mainland and from hundreds of islands, most of which have their own culinary styles. More offal is served in the restaurants of the city than can be found in the villages.

Athenian chefs can't seem to duplicate the *soudzoukakia* (hand-made sausages) from Greece's second-biggest, northern city of Thessaloniki. These hand-made sausages were invented by Greeks in Smyrna, part of Turkey. The secret ingredient is cumin. Corfu is a fine, cultured, European-style city, as well as an island. Its stewed fish, its *sofrito* (stewed steak), and its other methods of preparing fish are unlike those anywhere else in Greece.

Greece's largest island, Crete, also has culinary individuality. Its cities of Iraklion and Rethymnion produce pies and pastries unavailable elsewhere.

In the winter, *rathikia* (wild dandelion) seems, perhaps strangely, to be more popular on the tables of city eateries than in the country. The green leaves are similar to spinach, and it is served warm to cold, dressed with lemon and oil.

Dining is as relaxed in the cities as in the villages. Apart from during siesta time, city Greeks always seem to be eating out, which is one of their most popular pastimes.

## THE LAND

Greece is about 75 percent mountainous, and beef is not a prominent part of the cuisine because cattle are not as suited to the terrain as are goats and sheep. Goat's milk makes wonderful yogurt and cheeses including soft haloumi (great when grilled), semi-soft feta (which everyone knows is the crown on a Greek farmer's salad), and kefalotiri (which is a hard, biting cheese, an ingredient for main meal dishes, and a pasta topping). This kefalotiri is a better version of Parmesan. Myzithra (soft ewe's milk cheese) is a delicious cheese, especially the one from *Ios* island. Yogurt is often used in recipes as a marinade or as a dessert topped with honey (from the Peloponnese mainland).

No other people use lemons like the Greeks do, as a dressing, tenderizer or meat marinade, and in avgolemono (egg and lemon sauce). Poultry and pigs are farmed enthusiastically.

## OLIVES, HERBS AND WONDERFUL WINE

On the lower mountain slopes, olive groves are thick, none more famed than around Kalamata in the Peloponnese. Vines are tended on mainland plains, but excellent (non-resinated) wines also come from the lush, hilly hinterlands of the Ionian islands, notably Cephalonia, and

the drier, far-flung islands of Samos and Rhodes, near Turkey. Rhodian sparkling wine is superior to any other sparkling wine in Greece. Surprisingly, the stark, volcanic island of Santorini produces excellent wines, particularly rosé. Pine forests yield resin, which in ancient times infiltrated the wine while it was aging in pine wood barrels. Not to the taste of many foreigners, this wine (called retsina) is appreciated by most Greeks.

Corfu is the vegetable and herb garden of Greece, its slopes redolent with the perfume of 3500 plant species and 300 herbs. A specialty is kumquat liqueur processed at six distilleries.

In the Epirus region of Central Greece, one can enjoy freshwater fish from lakes and streams—trout, carp and eel. In preparing these fish, oregano, dill and rosemary are used—these are the most-used herbs throughout Greece.

## THE SEA

The fish of Greece are unparalleled, coming from waters surrounding the mainland and about 1600 islands. From the islands, *caique* (small boat) fishermen sell much of their catch to merchants who freeze the fish for dispatch to the high-paying restaurateurs and exporters in the cities of Athens, Piraeus, Patras and Kavala. Colorful island fish markets, although heavily frequented by tourists, still have enough to feed both their visitors and the local people who depend on this food source during Lent (when they fast from meat). In recent years, Greek cooks, usually fanatical about freshness, have become adept at preparing dishes from frozen produce. Those who dislike frozen fish still bargain with fishermen at the wharf for fresh produce.

# INTRODUCTION

## FISH FOR A DISH

Fish, prepared to perfection, tender, succulent, and retaining the fragrance of the sea, have pre-occupied Greeks for centuries. The Greeks introduced taramosalata (fish roe dip) to the world, and popularized calamari, the humble squid which is equally tender when barbecued, deep-fried in batter, or baked (after being stuffed with pine nuts, rice, tomatoes, raisins, mint and parsley). On the Ionian island of Kythera, squid is sensational in a stew with onions, wine and masses of parsley and tomatoes.

Pickled octopus is a nationally favored type of *mezethes*, as are *marides*. The latter are tiny whitebait fish (which can also be a meal on their own in the quantities often served in Greece). The Cretans prepare octopus with fennel and wine, and also serve snails superbly, fried with vinegar or braised with tomatoes, wheat or potatoes. On Ios island, as well as on Crete, snails are a speciality.

Fish soup, as an appetizer, or as a main course with bread and salad, is wonderful. Perch, cod and mackerel translate into super *stifado* (a stew which contains onions). Many islands offer versions of shrimp *saganaki* (shrimp baked with onions, tomatoes and cheese). Sardines, cuttlefish, swordfish and grey mullet are among dozens of fish varieties that are grilled with lemon juice or served with garlic sauce. Herbs, oil and tomatoes complement fish in different styles. Fish from the Saronic island of Spetsai, baked (again with garlic), is internationally renowned.

Lobster with long claws is served mostly in Piraeus and on the islands of Corfu and Mykonos. But lobster bows to the king of Greek fish, *barbounyi* (red mullet), as the most revered and most expensive seafood. *Barbounyi* is served untarnished by any sauce, purely pan-prepared, or grilled with olive oil and lemon juice.

## TRADITIONAL GREEK FOOD FOR THE NON-GREEK COOK

All dishes mentioned in this introduction, and the following recipes compiled and tested by Stephanie Souvlis, are authentic Greek recipes, traditionally derived. The wonderful thing about Greek food is that, although recipes have been re-named by conquerers who claimed them as their own, the food is essentially cooked the same way it was centuries ago.

Many Greeks in Greece are hesitant to try other cuisines. As an expatriate Australian on the island of Kythera, I tried to reciprocate the wonderful hospitality extended to me. I performed what (to me at least) were French-style miracles on a rare hare for my neighbors.

They ate little—mere mouthfuls in order to be polite. Later I was told, 'Your olive oil was inferior.' How was I to know that the vintage of the olives, the fields from which the olives grow, and even who processes them, are considered to be all-important in the taste test? My village friend Theohari told me to cook only Greek-style, and kindly offered lessons. I was to watch, smell and taste samples and then I was to return to my house to practice on my husband and child!

I never became an acclaimed cook in Greece. My *rathikia*, made of boiled dandelions, gathered from the mountainside, turned out to be boiled stinging nettles! Yet the way to my adopted people's hearts was through Brandy Alexanders, whipped up with Cypriot brandy, tinned milk and topped with cinnamon. At last, an offering that was acceptable to my new friends!

Tourism, and inter-marriage between Greeks and other nationalities, have made for some interesting culinary changes in recent years. Some Greek restaurateurs are adopting the influences of their foreign spouses. On the far-flung Cycladic island of Folegandros, I discovered a restaurant offering a fabulous combination of Swiss and Greek food in the main village square.

No recipes have been included in this introduction as you will find plenty of exciting recipes in the rest of this section. But I have tried to convey something of the depth, breadth and culinary evolution of Greek cuisine. Long may the old Greek traditions remain! And, as the Greeks would say: '*Kaliorexi!*' ('Good appetite!').

Kerry Kenihan

# appetisers

# MEZETHES

Start your Greek meal with dips and crusty bread. Greek dips include taramosalata (fish roe dip), which is very special when stuffed in artichokes, and tzatziki (cucumber with yogurt and mint). Purées include *melitzanasalata* (which directly translates as eggplant salad, but which is really a purée), and hummus (chickpea) with sesame butter. Pies of various sorts (cheese, spinach, mushroom and meat) are made with thin, layered filo pastry, fiddly to make, but available frozen in supermarkets.

*Mezethes* (appetizers) are as traditional to Greeks as antipasto is to Italians. Fresh cheeses, olives and salami (invented on the Greek island of Salamis, and not in Italy) appeal, as do pickled octopus and squid, dolmades (stuffed vine leaves), and tiny, marinated, spiced meatballs. Mussels, fried liver and stuffed eggs, which were introduced by Russian occupants of Corfu, can also begin the meal. The variation of omelette from Andros, with its spicy sausages, mint and potatoes, is outstanding, and makes a tasty brunch dish or appetizer.

### GREEK-STYLE CHEESES

Feta is a salty, crumbly cheese traditionally made from sheep's milk or goat's milk. It is both a table cheese and a cooking cheese, and is readily available in well-appointed supermarkets. Kefalotiri is often made from sheep's milk; it has a slightly oily quality and is mainly a grating cheese. Italian Parmesan is a satisfactory substitute. Kasseri is a soft, mild sheep's or goat's milk cheese similar to Italian mozzarella. It can be sliced and fried, or can be eaten as a table cheese. Mizithra is available as a fresh cheese reminiscent of Italian ricotta, as a salted cheese, and also as an aged cheese for grating.

Other popular cheeses include graviera, a yellow sheep's milk table cheese, and manouri, a very creamy cheese from Crete sometimes eaten with honey as a dessert.

## TARAMOSALATA (FISH ROE DIP)

(bottom right)

**Ingredients**

4 slices stale white bread, 3 days old
3 oz red caviar
6 oz vegetable oil
7 oz olive oil
juice of 1 lemon
1 tablespoon water

**Method**

1. Remove crusts from bread and soak the bread in water for 10 minutes. Squeeze bread dry until all excess water is gone, and place in food processor. Process for 1 minute. Add the caviar, and process for another minute.
2. With the processor still running, pour the oil in a continuous stream until all the oil has been added and the mixture is creamy and thick.
3. Add the juice of the lemon, and the water, and process until well combined. Remove and place in a bowl. It can be stored in the refrigerator for up to seven days.
4. Serve with toasted pita bread.

Makes approximately $2\frac{1}{2}$ cups

## ROASTED EGGPLANT AND GARLIC DIP (top opposite)

**Ingredients**

1 large eggplant
5 cloves garlic, roasted
olive oil, for drizzing, plus 1 tablespoon
1 tablespoon tahini
1 tablespoon lemon juice
salt and black pepper

**Method**

1. Preheat the oven to 400°F.
2. Place the eggplant and garlic on a baking tray, drizzle with olive oil and roast in the oven for 20 minutes. Remove from the oven, scoop the flesh out of the inside of the eggplant, and place the flesh and roasted garlic in the bowl of a food processor.
3. Process until puréed, then add the tahini, lemon juice and olive oil, and process for a few seconds to combine.
4. Season to taste with salt and pepper, and serve with bread.

Makes 2 cups

## TZATZIKI (CUCUMBER WITH YOGURT AND MINT) (middle opposite)

**Ingredients**

7 oz plain Greek yogurt
3 oz cucumber, grated
1 tablespoon lemon juice
1 clove garlic, crushed
salt and black pepper
1 tablespoon mint, chopped (optional)

**Method**

1. Combine all the ingredients in a bowl, and season with salt and pepper to taste. Cover with plastic wrap and refrigerate for at least one hour (to allow the flavors to develop).
2. Serve with pita bread as a dip, or as an accompaniment sauce.

Makes 1 cup

## DOLMADES (STUFFED VINE LEAVES)

### Ingredients

8 oz onion, minced

14 oz short-grain rice

⅔ cup oil

1 tablespoon dill, chopped

½ cup mint, chopped

1 tablespoon salt

5 oz lemon juice

40 small vine leaves

### Method

1. Mix the onion, rice, oil, herbs, salt and 4 oz of the lemon juice in a bowl. Boil some water and soak the vine leaves in boiling water for 15 minutes.
2. Place leaves under cold water for 10 minutes, and lie out on a tea-towel to dry.
3. To make the dolmades, place one tablespoon of the rice mixture in the center of each vine leaf and wrap like a parcel. (Use less mixture if the leaves are small.)
4. Place the dolmades in a saucepan and cover with boiling water. Add 2 oz of the lemon juice to the water. Place a plate over the top of them and cook for an hour (until the vine leaves are cooked).

Makes approximately 40 dolmades

## BABY OCTOPUS MARINATED IN OLIVE OIL AND OREGANO

**Ingredients**

1/3 cup olive oil
rind of 1 lemon
2 tablespoons lemon juice
1/3 cup shallots, finely sliced
2 teaspoons oregano, chopped
freshly ground pepper and salt
1 1/2 pound baby octopus, cleaned
salad leaves, for serving

**Method**

1. In a bowl, mix together the olive oil, lemon rind, lemon juice, shallots, oregano, and pepper and salt. Add the octopus and leave to marinate for one hour.
2. Heat a char-grill pan, lightly brush with oil, add octopus, and cook (basting with marinade) for 2–3 minutes, or until tender.
3. Serve on a bed of salad leaves.

Serves 4

## WHITEBAIT FRITTERS

**Ingredients**

1 pound smelt (whitebait)
1/3 cup shallots, finely sliced
2 teaspoons dill, chopped
rind of 2 lemons
2 teaspoons lemon juice
1/2 cup all-purpose flour
2 eggs, lightly beaten
freshly ground pepper and salt to taste
olive oil for frying
lemon wedges

**Method**

1. Place smelt in a food processor and process until well combined.
2. Transfer mixture to a bowl and add shallots, dill, lemon rind, lemon juice, flour, eggs, and pepper and salt, and mix together.
3. Heat oil in a pan and add mixture (one tablespoon per fritter) and cook for 2–3 minutes (or until golden).
4. Serve with wedges of lemon.

Serves 4 (makes 20 fritters)

## TIROPETES (CHEESE TRIANGLES)

**Ingredients**

10 oz ricotta cheese

10 oz feta cheese

4 eggs

white pepper

1 packet filo pastry

4 oz melted butter

**Method**

1. Preheat oven to 400°F.
2. Combine the ricotta, feta and eggs in a bowl and mix well. Season with the white pepper.
3. Brush one layer of filo pastry with melted butter, and place another layer on top. Cut the pastry lengthwise, into 4 strips.
4. To shape the triangles, place a heaping teaspoon of cheese mixture close to the bottom of the right hand corner of the strip. Fold this corner over the mixture, diagonally across to the left-hand edge to form a triangle. Continue folding from right to left in a triangular shape to the end of strip. Brush top of triangle with melted butter and place on a baking tray. Repeat until all mixture has been used.
5. Bake triangles in the oven for about 20 minutes (until they are golden).

***Note:*** To make larger triangles, cut the strips of pastry wider, and use more filling per triangle.

Makes approximately 25 triangles

## MARINATED MUSHROOMS (MANITARIA MARINATA)

### Ingredients

½ cup olive oil
⅓ cup lemon juice, freshly squeezed
½ teaspoon dried thyme
1 stalk fennel
1 clove garlic, crushed
1 stalk celery, finely chopped
10 black peppercorns
1 bay leaf
½ cup water
2 pounds fresh small mushrooms
1 lemon
2 tablespoons fresh parsley, chopped for garnish

### Method

1. In a medium saucepan, combine all of the ingredients down to, but not including, the mushrooms, and bring to a boil. Cover, reduce heat, and simmer until celery is just tender
2. Trim off mushroom stems. Cut lemon in halves and run the cut surface of the lemon over the mushrooms. Add mushroom caps to simmering liquid, and cook a further 5 minutes.
3. Remove mushrooms with a slotted spoon, and place on serving dish.
4. Increase heat, and boil liquid until it reduces and thickens. Pour sauce over mushrooms, cover, cool and place in refrigerator. Garnish with parsley before serving.

Serves 6–8

## SPANAKOPITA (SPINACH PIE)

### Ingredients

1 bunch spinach
½ cup olive oil
1½ cups chopped scallions
4 oz feta cheese, crumbled
4 oz tasty cheese, grated
1 tablespoon fresh dill, chopped
salt and pepper to taste
5 eggs, beaten
16 sheets filo pastry
¾ cup olive oil, for brushing

### Method

1. Preheat oven to 400°F. Cut root end off spinach and wash well. Shred spinach and place in a colander to drain. Shake in a tea-towel to dry. When dry, place spinach in a large bowl.
2. Heat oil in a small pan until very hot. Pour all (but a little) over spinach. This action will wilt the spinach sufficiently. Sauté scallions in remaining oil until soft, and then add to spinach. Mix in both the cheeses, and the dill, salt, pepper and beaten egg.
3. Oil a 12 x 10 inch baking dish. Lay out a sheet of filo pastry in dish and brush with oil. Repeat until eight sheets have been placed in dish. Spread in the spinach mixture, and turn in edges. Cover with eight more sheets, brushing each sheet with oil. Brush top with oil and trim edges. Score top layers of pastry into squares or diamond shapes with a sharp knife. Splash with a little water (to prevent curling).
4. Bake in preheated oven for ten minutes, then reduce heat to 350°F and bake for 30–35 minutes (until golden brown and puffed). The filling is cooked when the pie puffs up. Do not be deceived into thinking that the pie is cooked if it browns quickly on top. If this is the case, cover the pie with a sheet of brown paper and continue cooking until it comes up like a pillow.

Serves 8

## PAPOUTSAKIA (STUFFED EGGPLANTS)

### Ingredients

4 medium eggplants
salt
oil for frying
2 tablespoons olive oil
1 large onion, finely chopped
2 garlic cloves, crushed
1 pound ground beef or lamb
8 oz canned tomato pieces, peeled
2 teaspoons tomato paste
2 tablespoons parsley, chopped
⅛ teaspoon nutmeg
½ teaspoon sugar
salt and pepper

*Béchamel sauce*

1 tablespoon butter
3 tablespoons plain flour
1½ cups milk
1 egg
salt and pepper
pinch of nutmeg

### Method

1. Halve eggplants lengthwise. Cut around flesh, 2 inches in from the skin, then make cuts across and down flesh, taking care not to pierce skin.
2. Sprinkle cut surface with salt, and let stand for 30 minutes. Pat dry and shallow-fry in hot oil for two minutes on each side. Cool a little, then scoop out flesh carefully, leaving a thin wall. Reserve flesh, and place cases in a greased oven-proof dish.
3. Heat two tablespoons olive oil in a skillet, add onion and garlic, and then sauté until onion is soft. Add meat, and while the meat browns, add tomatoes (and their juice), tomato paste, parsley, nutmeg, sugar, salt and pepper. Cover and simmer for 20 minutes. Add chopped eggplant flesh.
4. Fill eggplant cases with filling mixture.
5. Prepare béchamel sauce. Preheat oven to 350°F. Melt butter in a saucepan, add flour, and stir for 1 minute. Gradually add milk, stirring to remove any lumps. Cook until it thickens. Remove from heat and quickly add egg while stirring vigorously. Add salt, pepper and nutmeg, and stir over very low heat for 30 seconds.
6. Spoon sauce neatly over meat filling. Place in preheated oven and cook for 30 minutes. Remove to serving dish and serve hot as an entrée, or as a main meal.

*Variation:* For large eggplants, the béchamel sauce may be omitted, and slices of fresh tomato placed on top of meat. Sprinkle lightly with grated Romano cheese and bake.

Serves 4–6

# soups

# Quick and EASY SOUP

Greece's simplest soup is avgolemono, and it is easy to prepare from bouillon, with rice, egg and lemon added. It's heartier when meat balls are added.

The oldest soup is the thick, fishy *kakavia* from which was derived the famous French *bouillabaisse* after the French observed ancient Greek mariners preparing it at the port of Marseilles.

Offal, which we have already noted in the preparation of the Easter soup *mayiritsa*, also features in the Turkish-named *patsa*, which is a lusty brew containing garlic, tripe and lamb's feet.

Beans are the basis for many warming soups, and soups made with haricot beans in *fassoulada* are a meal in one. Lentils feature in *faki*, which is one of the 'soul foods' eaten during Lent.

No tomato soup can compare with that prepared on Santorini for natural thickness, flavor and deep red color. But home cooks can be content with the peppered version textured with vermicelli outlined in these pages.

## MEATBALLS IN EGG AND LEMON SOUP (YOUVARLAKIA)

### Ingredients

1 pound ground beef
1 medium onion, minced
1/4 cup parsley, chopped
1/4 cup short-grain rice
1 egg
salt and pepper
1/3 cup cornstarch
4 cups beef bouillon
2 oz butter
1 egg
1/3 cup lemon juice

### Method

1. Combine the beef, onion, parsley, rice and egg in a bowl, and mix well with your hands. Season well with salt and pepper. Using one tablespoon of mixture for each meatball, shape mixture into balls, and roll in cornstarch (shaking off the excess).
2. Bring the bouillon and the butter to a boil, then reduce the heat and place the meatballs in the bouillon. Cover with a lid, and simmer for 45 minutes (until they are cooked). Let cool slightly.
3. Whisk the egg and lemon juice together in a bowl, then add 4 oz of warm bouillon to the egg and lemon juice. Pour this mixture back into the saucepan and heat very gently.
4. Season with salt and pepper before serving.

Serves 6

## CHILLED YOGURT SOUP

**Ingredients**

1 large seedless cucumber
1 cup light cream
7 oz natural yogurt
2 tablespoons white wine vinegar
1 tablespoon balsamic vinegar
2 tablespoons fresh mint, chopped
1 clove garlic, crushed
salt and freshly ground black pepper
extra mint and slices of cucumber, to garnish

**Method**

1. Peel and grate the cucumber.
2. Combine the cream, yogurt and vinegars together, and whisk lightly until smooth. Stir in the cucumber, mint, garlic and seasoning. Cover and chill for three hours.
3. Stir and taste for seasoning before serving chilled. Garnish with a slice of cucumber, a sprig of mint and cracked pepper.

Serves 4–6

## MIXED BEAN AND VEGETABLE SOUP

**Ingredients**

½ cup haricot beans, soaked overnight
½ cup chickpeas, soaked overnight
3 tablespoons olive oil
1 medium onion, diced
1 clove garlic, crushed
1 leek, white part only, diced
6 cups vegetable bouillon
2 sticks celery, sliced
1 carrot, diced
2 sprigs fresh thyme, chopped
1 small fennel bulb, grated
2 zucchini, grated
3 oz broad beans
3 medium tomatoes, peeled, seeded and chopped
salt and freshly ground black pepper
freshly grated Parmesan, for serving

**Method**

1. Drain the haricot beans and chickpeas. Place in a saucepan, cover with water and bring to a boil for 15 minutes. Cover and simmer for a further 30 minutes before draining again.
2. Heat the oil in a saucepan and add the onion, garlic and leek. Continue stirring until tender. Add the bouillon, haricot beans and chickpeas. Cover, and simmer for 45 minutes (until tender). Add the remaining ingredients and simmer for a further 15 minutes.
3. Taste for seasoning, and serve with freshly grated Parmesan.

Serves 4–6

## CHICKPEA, ROASTED TOMATO AND GARLIC SOUP

**Ingredients**

1 pound dried chickpeas

2 pounds plum tomatoes

1 bulb garlic

⅓ cup olive oil

salt

2 tablespoons dried oregano

2 leeks, sliced, white part only

1 quart chicken bouillon

2 tablespoons tomato paste

salt and pepper

fresh oregano leaves

**Method**

1. Soak chickpeas in cold water overnight. Place chickpeas in a saucepan covered with water and bring to a boil, then simmer for approximately one hour until chickpeas are cooked. Drain and set aside.
2. Preheat the oven to 400°F. Halve the tomatoes and place them on a baking tray. Cut the top off the garlic bulb and place on the baking tray.
3. Drizzle with olive oil, sprinkle with salt and dried oregano, and roast in the oven for 20–30 minutes.
4. Place the tomatoes and five peeled garlic cloves (reserve the rest) in a food processor, and purée for one minute.
5. Heat half the oil and sauté the leeks for three minutes. Add the bouillon, and bring to a boil, then reduce heat to simmer.
6. Add the tomato mixture, tomato paste and the chickpeas, season with salt and pepper, and heat through.
7. To serve, sprinkle with fresh oregano leaves just before serving.

Serves 4

## CHICKEN AND LEMON SOUP (SOUPA AVGOLEMONO)

**Ingredients**

6 cups chicken bouillon
12 oz chicken tenderloin, cut into thin strips
5 oz risoni (rice-shaped pasta)
1 egg
juice of 1 lemon
salt
ground black pepper

**Method**

1. Heat bouillon in a saucepan and bring to a boil. Reduce the heat until the bouillon is simmering, add the chicken pieces, and cook for 15 minutes (or until chicken pieces are cooked).
2. Add the risoni and cook for 10–15 minutes (until the risoni are cooked), then remove from the heat and let the mixture cool for 15 minutes.
3. Whisk the egg in a bowl, and continue whisking while pouring in the lemon juice. Add three ladles of hot soup to the egg mixture, still whisking.
4. Slowly pour the egg mixture back into the saucepan of soup, and heat, very gently, until soup has thickened slightly. Season with salt and pepper, and serve.

*Note:* Be careful not to heat the soup too fast as the egg will curdle.

Serves 4

## LENTIL SOUP (SOUPA FAKI)

**Ingredients**

1 pound lentils
olive oil
2 medium onions, chopped
2 stalks celery, chopped
2 small carrots, chopped
2 cloves garlic, crushed
2 tablespoons tomato paste
2 bay leaves
1 teaspoon oregano, dried
salt
black pepper, freshly ground
½ cup red wine

**Method**

1. Rinse lentils. Heat oil in a large heavy-based saucepan over medium heat.
2. Add onions, celery, carrots, garlic, tomato paste, bay leaves and oregano. Sauté until onions are translucent (4–5 minutes).
3. Add lentils and cover with water to a depth of 3 inches. Bring to boil, cover and reduce heat. Simmer until lentils are tender (about 30 minutes). Check while simmering to ensure lentils are completely covered with water (and add more if necessary).
4. Remove from heat, and discard bay leaves. Season with salt, pepper and wine.
5. It is best if left standing for a few minutes before serving (to allow flavors to blend).

Serves 4–6

# meat

# FAVORITE DISHES

As noted in the introduction, beef is less often offered on the Greek menu than are lamb, goat and game, because cattle are not bred prolifically in Greece. However, veal is available at many Greek eateries and makes the basis of delicious stews. Lamb is the preferred meat, followed by pork (which is usually grilled). Offal is prepared extensively; nothing goes to waste.

Many Greek dishes are based on ground meat combined with pasta, or with vegetables in layers. An example is moussaka with eggplant, zucchini or potatoes, or perhaps with all three. Ground meat is used as a popular stuffing for cabbage, zucchini, eggplant, tomato or bell pepper for economical main dishes. Alone, ground meat is made into *keftedes* (meat balls), which are eaten as appetizers or as a main dish, spiced with cinnamon and aniseed à la Smyrna. They can also be served with various sauces including avgolemono, wine or simply yogurt. *Rolo* (meat loaf) is a dinner-party dish. With a garlic-tomato sauce, it has a surprising center of boiled eggs.

## BEEF WITH ARTICHOKES, OLIVES AND OREGANO

**Ingredients**

2 tablespoons olive oil
1 ½ pound fillet of beef
1 clove garlic, crushed
1 bunch scallions, trimmed and halved
½ cup wine
1 cup beef bouillon
1 tablespoon tomato paste
2 teaspoons oregano, chopped
salt and freshly ground pepper
2 globe artichokes, trimmed, and cut into quarters
⅓ cup olives, pitted

**Method**

1. Preheat oven to 350°F.
2. In a large heavy-based oven-proof dish, heat one tablespoon olive oil, add meat and sear quickly on all sides. Take out and set aside.
3. Heat rest of olive oil, add garlic and onions, and cook for 2–3 minutes. Add white wine, cook for 1 minute, then add beef bouillon, tomato paste, oregano, and salt and pepper. Bring to boil, return meat to dish, add artichokes, cover, and bake for 30–40 minutes.
4. Add olives in the last 5 minutes of cooking time.
5. Slice the meat and arrange with vegetables; pour the sauce over meat and vegetables.

***Note:*** Trim artichokes of outer leaves and stems. Place in a bowl of water with lemon juice. This stops the artichokes from turning brown.

Serves 4.

## GREEK LAMB KEBABS

### Ingredients

12 oz ground lamb
1 cup fresh breadcrumbs
1 clove garlic, crushed
2 tablespoons onion, grated
1 teaspoon cumin, ground
1 tablespoon parsley, finely chopped
1 tablespoon mint, finely chopped
1 teaspoon oregano, chopped
rind of 1 lemon, finely grated
salt and freshly ground pepper
1 egg
1 oz olive oil
8 wooden kebab sticks (soaked in water for 30 minutes)

### Method

1. In a large bowl, combine all ingredients (until mixture is soft).
2. Roll mixture into sausage shapes, and place on kebab sticks. Place sticks on a tray and refrigerate overnight.
3. Heat some extra oil on a barbecue or in a char-grill pan, and cook kebabs for 5–6 minutes, turning frequently. Serve with tzatziki.

Makes 8

## LAMB SHANKS WITH BROAD BEANS, OLIVES AND RISONI

**Ingredients**

2 tablespoons olive oil
2 cloves garlic, crushed
4 lamb shanks
1 onion, chopped
2 cups beef bouillon
4 sprigs oregano
2 tablespoons tomato paste
2 cups water
1 cup risoni (rice-shaped pasta)
1 cup broad beans
½ cup olives
2 teaspoons fresh oregano, chopped
salt and freshly ground pepper

**Method**

1. Heat oil in a large saucepan, add garlic, lamb shanks and onion, and cook for five minutes (or until shanks are lightly browned).
2. Add the beef bouillon, sprigs of oregano, tomato paste and half the water, bring to a boil, reduce heat, and leave to simmer (with lid on) for 40 minutes.
3. Remove shanks, slice meat off bone, and set aside.
4. Add the risoni and water, cook for a further 5 minutes, then add broad beans, olives, meat, oregano, and salt and pepper, cook for 5 minutes more, and serve.

*Note*: If broad beans are large, peel off outer skin.

Serves 4–6

## MEATBALLS (KEFTEDES)

### Ingredients

1 pound onions, finely chopped
2 pounds ground beef
4½ oz packet breadcrumbs
2 eggs
1 tablespoon mint, chopped
¼ cup water
salt and freshly ground black pepper
all-purpose flour
2 cups vegetable oil, for frying

### Method

1. In a bowl, combine the chopped onion, beef, breadcrumbs, eggs, mint, water and salt and pepper. Using your hands, squeeze the mixture between your fingers making sure it is well combined.
2. Using 2 tablespoons of mixture for each meatball, shape into balls, and toss in a little flour, shaking off the excess. Flatten each ball slightly into the palm of your hand.
3. Heat the oil in a skillet and cook each meatball for approximately 3 minutes each side (see note below) until they are a dark brown color and cooked through.
4. Drain on paper towels.
5. Serve hot or cold with fresh tomato relish (see page 268).

*Note:* To test the oil for frying, toss a little flour into the oil: when it sizzles, the oil is ready for frying. The meatballs should be flattened out before cooking as they will puff up and rise whilst cooking.

Makes 40 meatballs

## RABBIT, OLIVE AND ONION CASSEROLE (LAGOS STIFADO)

### Ingredients

1½ pounds rabbit portions
1½ cup dry white wine
3 sprigs fresh oregano
3 bay leaves
⅓ cup olive oil
8 oz baby onions, peeled and halved
6 cloves garlic, unpeeled
1 tablespoon paprika
¾ cup chicken bouillon
½ cup black olives
salt and freshly ground black pepper
fresh oregano sprigs, to garnish
crusty bread

### Method

1. In a large bowl, combine rabbit, wine, oregano and bay leaves. Cover and refrigerate overnight.
2. Drain the rabbit and reserve the marinade. Preheat oven to 350°F.
3. Heat the oil in a large skillet and brown the rabbit a few pieces at a time on both sides. Remove the rabbit and place in a casserole dish.
4. Brown the onions and garlic in the skillet. Once golden, add the paprika. Stir continuously for two minutes, then add the bouillon and reserved marinade. Bring to a boil.
5. Pour onion and bouillon mixture over rabbit, add olives, and season with salt and pepper.
6. Cover and bake for one hour and 15 minutes (or until rabbit is cooked and tender). Garnish with fresh oregano, and serve with plenty of bread to mop up juices.

Serves 4

## LAMB'S LIVER WITH LEMON AND OREGANO

**Ingredients**

1 1/2 pounds lamb's liver
1/2 cup milk
1 tablespoon olive oil
1 clove garlic, crushed
1 medium red onion, sliced
8 oz bacon, cut into strips
1/4 cup olive oil, extra
1/3 cup all-purpose flour, seasoned
1 tablespoon parsley, chopped
1 teaspoon oregano, chopped
1/4 cup lemon juice
salt and freshly ground pepper

**Method**

1. Peel away membrane from liver, and cut out tubes and any green sections. Cut into thin slices, place in a large dish, pour milk over liver, and leave to soak for one hour.
2. Heat oil in a large pan, add garlic, onion and bacon, and cook for 2–3 minutes. Set aside in a dish.
3. Heat extra oil in pan, dip liver in seasoned flour, and cook quickly on both sides. Set aside and keep warm. Return onion and bacon to pan, add parsley, oregano, lemon juice, salt and pepper, and heat through.
4. Pour mixture over liver and serve.

Serves 4

## MARINATED LAMB KEBABS WITH PITA, SALAD AND YOGURT SAUCE (ARNI SOUVLAKIA)

**Ingredients**

¼ cup lemon juice
⅓ cup olive oil
1 clove garlic, crushed
1 teaspoon lemon thyme, chopped
salt and pepper
12 oz trim lamb, cubed
4 pieces of small pita bread

*Salad*

1 seedless cucumber, cubed
2 plum tomatoes, quartered
1 Spanish onion, sliced
2 oz feta cheese, crumbled
2 tablespoons olive oil
1 tablespoon vinegar
salt and pepper

*Yogurt sauce*

2 oz natural yogurt
1 clove garlic, crushed
4 oz cucumber, grated
1 teaspoon mint, chopped
salt and pepper to taste

*Method*

1. Combine lemon juice, olive, oil, garlic, lemon thyme, and salt and pepper in a bowl and marinate the lamb for at least 1–2 hours, or overnight (if time permits).
2. Combine all salad ingredients in a bowl and set aside.
3. Mix all the ingredients for the yogurt sauce together in a bowl, and set aside.
4. Char-grill the lamb pieces for a few minutes each side until lamb is cooked (but still slightly pink). Fill each pita bread with the lamb, salad and yogurt sauce and serve warm.

Serves 4–6 (depending on size of pita bread used)

## PORK CUTLETS WITH QUINCE

### Ingredients

1 tablespoon olive oil
4 pork cutlets

*Sauce*

1 oz olive oil
1 clove garlic, crushed
1 medium red onion, sliced
1 medium quince, peeled, cored and cut into thin wedges
1/2 cup white wine
juice of 1 orange (1/3 cup)
1/3 cup chicken bouillon
cinnamon stick
1 tablespoon honey
1 tablespoon parsley, chopped
salt and freshly ground pepper

### Method

1. Heat one tablespoon oil in a large skillet.
2. Add pork and brown quickly for 2–3 minutes each side. Set meat aside.
3. Heat extra oil in skillet. Add garlic and onion, and cook for 2–3 minutes. Add quince and cook for a further 3 minutes. Add white wine and cook for 2 minutes (or until reduced).
4. Stir in orange juice, chicken bouillon, cinnamon stick and honey, cook on low heat for 10–15 minutes (or until sauce has thickened slightly). Return pork to pan, and cook for a further 5–10 minutes. Stir in parsley, and salt and pepper. Spoon over cutlets, and serve.

Serves 4

# pastitcio

## PASTITCIO (LASAGNE)

**Ingredients**

1/4 cup oil
1 onion, sliced
2 pounds ground beef
2 tablespoons tomato paste
14 oz canned tomatoes
1 cup water
2 teaspoons oregano, chopped
1 teaspoon sugar
1 tablespoon Worcestershire sauce
1 cinnamon stick
salt and pepper
14 oz penne pasta, cooked
2 whole eggs
3/4 cup grated Romano cheese, for the top

***Béchamel sauce***

4 oz unsalted butter
3 tablespoons all-purpose flour
4 cups milk
8 oz Romano cheese
4 egg yolks

**Method**

1. Heat the oil and sauté the onion for 5 minutes. Add the meat and cook for 10 minutes, breaking up the meat with a fork as it cooks.
2. Add the tomato paste, tomatoes, water, oregano, sugar, Worcestershire sauce and the cinnamon stick, and bring to a boil. Simmer for 45 minutes or until mixture is cooked and sauce is thick. Add more water during cooking if needed. Season with salt and pepper.
3. To make the béchamel sauce, melt the butter in a saucepan, add the flour and cook for 3 minutes. Add the milk, and stirring continuously, bring to a boil, then simmer (until sauce thickens to a good coating consistency). Add the cheese and four egg yolks to the sauce, mixing well, then season with salt and pepper.
4. In a large ovenproof dish, mix the penne and the ground meat together, and add two eggs to the mixture. Pour the béchamel sauce over the top, sprinkle with the additional cheese, and bake in the oven for 30–45 minutes until the top is golden brown and the pastitcio is set.
5. Serve (cut into slices) hot or cold, with a Greek salad.

Serves 10

## ROASTED GARLIC LAMB WITH ROSEMARY AND RISONI

**Ingredients**

2–3 pound leg of lamb, trimmed
5 sprigs of rosemary
2 cloves garlic, sliced thinly
1/4 cup red wine
2 tablespoons olive oil
1 tablespoon rosemary, chopped
salt
black pepper

*Risoni*

2 oz olive oil
1 clove garlic
1 onion, chopped
1 cup risoni (rice-shaped pasta)
1 tablespoon rosemary, chopped
salt and pepper
14 oz canned tomatoes
1 cup water

**Method**

1. Preheat oven to 425°F.
2. Make incisions in the lamb, and place the pieces of sliced garlic, and little sprigs of rosemary in the incisions.
3. Pour the red wine and olive oil over the lamb, sprinkle with chopped rosemary, and season with salt and black pepper.
4. To make the risoni, heat oil in a saucepan and sauté the garlic and onion for 10 minutes (until the onion is cooked). Add the risoni and rosemary, season with salt and pepper, then take off heat and set aside.
5. Roast the lamb in the oven for 15 minutes, then reduce temperature to 400°F. Roast for a further 45 minutes. Take the lamb out of the oven and add risoni mixture (together with tomatoes and water), and mix well.
6. Return lamb to oven for a further 20 minutes until risoni is cooked. (A little more water can be added.)
7. Serve lamb on a bed of risoni.

Serves 6

## LAMB MOUSSAKA WITH CHAR-GRILLED EGGPLANT

**Ingredients**

2 tablespoons olive oil
1 clove garlic, crushed
1 onion, finely chopped
1 pound lamb, finely diced
1/4 cup white wine
2 tablespoons tomato paste
2 tablespoons parsley, chopped
1 tablespoon mint, chopped
fresh ground pepper and salt
2 medium eggplant, cut into 1/2 inch slices, char-grilled

*Cheese sauce*

3 tablespoons butter
3 tablespoons all-purpose flour
1 1/4 cup milk
1/4 cup kefalotiri cheese, grated
1/2 cup tasty cheese, grated
salt and pepper to taste

**Method**

1. Preheat the oven to 350°F.
2. In a large saucepan heat oil, add the garlic and onion, and cook for 3–5 minutes (or until soft).
3. Add the lamb in two batches and quickly brown on medium-high heat. Add the white wine and cook for 3 minutes (or until wine reduces a little). Add the tomato paste, parsley, mint, pepper and salt, and bring to a boil, reduce the heat, and simmer with the lid on for 30–40 minutes (or until lamb is tender). Set aside to cool.
4. To make the sauce, in a small saucepan heat the butter until it melts, take off the heat and add flour. Stir until well combined, add a little of the milk, and mix to a smooth paste. Then gradually add the rest of the milk, return to the heat, and stir until smooth. Add the cheeses, salt and pepper, and stir until the sauce is thick and smooth.
5. Lightly grease an 8 x 8 inch square baking dish. Place half of the eggplant slices on the bottom of the dish, top with half the lamb mixture, repeat with eggplant and lamb, then pour the cheese sauce over the eggplant and lamb.
6. Place in oven and bake for 30 minutes (or until sauce is brown on top).

Serves 4–6

## TOMATO RELISH (SALTSA DOMATA)

**Ingredients**

2 pounds plum tomatoes, chopped
2 onions, chopped
1 cup sugar
1/2 cup apple cider vinegar
2 tablespoons tomato paste
1 teaspoon salt
1/2 tablespoon dry mustard
1/2 teaspoon cayenne pepper (optional)

**Method**

1. Place all ingredients in a medium-sized saucepan and bring to a boil, then simmer for one hour until mixture becomes thick and pulpy. Check the seasoning and add salt and black pepper if desired.
2. Remove from the heat.
3. Serve with meatballs or with souvlakia. Can be stored in a sterilized jar in the refrigerator for up to one week.

Makes 2 cups

# seafood

# The taste OF GREEK

Many ingredients are used to enhance the taste of Greek fish or shellfish whether from the sea, the lake or the river. These include (not necessarily all together): tomatoes, garlic, parsley, onions, lemon juice, oil, oregano, rosemary, dill, vinegar, wine and feta cheese.

Fish are a high priority in Greece, even when it's not Lent. They may be baked, fried or grilled. Fish roe may be used in a dip or in rissoles (as traditionally in the Pelion region). Fried cod or grilled swordfish on skewers are particularly savory with *skordalia* (garlic pounded in a mortar with pestle, or blended electrically with either mashed potatoes or moist breadcrumbs, and oil and vinegar). The Northern Greek version contains thyme, tomatoes, bay leaves and bell pepper. Royal red mullet tends to be cooked with olive oil and lemon juice only. However, the stewed fish of Corfu, *bourtheto*, is flavored with paprika, black and cayenne peppers, and optional onions, for a really spicy kick.

Shellfish is magnificent baked in a casserole with tomatoes and feta. In the Epirus region, try skinned eel. It can be roasted with vinegar, garlic and bay leaves, or can be grilled and dressed with oil and lemon juice.

## MUSSELS WITH TOMATO SAUCE

### Ingredients

1 tablespoon olive oil
1 small onion, finely diced
1 clove garlic, crushed
2 x 14 oz canned tomatoes, drained
½ teaspoon sugar
½ teaspoon salt
freshly ground black pepper
3 large basil leaves, roughly torn
2 pounds mussels, scrubbed and bearded (see note)
extra basil, to garnish

### Method

1. Heat the oil in a large saucepan and sauté the onion and garlic over low heat until transparent. Add the tomatoes, sugar, salt and pepper. Simmer gently for 20 minutes. Add the basil and keep warm.
2. Place the mussels in a large pan with a little boiling water. Cover and cook over high heat (until the shells have opened).
3. Drain, and then spoon the mussels onto a serving platter accompanied with a bowl of warm sauce in which to dip. Garnish with extra basil leaves.

*Note:* When cleaning mussels, discard any that are already opened and any that don't shut when tapped gently. Also discard those that don't open when cooked.

Serves 4

## SWORDFISH KEBABS WITH TOMATO SAUCE

### Ingredients

1 tablespoon olive oil
1 small onion, finely diced
2 cloves garlic, crushed
2 x 14 oz canned tomatoes, drained
½ teaspoon sugar
½ teaspoon salt
freshly ground black pepper
1 ½ pounds swordfish
1 green bell pepper, seeded
1 medium eggplant
6 sprigs rosemary
2 oz olive oil
1 tablespoon rosemary, chopped
salt and freshly ground black pepper

### Method

1. Heat the oil in a large saucepan and sauté the onion and garlic over low heat until transparent. Add tomatoes, sugar, salt and pepper.
2. Simmer gently for 20 minutes. Add the basil and keep warm.
3. Preheat grill or barbecue to moderate.
4. Cut swordfish, green bell pepper and eggplant into large cubes.
5. Arrange on eight skewers (alternating with the rosemary sprigs). Brush with olive oil and chopped rosemary.
6. Grill kebabs, turning over at least once to brown the sides. Baste with a little more sauce. The swordfish should be golden, with the herbs and vegetables slightly charred.
7. Serve with extra sauce.

Serves 4

## PAN-FRIED SQUID WITH LEMON (KALAMARIA TIGANITA)

### Ingredients

1½ pounds squid tubes
½ cup fine semolina
1 teaspoon salt
1 teaspoon ground pepper
1 cup olive oil, for frying
1 lemon, cut into wedges

### Method

1. Cut each tube along one side. With a sharp knife, score inside skin diagonally in both directions. Cut squid into rectangles, each 2 x 1½ inches.
2. In a bowl, combine the semolina, salt and pepper.
3. Heat oil in a large skillet or wok. Dip squid into semolina, and when oil is hot, cook a few at a time until lightly brown and crisp. Drain on paper towels and serve with lemon wedges.

Serves 4

## SHRIMP WITH SPINACH

**Ingredients**

4 oz olive oil
1 medium onion, diced
1 red bell pepper, seeded and diced
1 clove garlic, crushed
2 tomatoes, peeled and diced
1½ bunches spinach, washed and roughly chopped
2 tablespoons dry white wine
juice of 1 lemon
salt and freshly ground black pepper
1 pound shrimp, shelled and deveined
lemon wedges to garnish

**Method**

1. Heat two tablespoons of olive oil in a saucepan, and brown onion. Add red bell pepper, garlic and tomatoes, and cook for 7 minutes. Add spinach, white wine, lemon juice and seasoning.
2. Cover and simmer gently for 8–10 minutes (until spinach is tender). Take off heat. Stir and keep warm.
3. Add the remaining oil to a large skillet. Once hot, add shrimp and sauté, stirring constantly, for 3 minutes (or until just cooked).
4. Spoon the shrimp into the spinach, fold to combine, and spoon onto a warm serving platter, garnished with lemon wedges. Serve immediately.

Serves 4

## SARDINES AND CHAR-GRILLED BELL PEPPER

**Ingredients**

1–2 tablespoons olive oil
8 oz sardine fillets (16 sardines)
1 tablespoon lemon juice
¼ cup virgin olive oil, extra
2 oz lemon juice, extra
1 tablespoon oregano, chopped
freshly ground pepper and salt
2 red bell peppers, roasted and thinly sliced
7 oz baby spinach or arugula, washed and trimmed

**Method**

1. Lightly brush char-grill pan with oil and heat. Lightly brush sardines with oil, then add to pan and cook for 1–2 minutes each side.
2. Set aside on a plate, and pour 1 tablespoon lemon juice over sardines.
3. Combine the olive oil, extra lemon juice, oregano, pepper and salt. Mix until well combined. On a plate (or bowl) add spinach or arugula, add slices of red bell pepper, place four sardines on top, and drizzle dressing over sardines.

Serves 4

## SEAFOOD CASSEROLE

**Ingredients**

1 tablespoon olive oil
1 medium onion, roughly chopped
1 leek, finely chopped
2 cloves garlic, crushed
7 oz canned tomatoes
2 bay leaves
1 tablespoon parsley, chopped
2 oz dry white wine
salt and freshly ground black pepper
2 pounds assorted fish and seafood (see note)
2 teaspoons oregano, chopped

**Method**

1. Heat the oil in a flameproof casserole dish. Sauté the onion, leek and garlic until softened and slightly golden.
2. Add the tomatoes, bay leaves, parsley, wine, salt and freshly ground black pepper. Bring to a boil, cover, and simmer gently for 20 minutes.
3. Stir in any firm-fleshed fish and simmer for 5 minutes. Stir in the remaining soft-fleshed fish, placing shellfish on the top.
4. Cover with a lid and continue cooking for 5–7 minutes (until the fish is tender) and the shellfish have opened (discarding any that remain closed).
5. Serve garnished with a fresh bay leaf.

***Note***: Suitable fish and seafood include red mullet, monk-fish, sea bream, cod, calamari, mussels, shelled shrimp and clams.

Serves 4–6

## BAKED FISH (PSARI PLAKI)

**Ingredients**

3 pound whole snapper or bream
salt and pepper
juice of 1 lemon
½ cup olive oil
1 large onion, sliced
3 cloves garlic, thinly sliced
½ cup celery, chopped
14 oz canned tomato pieces, peeled
½ cup dry white wine, optional
½ teaspoon sugar
1 teaspoon oregano

**Method**

1. Preheat oven to 350°F.
2. Prepare fish, leaving head and tail on. Make diagonal cuts on surface, sprinkle with a little salt and pepper and lemon juice. Set aside for 20 minutes.
3. Heat half the oil in a skillet, and sauté onion, garlic and celery for three minutes. Add tomatoes, wine, sugar and oregano, and season with salt and pepper. Sauté a further two minutes.
4. Spread mixture into an oiled baking dish and place fish on top. Drizzle remaining oil over fish. Bake in oven at 350°F for 30–40 minutes (depending on size). Baste fish during cooking.
5. Remove fish to serving platter, spoon sauce around fish, and serve with vegetable accompaniments or a salad.

Serves 4

## BAKED SARDINE FILLETS

### Ingredients

1 teaspoon olive oil
7 oz sardine fillets
2 tomatoes, peeled and diced
½ green bell pepper, seeded and finely diced
1 teaspoon capers, finely chopped
1 teaspoon fennel, finely chopped
2 teaspoons tomato paste
1 clove garlic, crushed
2 oz lemon juice
salt and freshly ground black pepper
1 tablespoon butter
lemon wedges, to garnish

### Method

1. Brush four sheets of aluminum foil with olive oil. Divide sardine fillets into four servings and arrange flat in center of each foil, skin side down.
2. Preheat oven to 350°F.
3. Combine in a bowl the tomato, green bell pepper, capers, fennel, tomato paste, garlic, lemon juice, salt and freshly ground black pepper. Mix well, and spoon this over the fillets. Dot with a little butter on the tops, and seal the foil over the fish.
4. Bake on a tray for 17 minutes. (Open one to check if the sardines are cooked.) Garnish with lemon wedges. Serve with a fresh salad.

Serves 4–6

## BABY SALMON IN VINE LEAVES

**Ingredients**

4 fresh baby salmon, cleaned, scaled and gutted
salt and pepper
4 sprigs lemon thyme
4 strips lemon zest
olive oil
8 vine leaves

*Sauce*

3 oz fruity olive oil
juice of half lemon
1 teaspoon capers, finely chopped
½ teaspoon parsley, finely chopped

**Method**

1. Wash and pat dry the salmon. Salt and pepper the cavity before placing a sprig of lemon thyme, and a strip of zest in each. Rub outside with olive oil, and lightly salt.
2. If using fresh vine leaves, trim off the tough part of the vine stem. Blanche in boiling water for 3 minutes, run under cold water and pat dry. (If using preserved vine leaves, drain, rinse under water and pat dry.)
3. Overlap two vine leaves. Place a salmon at one end and roll. Tie with a piece of water-soaked string. Continue with remaining salmon.
4. Cook on a preheated grill (or barbecue) for 8–12 minutes, turning once during this time.
5. Combine the sauce ingredients in a separate bowl, and whisk lightly, just before serving.

Serves 4

## SPINACH-STUFFED SQUID

**Ingredients**

4 large squid tubes (see note)
2 tablespoons olive oil
1 large onion, chopped
2 x 7 oz canned tomatoes, chopped
½ cup white wine
2 bay leaves
2 sprigs of rosemary
extra sprigs of rosemary, for garnish

*Stuffing*

2 tablespoons olive oil
1 medium onion, peeled and diced
8 oz cooked spinach, well drained
½ cup fresh breadcrumbs
2 oz ricotta cheese
1 clove garlic, crushed
salt and freshly ground black pepper

**Method**

1. To make the stuffing, heat the oil, and pan-fry the onion until softened.
2. Remove from the heat, and allow to cool a little before adding the remaining stuffing ingredients. Stir until well blended.
3. Rinse and pat the squid tubes dry. Divide the stuffing into four, and fill each tube. Secure the ends with metal skewers (or toothpicks).
4. Heat the oil in a skillet, and soften the onion. Add the tomatoes, wine and herbs. Cook over medium/high heat (until the mixture becomes pulpy in consistency). Lower the heat to a gentle simmer.
5. Add the squid, and spoon some of the mixture over the squid. Season, cover and simmer gently for 30 minutes.
6. Take out the skewers, and slice the squid.
7. Serve with sauce poured over, and garnished with a little extra rosemary.

*Note:* If large squid are unavailable, use 17 oz of small squid.

Serves 4

## BABY SNAPPER WITH TOMATOES AND POTATOES

**Ingredients**

4 baby snapper
¼ cup olive oil
¼ cup white wine
14 oz canned tomatoes
1½ pounds potatoes, peeled and chopped
1 tablespoon fresh oregano, chopped
salt and black pepper

**Method**

1. Preheat oven to 350°F.
2. Place the potatoes in a saucepan with cold water and boil for 10 minutes until potatoes are just starting to soften (but do not overcook).
3. Place all the ingredients in a baking pan.
4. Cover with foil and bake in oven for 20–30 minutes (until the fish is cooked and the potatoes are tender).
5. Serve the fish with fresh salad.

Serves 4

# chicken & poultry

# An old hen is worth FORTY CHICKS

Greeks don't boast about their chicken dishes, but it's a rare cook who fails with a recipe based on *kotopolo* (poultry or chicken). The Greek attitude to poultry is reflected in an old proverb that states, 'An old hen is worth forty chicks.' This is proved in many and varied ways.

An older hen may be stewed with celery, leeks, carrots and herbs to be placed in a pie, salad or fricassé, with its broth being savored separately. Roast poultry may be prepared by first stuffing a bird with pine nuts and herbs, or Cypriot-style with rice, currants and almonds. Roast poultry may also be offered as a pot roast in wine and bouillon, with peppers or figs. It may also be sautéed with onion, cinnamon, pepper, rice and tomatoes (which is Epirus-fashion), or with nutmeg and yogurt.

Poultry can also be braised in walnut sauce, or served sautéed or roasted with pine nuts and the ubiquitous (but never boring) avgolemono. Poultry is also super with spinach and feta, or in a filo pie with bacon, scallions, eggs and kefalotiri (or Parmesan) cheese. Other poultry respond well to these recipes. Quail is grilled with an olive oil, lemon and oregano baste, but is extra special when baked, wrapped in vine leaves, after marinating in honey, lemon and orange juices, brandy and thyme.

## ROASTED HERB-STUFFED CHICKEN (KOTA YEMISTA)

**Ingredients**

4 chicken breasts, skin on
2 tablespoons thick natural yogurt
1 clove garlic, crushed
1 teaspoon olive oil
2 tablespoons mint, minced
2 tablespoons Italian parsley, minced
2 tablespoons oregano, minced
2 tablespoons thyme, minced
2 tablespoons fennel, minced
2 scallions, minced
salt and finely ground black pepper

**Method**

1. In a small bowl, combine together all the ingredients (except the chicken) and mix well.
2. Using your finger tips, scoop up a quarter of the mixture and gently push under the skin of the chicken. Run your fingers over the skin to smooth the stuffing out. Repeat with the remaining pieces. Cover and refrigerate for 1½ hours.
3. Preheat the oven to 350°F, place the chicken on a roasting rack, and cook chicken for 15–17 minutes. (When juices run clear, the chicken is cooked.)

Serves 4–6

## CHICKEN KEBABS WITH YOGURT AND LEMON SAUCE

### Ingredients

10 oz plain yogurt
2 cloves garlic, crushed
$1\frac{1}{2}$ teaspoon paprika, ground
$1\frac{1}{2}$ teaspoon cumin seeds
$\frac{1}{4}$ cup lemon juice
2 tablespoons parsley, chopped
2 teaspoons oregano, chopped
freshly ground pepper
6 chicken thigh fillets, cubed
24 satay sticks

### Method

1. Soak satay sticks in cold water for 30 minutes.
2. Place (in a bowl) yogurt, garlic, paprika, cumin seeds, lemon juice, parsley, oregano and pepper, and mix until combined.
3. Place chicken on satay sticks and brush over with half the mixture. Leave to marinate in refrigerator for 2–3 hours.
4. Heat oil on barbecue (or char-grill pan), add chicken kebabs and cook 4–5 minutes each side.
5. Serve with remaining marinade mixture.

Serves 4

## RICE WITH CHICKEN LIVERS, PINE NUTS AND CURRANTS

**Ingredients**

2 pounds chicken livers
3 oz butter
12 shallots, chopped
1½ cups short-grain rice
2¼ cups chicken bouillon
½ cup parsley, chopped
4 oz pine nuts
4 oz currants

**Method**

1. Wash chicken livers and remove any sinew. Chop livers into bite-sized pieces.
2. Heat butter in a large saucepan and sauté the shallots for 5 minutes (until tender).
3. Add the chicken livers, and cook for a few more minutes (until they change color).
4. Add the rice and chicken bouillon to the saucepan, bring to a boil, then simmer (with the lid on), stirring occasionally, for approximately 30 minutes (until the liquid has been absorbed and the rice is cooked). If the rice is not cooked (and the mixture is looking a little dry) add another cup of water, and cook 5 minutes longer.
5. When rice is cooked, toss the chopped parsley, pine nuts and currants through the rice, and serve.

Serves 8

## CHICKEN, ROASTED BELL PEPPER, OLIVE AND FETA PIE

**Ingredients**

2 tablespoons olive oil
1 large leek, washed and sliced
1 clove garlic, crushed
1 pound chicken breasts, diced
1 bunch spinach, washed and blanched
2 red bell peppers, roasted and diced
2 oz black olives, pitted and halved
7 oz feta cheese, crumbled
2 tablespoons parsley, chopped
1 tablespoon oregano, chopped
3 eggs
1/4 cup cream
freshly ground pepper
8–16 sheets filo pastry
1 tablespoon olive oil, extra
1 tablespoon butter, melted
1 tablespoon sesame seeds

**Method**

1. Preheat oven to 350°F.
2. Heat one tablespoon oil in a large frying-pan, add leek and garlic, and cook for 5 minutes (or until soft). Set aside.
3. Heat extra oil, add chicken in batches, and cook for 6–8 minutes.
4. Drain spinach, squeeze out excess water, and chop roughly.
5. In a large bowl, combine chicken, spinach, bell pepper, olives, feta, parsley, oregano, eggs, cream and pepper. Stir until well combined. Set aside.
6. Lightly grease an 8 x 8 inch square baking dish. Combine the extra oil and butter. Lay out sheets of filo, put two together, and brush with the oil mixture. Put another two on top, and brush again. Continue to repeat this (until you have four double sheets). Line the baking dish with the filo, and trim around the edges. Fill with the chicken mixture. Brush the remaining sheets with oil (the same as before, using the same amount). Place the filo on top of the baking dish, tucking the edges inside.
7. Brush the top with the oil mixture, sprinkle with sesame seeds, and bake in the oven for 40–45 minutes.

Serves 4–6

## CHICKEN IN VINE LEAVES

**Ingredients**

2 young chickens, halved
2 oz honey
2 oz olive oil
2 oz orange juice
2 teaspoons lemon thyme, finely chopped
½ cup white wine
8–10 vine leaves

**Method**

1. Rinse out the chicken, and pat dry. Combine the honey, oil, juice, thyme and wine. Place the chickens in a bowl and pour half the liquid over them. Cover and refrigerate overnight. Turn poultry over once or twice during its marinating time.
2. Preheat the oven to 350°F.
3. Wrap the chicken in vine leaves and secure with skewers. Bake in a roasting dish for 25–30 minutes. Remove leaves, and return chicken to oven for 10 minutes (or until cooked and brown).
4. Remove the skewer, and place the chickens on their leaves.
5. Heat remainder of marinade in pan, and pour it over the chicken before serving.

Serves 2

## CHICKEN WITH OREGANO AND LEMON

**Ingredients**

4 chicken breasts
2 teaspoons oregano, dried
freshly ground pepper and salt
2 tablespoons olive oil
1½ pounds thick potatoes, sliced 2 inches thick
1 bunch scallions (trimmed and halved)
½ cup chicken bouillon
⅓ cup lemon juice
2 sprigs oregano, chopped
salt and pepper to taste

**Method**

1. Season chicken with dried oregano, pepper and salt.
2. Heat oil in a large skillet.
3. Add chicken, potatoes and onions, and brown quickly for 2–3 minutes.
4. Pour in bouillon, cover and simmer for 10–15 minutes (or until chicken is cooked).
5. Add lemon juice and fresh oregano. Cook for a further 3 minutes. Serve immediately.

Serves 6

## GREEK-STYLE CHICKEN RISSOLES IN TOMATO SAUCE

**Ingredients**

*Rissoles*

1 pound ground chicken
1 medium onion, grated
2 tablespoons parsley, finely chopped
½ teaspoon salt
pepper
1 egg
½ cup breadcrumbs, dried
1 tablespoon water
oil for frying

*Tomato sauce*

1 medium onion, finely chopped
1 clove garlic, crushed
1 tablespoon oil
14 oz canned tomatoes
1 tablespoon tomato paste
½ cup water
½ teaspoon oregano, dried
1 teaspoon sugar
salt and pepper
1 tablespoon parsley, chopped

**Method**

1. Place ground chicken in a bowl, grate onion into the chicken and add remaining ingredients. Mix well to combine, and knead a little by hand. With wet hands, roll into balls. Heat oil ½ inch deep in a skillet, and sauté the rissoles (until they change color on both sides). Remove to a plate.
2. For the sauce, add the onion and garlic to the skillet, and sauté a little. Add remaining sauce ingredients, and bring to a boil. Return rissoles to the pan, reduce heat, and simmer (covered) for 30 minutes.
3. Serve over boiled spaghetti (or pasta of your choice).

Serves 4–6

# vegetables

# FRESKA

'*Freska*!' That's all that vegetable lovers in Greece seek—that vegetables be fresh. Every vegetable used in Greece is available to readers of this book, with the exception of wild dandelion, which is not commercially marketed, but can be harvested wild.

Fresh okra, introduced to Greece from West Africa, may be hard to find outside metropolitan markets, but it is often included in canned tomato purée imported by Greek merchants. Artichokes are well loved in many forms by Greeks, as is asparagus, valued from ancient times for its healing powers and flavor. Lettuce is not just a salad vegetable. It is used in a casserole with dill to blend with cheap lamb cuts. Finished with avgolemono (egg-lemon sauce), this is also a delicious dinner party surprise.

What would the Greeks do without spinach, eggplant and especially tomatoes as pie fillers? And how would they do without beans served in so many ways? Cauliflower and zucchini are delicious when fried, and leek is lovely in an open-baked pie.

## FENNEL AND ZUCCHINI CAKES

**Ingredients**

$\frac{2}{3}$ cup all-purpose flour
1 egg, separated
1 tablespoon olive oil
$\frac{1}{3}$ cup cold water
$\frac{1}{4}$ teaspoon salt and freshly ground black pepper
8 oz fennel bulb
8 oz zucchini
1 tablespoon mint, chopped
oil for shallow-frying
garlic-flavored natural yogurt

**Method**

1. Sift the flour into a bowl and make a well in it. Into the well add the egg yolk, olive oil and cold water. Whisk the center, gradually incorporating the flour (until a smooth batter has formed). Season with salt and pepper, cover and leave to thicken for 30 minutes (in a cool place).
2. Grate the fennel and zucchini. Stir, along with the mint, into the batter. Whisk the egg white until soft peaks form, and fold gently into the batter mixture.
3. Shallow-fry dessert spoonfuls of mixture (a few at a time). Cook until golden on both sides and cooked in the center. Drain on paper towels.
4. Serve warm with garlic-flavored natural yogurt.

Serves 6

## DEEP-FRIED OKRA

**Ingredients**

8 oz okra

1 egg

1 cup all-purpose flour

1 cup ice-cold water

oil, for frying

**Method**

1. Wash and trim okra. In a large bowl, whisk egg until frothy, add flour and water, and whisk together until batter is also frothy.
2. Heat the oil in a large skillet, dip okra in batter, cook in oil for 1–2 minutes or until lightly brown.
3. Drain on paper towels and serve with lemon wedges and garlic walnut sauce.

Serves 4

## GARLIC WALNUT SAUCE

**Ingredients**

2 slices bread

⅔ cup water

2 oz walnuts

2 cloves garlic, roughly chopped

1 oz white wine vinegar

1½ oz olive oil

salt and pepper, to taste

**Method**

1. In a small bowl, soak bread in water for 5 minutes, squeeze out water.
2. Place walnuts in a food processor and process until finely chopped. Add bread, garlic and white wine vinegar, and process until combined. While motor is running, add olive oil and salt and pepper, process until paste is formed. Serve with chicken, fish or vegetables.

## SPINACH, OLIVE AND FETA FRITTATA WITH ROASTED BELL PEPPER SAUCE

**Ingredients**

10 eggs
1 tablespoon fresh oregano, chopped
black pepper, freshly crushed
1/4 cup olive oil
8 oz potatoes, peeled and diced
1 onion, diced
1 clove garlic, crushed
5 oz baby spinach
2 oz pitted Kalamata olives, halved
3 oz feta, crumbled
2 oz semi-dried tomatoes
3 large red bell peppers

**Method**

1. Lightly whisk together the eggs and oregano in a bowl, and season with black pepper. Set aside.
2. Heat the oil in a 9 inch skillet and sauté the potato, onion and garlic for a few minutes (until soft).
3. Add the spinach and cook (until spinach begins to wilt). Remove the skillet from the heat, then add olives, feta and semi-dried tomatoes.
4. Return the skillet to a very low heat, pour in the egg mixture, and cook for 10–15 minutes. Run a spatula around the sides of the skillet as the frittata is cooking, and tilt it slightly while cooking (so that the egg mixture runs down the sides a little).
5. When frittata is almost cooked through the middle, place under a broiler for five minutes to cook and brown the top.
6. Serve in wedges with the roasted bell pepper sauce.
7. To make the sauce, halve the bell peppers and remove the seeds. Char-grill the bell peppers (or broil) until black. Let them cool, and remove the skins. Place into a food processor and process until puréed. Transfer to a bowl. Makes 1 cup.

Serves 4–6

## POTATO FETA FRITTERS

**Ingredients**

$1\frac{1}{2}$ cups cooked potato, mashed
4 oz feta cheese, crumbled
1 egg beaten
3 scallions, chopped
3 tablespoons fresh dill, chopped
1 tablespoon lemon juice
rind of half a lemon, finely grated
freshly ground black pepper
plain flour for dredging
olive oil
extra dill and lemon, to garnish

**Method**

1. In a medium bowl, add the potato, feta, egg, scallions, dill, lemon juice, lemon rind and black pepper. Mix until well combined. Cover and chill for 1–2 hours (until firm).
2. Using your hands, roll the mixture into golf ball size balls and flatten slightly. Dredge lightly in flour.
3. Heat a little oil in a skillet, and cook a few at a time (until golden brown on both sides). Drain on paper towels and serve at once. Garnish with extra dill and lemon.

Serves 4

## ZUCCHINI AND FETA PIE (CRUSTLESS)

### Ingredients

1½ pounds zucchini
8 oz feta cheese
4 eggs, beaten
2 tablespoons toasted walnuts, chopped
2 tablespoons fresh dill, finely chopped
2 tablespoons fresh Italian parsley, finely chopped
¼ cup Parmesan, freshly grated
black pepper, freshly ground
1 tablespoon extra Parmesan, grated

### Method

1. Trim and wash zucchini before steaming in a colander for 12–15 minutes (until tender). Press out any excess moisture with the back of a wooden spoon.
2. Finely chop the zucchini, and place in a large mixing bowl. Preheat oven to 350°F, and grease a 8–10 inch pie dish with butter.
3. Soak the feta in warm water for 10 minutes, drain. Mash cheese until you have a paste-like consistency, and add to zucchini. Combine with the remaining ingredients, and stir well.
4. Pour into the prepared pie dish, sprinkle with a little extra Parmesan and bake for 45 minutes (or until set). Test the center with a skewer before serving.

Serves 6

## FETA AND RICOTTA STUFFED TOMATOES

### Ingredients

6 large firm tomatoes
5 oz feta cheese, crumbed
5 oz ricotta cheese
2 oz pine nuts, chopped
10 pitted black olives, chopped
1½ tablespoons fresh oregano, chopped
3 tablespoons whole wheat breadcrumbs
freshly ground black pepper
6 black olives, to garnish
oregano leaves

### Method

1. Preheat oven to 350°F.
2. Cut the top quarters off each tomato, and scoop the centers into a bowl. Dice the tops and add to the bowl. Combine half the tomato mixture with the feta, ricotta, pine nuts, olives, oregano, breadcrumbs and pepper. Beat mixture together, and spoon into the tomato shells (piling the tops high).
3. Place in a shallow ovenproof dish and bake for 20–25 minutes.
4. Garnish with an olive and oregano to serve.

Serves 6.

## ROASTED RED BELL PEPPERS WITH FETA, EGGPLANT, OLIVES AND SUN-DRIED TOMATOES

**Ingredients**

2 large red bell peppers, halved and seeded
2 baby eggplants, sliced
2 oz semi-sun-dried tomatoes
2 oz olives
4 oz Greek feta, cubed
2 tablespoons olive oil
2 teaspoons oregano
1 clove garlic, crushed

**Method**

1. Preheat oven to 350°F.
2. Place bell peppers on a baking tray. Place eggplant slices, tomatoes, olives and feta in bell peppers. In a jar, mix together olive oil, oregano and garlic. Drizzle this oil mixture over bell peppers, and bake for 20–25 minutes.

Serves 4

## EGGPLANT ROLLS

### Ingredients

2 x 8 oz eggplant

3 tablespoons olive oil

3 medium tomatoes, seeded and diced

5 oz mozzarella cheese, finely diced

2 tablespoons fresh basil, chopped

salt and freshly ground black pepper

fresh basil leaves, for serving

### *Dressing*

¼ cup olive oil

1 tomato, diced

1 tablespoon balsamic vinegar

2 tablespoons pine nuts, toasted

### Method

1. Remove the stalks from eggplants, and slice the eggplants lengthwise thinly to ½ inch thick. Brush the slices on both sides with oil, and grill on both sides (until soft and beginning to brown).
2. Preheat the oven to 350°F. Combine together in a bowl the tomatoes, mozzarella, basil and seasoning. Spoon a little onto the end of each slice of eggplant, and roll up. Place seam-side down in a greased oven-proof dish and bake for 15–17 minutes.
3. In a small pan, using a little of the dressing oil, sauté the tomato until softened. Add the remaining oil, balsamic vinegar and pine nuts, and gently warm. Season to taste. Arrange the rolls on a platter, and spoon the dressing over the rolls.
4. Garnish with fresh basil leaves to serve.

Serves 4

## BRAISED LEEKS WITH TOASTED ALMONDS

**Ingredients**

4 leeks, trimmed top and tail
3 tablespoons parsley, chopped
2 tablespoons mint, chopped
2 tablespoons oregano, chopped
2 tablespoons dill, chopped
salt and ground black pepper
½ cup olive oil
1 cup water, boiling
⅓ cup breadcrumbs, fresh
3 tablespoons almond flakes

**Method**

1. Split the leeks lengthwise down the center. Wash well, removing any dirt between layers.
2. Preheat oven to 350°F.
3. Place leeks in an ovenproof baking dish, sprinkle with all herbs, salt and pepper.
4. Pour in the olive oil and boiling water. Cover the dish and bake for 40 minutes until tender.
5. Remove the cover and drain half the excess liquid away. Sprinkle the tops of the leeks with breadcrumbs and a sprinkle of almonds, and bake for a further 15–17 minutes (until the breadcrumbs and almonds are golden). Serve at once.

Serves 4

## OKRA WITH VEGETABLES

**Ingredients**

12 oz small okra
2 oz olive oil
1 small red bell pepper, seeded and diced
1 medium onion, chopped
1 clove garlic, crushed
14 oz tomatoes, peeled and chopped
½ cup black olives
1 oz sun-dried tomatoes, shredded
2 tablespoons white wine
1 tablespoon oregano, freshly chopped
1 teaspoon sugar
salt and ground black pepper
fresh oregano, for garnish

**Method**

1. Trim the stems off the okra, wash pods, and pat dry with a paper towel.
2. Heat the oil in a large skillet. Add the red bell pepper, onion and garlic. Cook until softened and lightly brown. Add the okra and cook for a further 6 minutes. Stir in tomatoes, olives, sun-dried tomatoes, wine, oregano, sugar, and salt and pepper. Cover and simmer on low heat for 20 minutes. Remove lid and continue to cook for a further 7–10 minutes until the okra is tender, and the sauce is reduced and thickened.
3. Garnish with fresh oregano.

Serves 4

## GREEN BEANS IN TOMATO SAUCE (FASOLIA YAHNI)

**Ingredients**

1 pound fresh green beans
2 oz olive oil
1 medium onion, chopped
1 clove garlic, crushed
1 cup water
14 oz canned tomato pieces, peeled
1 tablespoon tomato paste
1 teaspoon sugar
½ teaspoon salt
1 teaspoon oregano, dried

**Method**

1. Wash beans, top and tail.
2. Heat oil in a saucepan, and sauté onion and garlic until onion is soft, but not brown.
3. Add water, bring to a boil, add beans and boil for 5 minutes.
4. Add tomatoes, tomato paste, sugar, salt and oregano. Turn down heat and simmer for 25–30 minutes (until beans are tender and sauce has reduced).

## OLIVE TAPENADE

**Ingredients**

4 oz black olives, pitted
⅓ cup parsley
2 cloves garlic, chopped
1 tablespoon capers
¼ cup shallots, sliced
2 tablespoons lemon juice
2 teaspoons oregano
⅓ cup olive oil
salt and ground pepper

**Method**

1. Place olives, parsley, garlic, capers, shallots, lemon juice and oregano in a food processor. Process until well combined.
2. With motor running, add olive oil in a slow stream, and process (until a paste has formed). Season with salt and pepper.

Serves 4

## RICE WITH LEMON, DILL AND SPINACH

**Ingredients**

2 tablespoons olive oil
1 onion, chopped
1 clove garlic, crushed
1 large bunch beet greens, washed and shredded
1 cup short-grain rice
1½ cup chicken bouillon
1 bunch dill, chopped
juice and rind of 1 lemon

**Method**

1. Heat oil, add the onion and garlic, and cook for one minute. Add the greens, and cook until the greens just wilt.
2. Add the rice and stir through. Add the bouillon, reduce the heat and cook covered for 10 minutes. If liquid has evaporated (and rice needs more cooking), add a little more water and cook for a further few minutes.
3. When rice is cooked, add chopped dill and lemon juice, season before serving.

Serves 4

# salads

# Horiatiki and OTHER SALADS

*Horiatiki salata*, the Greek farmer's colorful village salad, is very popular with visitors to Greece and with Hellenic food cooks at home. A spring salad is refreshing. Try a salad of finely chopped lettuce, shallots, fennel, fresh parsley (or dill) and garlic, topped with oil and vinegar dressing. *Rathikia* (boiled dandelion) is the Greeks' most favored winter salad, and artichokes and beets (with garlic) salads are only made from fresh ingredients. Consider serving broccoli and cauliflower (just tenderized by boiling) as salads, draped with oil and lemon juice.

Rice salad with shallots, chopped hard-boiled eggs, bell pepper, pimentos and dill pickles, mixed with oil and lemon, optional mayonnaise and prepared mustard is chilled in a mold, turned onto lettuce leaves, and garnished with black olives and pimentos. This salad is little known outside Greece, but is often served with fish.

Tomatoes, drizzled with oil, peppered and sprinkled with oregano, comprise a simple salad. Easier than *horiatiki*, it becomes special with a garnish of crumbled feta, black olives and decorative sprigs of parsley. Slice the tomatoes if you are in northern Greek or Cretan mode, otherwise quarter them.

## BROILED GOAT'S CHEESE SALAD

**Ingredients**

4 small fresh goat cheeses
1 clove garlic, crushed
1 sprig thyme, chopped
½ lemon, halved and thinly sliced
cracked pepper
⅓ cup extra virgin olive oil
10 oz mixed salad leaves
toasted bread

**Method**

1. Place the cheese on a plate. Combine together the garlic, thyme, lemon, pepper and oil. Spoon this over the cheese. Cover and place in fridge to marinate for 4–6 hours.
2. Pre-heat the broiler. Broil both sides of the cheese for 3–4 minutes. Also grill the lemon (until softened).
3. Arrange salad leaves on four plates. Place a cheese on each (with a little lemon), and drizzle some of the marinade oil over the cheese.
4. Serve with warm toasted bread.

Serves 4

## GREEK SALAD (HORIATIKI SALATA)

### Ingredients

2 seedless cucumbers, sliced
4 plum tomatoes, quartered
2 red onions, sliced or quartered
3 oz feta cheese, crumbled
½ cup Kalamata olives, left whole
3 tablespoons olive oil
2 tablespoon apple cider vinegar
salt
black pepper, freshly ground
oregano leaves, for garnish

### Method

1. Place all ingredients for the salad in a bowl.
2. Combine olive oil and vinegar in a bowl and whisk. Pour over the salad, then season with salt and ground black pepper.
3. Serve salad on its own, or with fresh bread. Garnish with oregano leaves.

Serves 4

## BABY SPINACH, FETA, ARTICHOKE AND WALNUT SALAD

**Ingredients**

1 red bell pepper, quartered and seeded
1 oz olive oil
4 oz walnuts
7 oz baby spinach, washed
7 oz Greek feta, cubed
10 oz artichoke hearts, quartered
½ cup black olives, pitted
pita bread, for serving

*Dressing*

½ cup extra virgin olive oil
¼ cup lemon juice
2 teaspoons honey
2 teaspoons oregano, chopped
pepper, freshly ground

**Method**

1. Preheat broiler. Place bell pepper under broiler, and leave to cook (or until it turns black on top). Cut into strips and set aside.
2. In a small jar, combine all ingredients for dressing, and shake well.
3. In a skillet, heat 1 tablespoon olive oil, add walnuts, and cook for 1–2 minutes (or until lightly browned). In a large salad bowl combine all salad ingredients, drizzle dressing over ingredients, and serve with pita bread.

Serves 4–6

*Note:* If artichoke hearts are not available fresh, use marinated canned or frozen.

## BROAD BEANS WITH GRILLED HALOUMI AND LEMON

**Ingredients**

4 oz haloumi or kassery cheese, halved
oil for brushing
8 oz broad beans, fresh or frozen (see note)
1/3 cup lemon juice
1/3 cup olive oil
salt and ground black pepper
4 rounds pita bread

**Method**

1. Slice cheese very thinly, then brush with olive oil, and broil under a broiler (until starting to brown).
2. Place the broad beans and cheese in a bowl, and add the lemon juice, olive oil, salt and ground black pepper, and serve. Serve with toasted pita bread.

Serves 4

***Note:*** If broad beans are large, peel off outer skin.

## ARTICHOKES LA POLITA (ANGINARES POLITIKA)

### Ingredients

6 globe artichoke hearts
½ cup olive oil
½ cup scallions, chopped
2 tablespoons fresh dill, chopped
12 pickling onions, peeled
1 pound baby carrots, peeled
12 small new potatoes
juice of 1 lemon
water
salt, pepper
2 tablespoons arrowroot, blended

### Method

1. Prepare artichoke hearts. Strip away outer leaves and trim around base. Cut off top ⅓ of artichoke and scoop out center. Cut in half. Place in a bowl of cold water with a squeeze of lemon juice (to prevent discoloring).
2. Heat half the oil in a large saucepan. Add scallions and dill and sauté until soft.
3. Cross-cut root end of onions, and place in saucepan. Arrange carrots and potatoes. Add lemon juice, remaining oil, salt and pepper (and enough water to cover), then cook for 15 minutes.
4. Place artichoke hearts over vegetables and cook for 15 minutes more (or until tender).
5. With a slotted spoon, remove vegetables to a heated platter. Arrange attractively, displaying the various vegetables. Keep warm.
6. Taste cooking liquid, and add salt, pepper and lemon juice, and adjust seasoning (if necessary). Stir in blended arrowroot, and stir over heat to thicken sauce. Spoon over vegetables. Serve hot with crusty bread as a main course.

Serves 6

# desserts

# GREEK FRUITS

*Frouta* (fruit) is an expected dessert in Greece. In a home, it is peeled and divided. The host spears the first portion and offers it to a guest who is the one privileged to taste first. Most Greek fruits will be familiar to readers, with the possible exception of the prickly pear cactus fruit, which is similar to peach or pear in texture and flavor. Fresh figs with walnuts are adored. For a sensationally simple dessert, soak preserved figs in Greek brandy, sprinkle with walnuts and top with whipped cream.

Cooked desserts must start with halva, which is the Turkish name for a baked semolina cake/pudding flavored with cloves, cinnamon, almonds and lemon juice with sugar syrup. It's so easy to make. *Kadaifi* is swirly-surfaced filo pastry, available in many supermarkets. With cream, nut or custard fillings, it's a fantastic finisher. *Loukoumathes* (honey puffs) are well-known to many non-Greeks and are always served hot. Milk pies, rice pudding and baklava stuffed with nuts and spices are also popular. *Thiples* (fried bow-knots) are offered to visitors at celebrations, or as part of a dessert.

## ALMOND SHORTBREAD COOKIES

**Ingredients**

14 oz butter, clarified
2 oz superfine sugar
1 tablespoon vanilla extract
4 oz roasted blanched almonds
1 egg yolk
5 cups all-purpose flour
cloves
confectioner's sugar

**Method**

1. Preheat the oven to 325°F.
2. Beat the butter with the sugar until pale and creamy, then add the vanilla and yolk and mix until well combined. Sift flour and fold into the mixture with a metal spoon (until well combined). Bring the dough together with your hands, and knead lightly for two minutes (until smooth). Wrap in plastic, and refrigerate for 15 minutes.
3. Flatten out the dough with your hands (to a thickness of ½ –¾ inch), and roll into half moon shapes. Place a clove in the center of each cookie, and bake on a baking sheet for 15 minutes or until cookies are golden.
4. Remove from the oven, place on a sheet of baking paper, and while still hot, sift confectioner's sugar over cookies until well covered. Let them cool, and store in an airtight container.

Makes 20 cookies.

## LEMON AND YOGURT SEMOLINA CAKE

**Ingredients**

4 oz butter, softened
$^{3}/_{4}$ cup superfine sugar
rind from 1 lemon, finely grated
4 eggs
1 cup fine semolina
2 teaspoons baking powder
1 cup almond meal
1 cup raisins
$^{1}/_{2}$ cup almonds, flaked
7 oz yogurt

*Syrup*

1 cup superfine sugar
1 cup lemon juice
$^{1}/_{2}$ cup honey

**Method**

1. Preheat oven to 350°F.
2. Grease a 8 inch cake tin, and line with paper.
3. In a large bowl, add butter, sugar and rind. Using an electric beater, cream butter, sugar and rind until light and soft.
4. Add eggs one at a time, and beat well after each egg.
5. Fold in semolina, baking powder and almond meal. Lightly fold in raisins, almonds and yogurt.
6. Pour mixture into prepared cake tin and bake for 35–45 minutes (or until cake is lightly browned on top).
7. To make the syrup, in a small saucepan combine sugar, lemon juice and honey. Cook on low heat for 15–20 minutes (or until it forms a syrup).
8. Using a skewer, poke cake evenly. Cool syrup slightly, and pour over cake. Serve with cream.

Serves 6–8

## BAKED FRESH DATES AND APPLES

**Ingredients**

5 large cooking apples
butter for greasing
7 oz fresh dates, stoned and halved
juice of half lemon
juice of 2 oranges
rind of 1 orange, finely grated
2 cinnamon sticks
3 tablespoons clear honey
natural yogurt, to serve
ground cinnamon, to garnish

**Method**

1. Preheat oven to 350°F.
2. Peel and slice the apples (thinly). Place in a shallow oven-proof dish (greased with butter). Stir in the dates, juices, rind and cinnamon sticks. Drizzle the honey over the mixture.
3. Cover and bake for 45–55 minutes (until tender and flavors are absorbed).
4. Serve warm or chilled with Greek yogurt, dusted with cinnamon.

Serves 4

## BAKLAVA

### Ingredients

8 oz unsalted butter, melted
14 oz blanched roasted almonds, ground
1 ½ teaspoons cinnamon
½ cup superfine sugar
1 ½ pounds filo pastry

*Syrup*

3 cups superfine sugar
1 ½ cups water
1 cinnamon stick
1 piece of orange or lemon rind
1 tablespoon honey

### Method

1. Preheat oven to 475°F.
2. Melt butter, set aside.
3. Mix nuts in a bowl with cinnamon and sugar.
4. Brush 10 x 14 inch baking tray with butter.
5. Place one sheet of filo on bottom of dish with ends hanging over sides. Brush with melted butter and add another layer of filo. Repeat with 8 more filo sheets.
6. Sprinkle nut mixture generously over the filo. Continue the layering of filo pastry (3 sheets) and one layer of nuts until all nuts are used.
7. Top with 8 reserved sheets of filo, making sure the top sheet is well buttered. Cut the top lengthwise in parallel strips.
8. Bake in oven at 475°F for 30 minutes, then reduce heat to 325°F and bake for a further hour.
9. To make the syrup, place ingredients in saucepan and bring to a boil. Reduce heat and let simmer for 10–15 minutes. Leave to cool before use. Pour cold syrup over baklava and cut into diamond shapes.

# almond

## ALMOND CAKES

**Ingredients**

1 pound almonds, blanched
1 cup superfine sugar
2 medium eggs
$\frac{2}{3}$ oz soft white breadcrumbs
$\frac{1}{3}$ cup honey

**Method**

1. Grind almonds in a food processor (with a little of the sugar). Combine the remaining sugar with the eggs, and whisk until pale and creamy. Add the ground almonds to the breadcrumbs, and stir until well combined.
2. Preheat oven to 350°F.
3. Shape, using a tablespoon, roughly into diamond shapes, and place on a non-stick baking tray. Bake for 15 minutes.
4. While warm, place on wire cooling racks, and brush with warm honey. Leave to cool a little before serving.

Makes 38–40 cakes

## GREEK SHORTBREAD (KOURABIETHES)

**Ingredients**

8 oz unsalted butter
2 tablespoons confectioner's sugar
1 tablespoon brandy
½ cup almonds, chopped
2½ cups all-purpose flour, sifted
1 teaspoon baking powder
whole cloves
rose water
1 pound confectioner's sugar, sifted

**Method**

1. Preheat oven to 350°F.
2. Cream butter (until white and fluffy). Add confectioner's sugar, and brandy.
3. Stir in almonds and half the sifted flour. Use your hand to mix in remaining flour (a little at a time), and mix to a soft dough. If dough is sticky, add a little more flour.
4. Break off pieces and roll into a ball, flatten slightly in the palm of your hand, then pinch twice leaving four fingerprints. Insert a clove in top of each, place on ungreased baking sheet.
5. Bake in oven for 15–20 minutes until lightly colored, but do not brown. Remove from oven, and let stand for 5 minutes. Splash a little rose water over the cookies.
6. Sift confectioner's sugar onto a large sheet of grease-proof paper or a large tray. Lift warm cookies onto this, then completely cover with confectioner's sugar. Allow to cool in confectioner's sugar.

Makes approximately 25

## BUTTER COOKIES (KOULOURIA)

**Ingredients**

4 oz butter
4 oz ghee
1¼ cups superfine sugar
½ teaspoon cinnamon, ground
3 eggs
⅓ cups brandy
1½ teaspoons baking powder
4–5 cups all-purpose flour
egg glaze
sesame seeds

**Method**

1. Preheat oven to 375°F.
2. Cream butter, ghee and sugar well, and add cinnamon. Gradually add eggs, beating mixture well.
3. Add brandy and baking powder, then begin to add flour. Add as much as is needed to make a stiff (not dry) dough. It is safer to add half the flour, then mix in a little at a time (until desired consistency is reached). Test to see if dough is right by rolling a little in your hands: if it is not sticky, and rolls well, enough flour has been added.
4. Shape pieces of dough into slim pencil-shapes, roll into sesame seeds, form into twists, circles or scrolls. Place on greased baking sheet, glaze with egg glaze, and bake in oven for 15–20 minutes. Cool on wire rack.

Makes approximately 48

## ORANGE ROLL PRESERVE (GLYKO PORTOKALI)

**Ingredients**

6 large thick oranges, skinned
3 cups sugar
3 cups water
1 tablespoon lemon juice

**Method**

1. Lightly grate oranges all over (just enough to scratch the surface).
2. Score, peel into six segments lengthwise, and carefully remove peel. Roll up peel, and thread onto a long strand of cotton (12 rolls to each strand).
3. Place rolls in a large pan of cold water, and bring to a boil. As soon as they boil, drain (and discard water), refill with fresh water, and boil again. Repeat this process twice more to remove bitterness from peel.
4. Cover with cold water again, and allow rolls to boil (until tender); then drain.
5. In a clean saucepan, bring sugar and water to a boil, and stir to dissolve sugar. Add lemon juice and orange rolls. Simmer gently for 20–30 minutes (or until syrup gels when tested on a cold saucer). Cool a little. Remove thread, and place rolls and syrup in sterilized jars.
6. Serve a roll on a small dish with a spoon. Ideal to serve with after-dinner coffee.

## BAKED STUFFED PEACHES

**Ingredients**

4 large firm peaches
2 tablespoons superfine sugar
1 egg yolk
1 oz softened butter
1 cup cake crumbs
¼ cup almonds, ground
1 cup sweet white wine
⅓ cup almonds, slivered

**Method**

1. Preheat oven to 350°F.
2. Cut the peaches in half (and discard the stones). Spoon a little of the flesh out, roughly chop, and place in a bowl. Add the sugar, egg yolk and butter, and beat (until smooth). Stir in the cake crumbs and almonds.
3. Divide the mixture into eight, and spoon into center of each peach. Place in a greased ovenproof dish, and pour the wine over mixture and peaches. Sprinkle slivered almonds on top.
4. Bake for 30 minutes or until peaches are tender, but still holding their shape.
5. Serve warm with baking juices drizzled over.

Serves 4

# GLOSSARY

**Abocado (Spanish):** sweet

**Aceite (Spanish):** oil

**Affettati (Italian):** a commonly used term referring to thinly cut slices of processed pork, such as prosciutto, salami and a variety of sausages.

**Agneau (French):** lamb

**Agrodolce (Italian):** sweet and sour; lemon and/or vinegar, sugar and/or golden raisins are mixed to make basic *agrodolce* sauces (from agro 'bitter, sour' and dolce 'sweet')

**Aioli (French, Italian):** a golden-colored mayonnaise from Provence made of olive oil, garlic and egg yolks

**Ajo:** garlic

**Al fresco:** a term used in English to indicate that section of restaurants or cafés out in the open air; (but note that this particular expression has a very different meaning in Italian where it means 'to be in jail' or 'in the cooler'!; in Italy you must use the expression all'aperto—'in the open')

**Alcachofas (Spanish):** globe artichokes

**Alioli (Spanish):** garlic and olive oil sauce

**Almejas (Spanish):** clams

**Almendras (Spanish):** almonds

**Anchoas (Spanish):** anchovies

**Anguila (Spanish):** eel

**Antipasti (Italian):** appetizers; a general term for what is served before a meal to stimulate the appetite

**Antipasto di mare (Italian):** seafood appetizers; may include fish and crustaceans

**Antipasto misto di mare (Italian):** mixed seafood appetizers; includes all types of seafood

**Antipasto misto (Italian):** mixed appetizers; made up of a variety of different appetizers: seafoods; cheeses; fresh, cooked and pickled vegetables; cured meats; hot and cold savories

**Arenques (Spanish):** herrings

**Armagnac:** a French brandy/cognac from Armagnac (France)

**Arroz (Spanish):** rice

**Asperge (French):** asparagus

**Atun (Spanish):** tuna

**Aves (Spanish):** poultry

**Avgolemono (Greek):** egg and lemon sauce

**Bacalao (Spanish):** cod

**Baklava:** honey and almond pastries, sometimes stuffed with spices

**Barbounyi:** red mullet—the most revered and most expensive Greek seafood

**Bardolino:** light, dry, red wine from the shores of Lake Garda (not far from Verona)

**Barolo:** austere, full-bodied red wine from Piedmont

**Bartolillos (Spanish):** little almond tarts

**Bearnaise sauce (French):** rich sauce made with egg yolks and flavored with wine, onion and tarragon

**Beaujolais:** red table wine made in Southern Burgundy in France.

**Berberechos (Spanish):** cockles

**Berenjena (Spanish):** eggplant

**Beurre (French):** butter

**Bianchetti (Italian):** (literally 'little white ones') name given to tiny, translucent fish; hooks are of no use, nets are used to catch them

**Bisque (French):** thick cream soup, especially one made with shellfish or game.

**Bistec (Spanish):** steak

**Blanco (Spanish):** white

**Bocconcini (Italian):** (literally 'morsels') a term used to indicate small, fresh mozzarella cheeses, no bigger than a walnut

**Bodega (Spanish):** wine bar

**Bœuf (French):** beef

**Bollito misto (Italian):** different types of meat that have been boiled in salted water; the boiled meats can be served separately, usually with green sauce; the broth can be used on its own for noodle soup, as a base for rich vegetable soups, or to make risotto

**Boquerones (Spanish):** whitebait

**Bouillabaisse (French):** seafood and fish stew from Marseilles.

**Bourguignon (French):** quintessential French stew containing red wine and onions

**Bourtheto:** the stewed fish of Corfu, often served with peppers and onions

**Bouzouki:** traditional Greek folk band music featuring the stringed instrument of the same name

**Brazo de gitano (Spanish):** 'Gypsy's arm' (sponge roll filled with jam or fruit)

**Brioche (French):** a butter-rich dough baked in a loaf pan.

**Brodi (Italian):** general term for broths

**Brodo di carne (Italian):** beef broth

**Brolio chianti:** name of a wine from the Brolio Castle, of the famous Ricasoli family; vines grow on the hills between Florence and Siena in Tuscany

**Brunello:** an orange-red, dry wine from Montalcino (near Siena)

**Bruschetta (Italian):** a thick slice of bread, usually grilled and rubbed with garlic, with a few drops of olive oil on top

**Buckwheat groats:** hulled crushed buckwheat grains used in French cooking. They are usually cooked in a similar manner to rice and may be served as a side-dish with vegetables or used as a thickener for soups

**Buey (Spanish):** beef

**Bon appetito! (Italian):** literally 'good appetite' (used at the beginning of a meal)

**Burgundy:** a red or white table wine from the Burgundy region of France

**Caballas a la parilla (Spanish):** grilled mackerel in parsley sauce

**Caille (French):** quail

**Calabacines rellenos (Spanish):** stuffed zucchini (courgette) in sauce

**Calamares (en su tinto) (Spanish):** squid cooked in its own ink

**Caldeirada (Spanish):** thick fish and onion soup

**Caldo de pescado (Spanish):** clear fish soup

**Callos a la asturiana (Spanish):** tripe in wine sauce

**Calvados:** fragrant apple brandy

**Camarones (Spanish):** shrimp

**Camembert:** one of the great cheeses of Normandy

**Canalones (Spanish):** stuffed tubes of pasta

**Canard (French):** duck

**Cangrejo (Spanish):** crab

**Cannelloni (Italian):** stuffed pasta; large squares of pasta cooked in boiling salted water and stuffed, rolled up and browned in the oven

**Cappellini (Italian):** long, thin spaghetti pasta, cooked in clear soups or meat broths

**Capri:** a straw-colored, dry, white wine from the Isle of Capri

**Caracoles en salsa (Spanish):** snails in wine sauce

**Carne (Spanish):** meat

**Carni (Italian):** general term for all types of meat

**Carpaccio (Italian):** thin slices of raw meat dressed in oil, salt and shavings of Parmesan cheese (so-called because the dish was prepared to celebrate the exhibition, held in Venice, of the Italian painter Carpaccio)

**Carta da musica (Italian):** flat Sardinian bread that looks like round sheets of paper (origin of name is uncertain: perhaps called 'music paper' because it is so thin that when it breaks it looks like the ruled staffs on music paper; another explanation is that the sound made when the bread is broken is like music)

**Cassoulet (French):** bean stew

**Celeriac:** a type of celery grown for its thick turnip-like edible root.

**Centolla a la vasca (Spanish):** stuffed spider crabs

**Cepa:** wine, Spanish grape variety

**Cèpe mushrooms:** also known as porcini mushrooms. These are pale brown wild mushrooms. If you can't buy fresh cèpes, dried cèpes are usually available from speciality food stores. The dried variety need to be soaked before use.

**Charcuterie (French):** seasoned, smoked or aged meats and sausage often filed in the 'red meat' category, and automatically served with red wines

**Chipirones a la plancha (Spanish):** grilled baby squid

**Chipura (Spanish):** alcoholic drink made from grape skins

**Chocha a la vizcaina (Spanish):** stewed woodcock

**Chorizo:** dried pork sausage that is highly seasoned with paprika, pimientos, garlic and spices

**Chronia polla (Greek):** 'long life'

**Chufas (Spanish):** tiger nuts

**Chuletas a la parilla (Spanish):** grilled pork chops

**Churrasco (Spanish):** charcoal-grilled steak

**Churros (Spanish):** fried pastry cut into lengths

**Cincin! (Italian):** (a toast) 'Cheers—to your health!'

**Cinqueterre:** name of a golden colored wine from Liguria

**Clarete (Spanish):** light red wine

**Coca Mallorquina (Spanish):** Majorcan pizza

**Cochida de lenteja (Spanish):** lentil stew

**Cochinillo asado (Spanish):** roast sucking pig

**Codornices asadas (Spanish):** pot-roasted quails

**Col hervido (Spanish):** crisp steamed cabbage

**Coliflor (Spanish):** cauliflower

**Compote:** a dessert of fruit cooked in syrup and usually served cold.

**Conejo (Spanish):** rabbit

**Consommé:** clear soup

**Coppa ham:** similar to Parma ham

**Coq au vin:** chicken in a red wine sauce with button mushrooms and onions

**Coquilles (French):** scallops

**Coquinas (Spanish):** cockles

**Cordero a la pastora (Spanish):** lamb casserole with herbs

**Crema Catalana (Spanish):** crème brulée

**Crème (French):** cream

**Crème fraîche:** thick, velvety cream, with a subtle, nutty flavor. Plays a major role in the French kitchen.

**Crêpe:** thin folded or rolled pancake.

**Crevettes (French):** shrimp

**Crudités:** raw, fresh vegetables served with usually just one mousse or dip as an appetizer

**Datiles (Spanish):** dates

**Dolci (Italian):** general term for sweets

**Dolmades (Greek):** stuffed grape leaves

**Dulce (Spanish):** sweet

**Duxelles (French):** a finely chopped mixture of mushrooms, onions, shallots and herbs sautéed in butter

**Empanadas (Spanish):** pastries fried in oil

**En croûte (French):** wrapped in pastry

**Ensalada de arroz (Spanish):** rice salad

**Entrecôte:** rib steak

**Entremeses (Spanish):** starters

**Erbe e Spezie (Italian):** herbs and spices (fresh and dried)

**Escargots (French):** snails

**Esparragos (Spanish):** asparagus

**Espinacas (Spanish):** spinach

**Fabada asturiana (Spanish):** stew made from black smoked sausage and haricot beans

**Faisan (Spanish):** pheasant

**Faki (Greek):** lentils

**Falerno:** dark, ruby-red and subtly scented wine from the Campi Flegrei (near Naples)

**Falerno laziale:** a different wine from the Falerno (above); the Falerno laziale is lighter in color, rather like liquid-amber

**Fassoulada (Greek):** bean soup

**Fava beans:** it is preferable to choose the medium-sized pods, since they have a small seed with a more delicate flavor.

**Feta:** popular soft Greek cheese

**Fettuccine (Italian):** long strips of fresh pasta (about ⅕ inch-wide)

**Filo:** tissue-thin, layered pastry

**Fougasse (French):** a French flatbread that was once served sweetened with sugar and orange water. It is now more commonly eaten with savory dishes.

**Fraise (French):** strawberry

**Frambuesas (Spanish):** raspberries

**Frangelico:** popular Italian liqueur (the name possibly being derived from *fratello*, 'brother'—a term used by friars, and *angelico*—'angel')

**Frappé:** iced coffee

**Fritos (Spanish):** chicken and ham croquettes

**Frittata (Italian):** a more sophisticated version of the omelette; is cooked slowly (over very low heat) with cheese, vegetables and other ingredients being beaten into the eggs before cooking; it is not folded but it is served flat and round

**Fritura de pescado (Spanish):** mixed fried fish

**Fromage (French):** cheese

**Frouta (Greek):** fruit

**Galaktopoleia (Greek):** a milk-shop serving dairy products, ice cream, pastries, tea and coffee

**Gambas a la plancha (Spanish):** grilled prawns

**Ganso (Spanish):** goose

**Garbanzos (Spanish):** chickpeas

**Garum (Italian):** a Latin word describing an ancient Roman condiment; a very expensive fish sauce

**Gâteau (French):** cake

**Gattinara:** a full-bodied red wine with a distinctive aroma; originally from the Vercelli area, in Piedmont

**Gazpacho (Spanish):** iced cucumber, pepper and tomato soup

**Gorgonzola:** the blue-veined cheese with a slightly spiced and sharp flavor; first produced in the city of Gorgonzola, in Lombardy

**Gratin (French):** brown crust formed on food that has been cooked with a topping of breadcrumbs or grated cheese.

**Guisantes (Spanish):** peas

**Habas (Spanish):** broad beans

**Haloumi:** soft Greek cheese, often served grilled

**Helado (Spanish):** ice cream

**Higado (Spanish):** liver

**Higos (Spanish):** figs

**Horchata (Spanish):** non-alcoholic drink made from chufas or tiger nuts

**Horiatiki salata (Greek):** a village mixed salad

**Huevos (Spanish):** eggs

**Hummus:** chickpea spread

**Insalate (Italian):** salads

**Jabali estofado (Spanish):** stewed wild boar

**Jamon con habas (Spanish):** ham with broad beans

**Judias verdes (Spanish):** French beans

**Kadaifi (Greek):** a swirly-surfaced, filo, nut pastry

**Kafenion (Greek):** a coffee house; a haven for men (and, more recently, women) to talk, play cards and backgammon, drink coffee or take ouzo with *mezethes*

**Kakavia (Greek):** thick fish soup

**Kalamari (Greek):** squid

**Kaliorexi! (Greek):** 'good appetite!'

**Kefalotiri (Greek):** a hard, biting Greek cheese similar to Parmesan; an ingredient for main meal dishes, and a pasta topping

**Keftedes (Greek):** fried (sometimes boiled) mince balls with herbs

**Koboloi (Greek):** worry beads

**Kokoretsi (Greek):** offal-stuffed lamb entrails

**Kotopolo (Greek):** poultry or chicken

**Koulouria (Greek):** special Easter cakes

**Laghos stifado (Greek):** stewed hare

**Lamprea (Spanish):** lamprey

**Langosta (Spanish):** lobster

**Lapin (French):** rabbit

**Lechazo asado (Spanish):** roast baby lamb

**Lechona asada (Spanish):** roast piglet

**Legumbres asadas (Spanish):** mixed baked vegetables

**Lengua de ternera (Spanish):** calf's tongue

**Lenguado (Spanish):** sole

**Lentejas y anchoas (Spanish):** lentils with anchovies

**Liebre (Spanish):** hare

**Linguine (Italian):** dried pasta; long, flat noodles, about the size of spaghetti

**Lomo de cerdo (Spanish):** roast loin of pork

**Loukoumathes (Greek):** cinnamon and honey fritters (or puffs)

**Manitas de cerdo (Spanish):** pig's trotters

**Marides (Greek):** tiny whitebait fish (an appetizer or a main dish)

**Mascarpone:** a very rich and creamy cheese from Lombardy

**Mayiritsa (Greek):** easter soup

**Mejillones (Spanish):** mussels

**Melitzanasalata (Greek):** directly translates as eggplant salad, but is really a purée

**Menudos (Spanish):** tripe

**Mezethes (Greek):** appetizers

**Minestrone alla genovese:** very thick minestrone with some typical Genoese pesto added before serving

**Minestrone:** a very hearty vegetable soup

**Monica:** a sweet, velvety, red wine with amber highlights; originally from the area near Cagliari, on the isle of Sardinia

**Moscato di Pantelleria:** a sweet, soft, white wine from the isle of Pantelleria

**Moules (French):** mussels

**Moussaka:** layered dish containing eggplant, zucchini, potatoes, beef and béchamel sauce

**Moutarde (French):** mustard

**Mozzarella:** a typical Neapolitan fresh cheese, roundish in shape, made from the milk of cows or water buffaloes; can be used in cooking

**Mujol (Spanish):** mullet

**Myzithra:** soft ewe's milk cheese

**Naranja (Spanish):** orange

**Noisette (French):** a small round thick boneless slice of meat, usually from the boned and rolled best end of neck of loin

**Okra:** green pod vegetable, originally from Africa

**Osso buco (Italian):** (literally 'bone with a hole') joint of hind leg of a calf; a popular Milanese dish

**Ostras (Spanish):** oysters

**Ouzeri (Greek):** a small restaurant selling ouzo and, sometimes, evening meals

**Ouzo:** aniseed-flavored spirit from Greece that is diluted with water and turns cloudy on contact

**Paella (Spanish):** dish of rice and vegetables, meat or shellfish

**Pan (Spanish):** bread

**Pancetta (Italian):** meat similar to bacon

**Panetteria (Italian):** bread shop where bread is baked fresh daily

**Panettieri (Italian):** bakers

**Pappardelle (Italian):** fresh pasta (wide and rectangular)

**Parfait (French):** a rich frozen flavored dessert that resembles custard and contains whipped cream and eggs.

**Pargo (Spanish):** sea bream

**Parmesan cheese:** a favorite Italian cheese used both as a table cheese and for seasoning (originally from the city of Parma, in Emilia, but also from other officially designated places in the north, and made under carefully controlled conditions)

**Pasta dura (Italian):** (literally 'tough dough') one of the oldest types of bread; a large bread made from the same sort of dough used to make small bread rolls; typical of the Emilia–Romagna region

**Pasta e riso (Italian):** pasta and rice

**Pasticceria (Italian):** a pastry shop that bakes and sells all sorts of cakes; often doubles as a coffee bar; a very popular place for meeting friends

**Pastitcio:** baked dish of pasta, beef, cheese and tomatoes from Greece

**Patatas (Spanish):** potatoes

**Pato (Spanish):** wild duck

**Patsa (Greek):** a soup brew with garlic, tripe and lamb's feet

**Pavo asado (Spanish):** roast turkey

**Pecorino (Italian):** (from *pecora*: 'sheep') a cheese with a rather sharp flavor; made from sheep's milk

**Penne (Italian):** (from *penna*: 'pen') short, hollow dried pasta, the thickness of a finger

**Perdiz (Spanish):** partridge

**Persil (French):** parsley

**Pescado (Spanish):** fish

**Pesci e frutti di mare (Italian):** (literally: 'fish and fruit of the sea') all types of fish and crustaceans

**Pesto alla genovese (Italian):** the green sauce from Genoa, Liguria

**Pesto:** green sauce typical of Liguria (so-called because the traditional recipe required that all ingredients be 'crushed' and 'pounded' with a pestle in a mortar, preferably in a marble mortar!)

**Pez espada (Spanish):** swordfish

**Pichones (Spanish):** pigeons

**Pimientos (Spanish):** peppers

**Pinchos (Spanish):** kebabs

**Pita:** a flat, round, Middle Eastern bread, often split open to form a pocket for fillings

**Pois (French):** peas

**Polenta:** a kind of savory cornmeal pudding; can be a first course or an accompaniment to many other dishes

**Pollame e cacciagione (Italian):** poultry and game

**Pollo (Spanish):** chicken

**Pomme de terre (French):** potato

**Pomodori (Italian):** tomatoes

**Porc (French):** pork

**Porcini mushrooms:** crepes's mushrooms of the Boletus family

**Pot au feu (French):** this is a simple stockpot soup made of blanched meat and fowl, cooked with vegetables and served with traditional side dishes. It is made with care to obtain a rich, clear, well-flavored consomme

**Poule, poulet (French):** chicken

**Poussin (French):** baby chicken

**Primo piatto (Italian):** first course; pasta, rice or soups

**Prosciutto:** ham; pig's hind-thigh that is seasoned and cured in carefully ventilated rooms; the prosciutto from Parma and the prosciutto from Friuli (the San Daniele) are considered to be the best in Italy

**Provençal:** originating from the French region of Provence.

**Pulpo (Spanish):** octopus

**Queso (Spanish):** cheese

**Ragoût (French):** stew

**Raki (Greek):** resin-flavored alcoholic liquor (similar to chipura) favored by Cretans and Greeks living close to Turkey

**Ratatouille:** a cooked vegetable dish of eggplant, onions, tomatoes and zucchini.

**Rathikia (Greek):** wild dandelion; similar to spinach, it is green, and is served warm to cold, dressed with lemon and oil.

**Ravioli:** small squares of stuffed fresh pasta

**Raya (Spanish):** skate, a type of fish

**Rembetika:** folk music somewhat like the American blues, but Greek-style

**Remoulade (French):** a mayonnaise sauce flavored with herbs, mustard and capers

**Retsina:** traditional, dry Greek wine treated with pine resin

**Ricotta:** a fresh, moist, unsalted cheese, similar to cottage cheese

**Rinones al jerez (Spanish):** kidneys in sherry

**Risotto:** famous Italian dish made by boiling rice in stock and flavoring it with onion, cheese, mushrooms, kidneys, white wine, etc.

**Rolo (Greek):** meat loaf with garlic sauce and a center of boiled eggs

**Romano cheese:** a typical Roman cheese; made with sheep's, goat's or cow's milk; see pecorino

**Roquefort:** a blue cheese made from sheep's milk. A good cheese has a creamy pale and well marbled blue veins

**Sabalo (Spanish):** shad fish

**Saganaki (Greek):** a dish baked (or fried) with onions, tomatoes and kasseri cheese

**Salade niçoise (French):** salad originating from Nice. Typically contains tomatoes and tuna and is garnished with black olives and green beans

**Salchica (Spanish):** pork sausage

**Salmonete (Spanish):** red mullet

**Salsa (Italian):** sauce

**Saltimbocca alla romana (Italian):** a typical Roman meat dish; thin slices of veal so delicious that 'they jump into the mouth'

**San Pedro (Spanish):** John Dory

**Sardinas (Spanish):** sardines

**Saumon (French):** salmon

**Seco (Spanish):** dry

**Secondo piatto (Italian):** second course; meat, fish, poultry, accompanied by vegetables

**Skordalia (Greek):** thick garlic sauce, with oil, vinegar and mashed potatoes or moist breadcrumbs

**Sofrito (Greek):** stewed steak with vinegar and garlic (from Corfu)

**Sopa (Spanish):** soup

**Soudzoukakia (Greek):** hand made sausages containing cumin (from Thessaloniki)

**Soufflé:** a light fluffy dish made with egg yolks and stiffly beaten egg whites.

**Spaghettini (Italian):** very thin spaghetti for thin soups and clear broths

**Stifado (Greek):** a stew that contains onions

**Suprême de volaille (French):** chicken breast

**Tahini:** sesame paste

**Tapas (Spanish):** snacks, canapés

**Taramosalata (Greek):** fish roe dip

**Tartufi (Italian):** truffles

**Tenca (Spanish):** tench

**Ternasco (Spanish):** roast lamb

**Ternera (Spanish):** veal

**Terrine:** a pâté baked in an earthenware casserole

**Thiples (Greek):** fried bow-knots dessert or welcoming sweet

**Tiramisù (Italian):** a sweet, similar to the English trifle (in fact, an older and less sophisticated version of tiramisù is called zuppa inglese—'English soup')

**Tortilla:** Spanish omelette

**Trucha (Spanish):** trout

**Tzatziki:** Greek dip (or salad) containing cucumber with yogurt and mint

**Uvas (Spanish):** grapes

**Verduras (Spanish):** green vegetables

**Via Salaria:** the name of one of the main roads leading to Rome, originally used by Roman salt exporters

**Volaille (French):** poultry

**Vongole (Italian):** clam

**Zabaglione (Italian):** a dish incorporating whipped egg-yolk with sugar and Marsala wine

**Zaharoplasteia (Greek):** a sweet shop offering biscuits, cakes, chocolate and beverages (including bottled alcohol)

**Zampone (Italian):** a specialty sausage of Modena; (the name coming from the *zampa*—pig's foot—used as casing)

**Zanahorias (Spanish):** carrots

**Zesty parakalo (Greek):** 'hot, please'

**Zuppa di pesce (Italian):** fish soup

**Zuppa di verdura (Italian):** vegetable soups

# INDEX

# INDEX

# NOTES

North S
Ireland
United Kingdom
Atlantic Ocean
Seine
Paris
France
Swi
Lyon
Bordeaux
Marseille
Corsica
Spain
Barcelona
Madrid
Portugal
Algeria
Morocco